TRAUMA AND ORGANIZATIONS

NEW INTERNATIONAL LIBRARY OF GROUP ANALYSIS

Series Editor: Earl Hopper

Other titles in the Series

Contributions of Self Psychology to Group Psychotherapy
  by Walter N. Stone

Difficult Topics in Group Psychotherapy: My Journey from Shame to Courage
  by Jerome S. Gans

Resistance, Rebellion and Refusal in Groups: The 3 Rs
  by Richard M. Billow

The Social Unconscious in Persons, Groups, and Societies:
Volume I: Mainly Theory
  edited by Earl Hopper and Haim Weinberg

TRAUMA AND ORGANIZATIONS

Edited by

Earl Hopper

KARNAC

First published in 2012 by
Karnac Books Ltd
118 Finchley Road, London NW3 5HT

British Library Cataloguing in Publication Data

A C.I.P. for this book is available from the British Library

ISBN 978 1 85575 779 0

Edited, designed and produced by The Studio Publishing Services Ltd
www.publishingservicesuk.co.uk
e-mail: studio@publishingservicesuk.co.uk

Printed in Great Britain

www.karnacbooks.com

CONTENTS

ACKNOWLEDGEMENTS   ix

ABOUT THE EDITOR AND CONTRIBUTORS   xi

FOREWORD: Earl Hopper, Editor of NILGA   xvii

INTRODUCTION: The theory of Incohesion: Aggregation/   xxxi
Massification as the fourth basic assumption in the
unconscious life of groups and group-like social systems
   Earl Hopper

PART I: PROCESSES AND SYSTEMS

CHAPTER ONE
A study in institutional change: the experience of trauma   3
and the role of rumour in a case of paranoiagenesis
   Howard D. Kibel

CHAPTER TWO
Traumatogenic processes in a psychiatric hospital: 23
unconscious destructiveness of leadership change
   Bent Rosenbaum and Gerda Winther

CHAPTER THREE
Trauma as cause and effect of perverse organizational   45
process
    Susan Long

CHAPTER FOUR
Baked beans and mashed potato: the basic assumption of   65
Incohesion: Aggregation/Massification in organizations
treating adolescents with eating disorders
    David Wood

CHAPTER FIVE
A study of trauma and scapegoating in the context of   89
incohesion: an example from the oil industry
    Ellen I. McCoy

CHAPTER SIX
The survival and development of a traumatized clinic   111
for psychotherapy for people with intellectual
disabilities
    Alan Corbett, Tamsin Cottis, and Elizabeth Lloyd

PART II: LEADERS AND LEADERSHIP

CHAPTER SEVEN
Personal trauma and collective disorder: the example   129
of organizational psychodynamics in psychiatry
    Robert D. Hinshelwood

CHAPTER EIGHT
Disorganized responses to refusal and spoiling   151
in traumatized organizations
    Christopher Scanlon and John Adlam

CHAPTER NINE
Trauma and leadership succession: congregational   173
leadership transition in the context of socio-cultural
change
    Louis B. Reed

CHAPTER TEN
Leaders and groups in traumatized and traumatizing   195
organizations: a matter of everyday survival
   Gerhard Wilke

CHAPTER ELEVEN
Organizations in traumatized societies: the Israeli case   215
   Orit Nuttman-Shwartz and Haim Weinberg

CHAPTER TWELVE
Two perspectives on a trauma in a training group: 233
the systems-centred approach and the theory of
incohesion
   Susan P. Gantt and Earl Hopper

CHAPTER THIRTEEN
Building individual resilience and organizational   255
hardiness: addressing post-trauma worker's block
   Jeffrey Kleinberg

INDEX   277

As the Editor of Trauma *and* Organizations, *I would like to dedicate this book to my wife, Cicely Cawthorne Hopper, who has helped hold the "organization" together.*

ACKNOWLEDGEMENTS

I am grateful to my colleagues with whom I have worked on the topic of trauma and organizations, and especially to those who have contributed chapters to this book. I have learnt from them and I have enjoyed their company. I am pleased to thank once again my assistant, Céline Stakol, for her invaluable administrative help in the production of this book and for her general support in working with an international collection of creative colleagues who slowly became an authorial team. I am sure that my colleagues very much appreciate the tolerance and patience of their families and friends during these years of consultation to organizations and our prolonged efforts to write about it as clearly and as discreetly as possible.

John Adlam, MA (Cantab), is Consultant Adult Psychotherapist in Reflective Practice and Team Development for forensic secure services in South London and Maudsley Foundation NHS Trust. He is also Principal Adult Psychotherapist and Lead for Group Psychotherapies at the South West London and St George's Adult Eating Disorders Service. He trained in Psychoanalytical Group Psychotherapy at the Tavistock Centre and in Forensic Psychotherapeutic Studies at the Portman Clinic. He is a member of the Psycho-Social Studies Network Steering Group; a member of the Faculty for Homeless Health and an Associate Editor of the journal *Free Associations*. He is also a group psychotherapist in private practice and a freelance organisational consultant.

Alan Corbett, DClinSci, is a psychoanalytic psychotherapist and supervisor in private practice in Dublin and London. A clinical director of the Immigrant Counselling and Psychotherapy (ICAP), a Council Member of the Guild of Psychotherapists, and a trustee of the Institute of Psychotherapy and Disability, he is also a Board member of the International Association for Forensic Psychotherapy.

Tamsin Cottis, CertEd, MA, UKCP is a Child Psychotherapist working in schools, in private practice and at Respond, where she is Clinical Lead for the Young People's Sexually Harmful Behaviours Project.

Susan Gantt, PhD, ABPP, CGP, FAGPA, FAPA, is a psychologist in private practice in Atlanta, Assistant Professor in Psychiatry at Emory University School of Medicine, and Director of the Systems-Centered Training and Research Institute. She is also a Diplomate in Group Psychology for the American Board of Professional Psychology, a consultant to organizations, and a supervisor and conference director in systems-centred training in the USA and Europe.

Robert Hinshelwood, Bsc, MB.BS, FRCPsych, is a Fellow of the British Psychoanalytical Society. He is a former consultant psychotherapist in the NHS, a former clinical director of the Cassel Hospital (1993–1994), and currently professor in the Centre for Psychoanalytic Studies, University of Essex.

Earl Hopper, PhD, is a psychoanalyst, group analyst, and organizational consultant in private practice in London. He is a Fellow of the British Psychoanalytical Society, a member of the Institute of Group Analysis, a full member of the Group Analytic Society (London), and a Fellow of the American Group Psychotherapy Association. He is also a supervisor and training analyst for the Institute of Group Analysis, the British Association of Psychotherapists and the London Centre for Psychotherapy. An honorary tutor at The Tavistock and Portman NHS Trust, and a member of the Faculty of the Post-Doctoral Program at Adelphi University, New York. He is a former President of the International Association for Group Psychotherapy and Group Processes (IAGP), and a former Chairman of the Association of Independent Psychoanalysts of the British Psychoanalytical Society.

Howard D. Kibel, MD, is a clinical professor of psychiatry at New York Medical College in Valhalla, New York, and Adjunct Clinical Professor of Psychiatry at the Weill Medical College of Cornell University, Westchester Division. He is a former President of the American Group Psychotherapy Association and a Distinguished Life Fellow of AGPA. A former member of the Board of the International Association for Group Psychotherapy and Group Processes, and the Secretary of IAGP during 2003–2006.

Jeffrey Kleinberg, PhD, is a psychoanalyst, group analyst, and organizational consultant in private practice in New York. He is also a Professor Emeritus of LaGuardia Community College, of the City University of New York, the former President of the American Group Psychotherapy Association, a former President of the Eastern Group Psychotherapy Society, and a former editor of *GROUP*.

Elizabeth Lloyd studied French at the University of Sussex and subsequently did post-graduate training there in social work and in counselling. She is a member of the Guild of Psychotherapists, a psychoanalytic psychotherapist in private practice at Respond and at the Clinic for Dissociative Studies. She lives in mid-Wales and is involved in setting up conferences and workshops on the issue of access to Welsh language psychotherapy in Welsh-speaking parts of Wales.

Susan Long, BAMed, PhD, is an organizational consultant in Melbourne. A former professor of Creative and Sustainable Organis ation at RMIT University, now an adjunct professor, she is President of the Psychoanalytic Studies Association of Australasia, and a former president of the International Society for the Psychoanalytic Study of Organizations and of Group Relations Australia.

Ellen I. McCoy, MS, was a senior executive in the oil industry where she held general management positions for multi-national and global portfolios. She has studied psychoanalytic psychology and group analysis, focusing on organizational life and leadership. She teaches courses in this subject area at Birkbeck College, University of London.

Orit Nuttman-Shwartz, PhD, MSW, CGP & GA. Associate Professor, Founder and Director of the School of Social Work at Sapir College in Israel. Chairperson, The Israeli National Council for Social Work. Her research concerns personal and social trauma, group work and therapy, life transitions and occupational crises. Located near the Israeli border, she has a particular interest in the effects of continuous exposure of individuals, communities, and organizations to the impact of an environment of collective trauma on students, supervisors, and social workers.

Louis B. Reed, DMin, is a pastoral psychotherapist residing in Charlotte, North Carolina. He has served as director of pastoral counselling centres and training programmes in south-eastern America, and currently provides education and consultation for ministers at a clergy resource centre and clinical supervision at an interdisciplinary psychotherapy institute. His clinical training was at the Institute for Religion and Health and the Washington School of Psychiatry.

Bent Rosenbaum, MDsci, is a specialist in psychiatry, and Professor at the Institute of Psychology, University of Copenhagen. He is a training analyst and a former President of the Danish Psychoanalytic Society, and the European Chair of the IPA New Group Committee as well as a member of the International Executive Committee of the International Society for the psychological treatments of schizophrenia and other psychoses (ISPS).

Christopher Scanlon, MSc, is a consultant psychotherapist in general adult and forensic mental health and organizational consultant in the NHS, and in private practice in London. He is also training group analyst and member of faculty at The Institute of Group Analysis (London); Senior Visiting Research Fellow, Centre for Psychosocial Studies, University of West England, visiting senior lecturer in Forensic Psychotherapy, St George's University of London, associate member of the Organisation for the Promotion of the Understanding of Society (OPUS); member of the International Society for Psychoanalytic Study of Organisations (ISPSO) and associate editor of *Psychoanalysis, Culture and Society* and *Free Associations*.

Haim Weinberg, PhD is a clinical psychologist and group analyst in private practice in California. He is Director of The International Program at the Professional School of Psychology, Sacramento, California, Adjunct Professor at the Wright Institute, Berkeley and at the Alliant International University, Sacramento. A faculty member of the Group Facilitators Training Program in Tel-Aviv University, he is also current President of the Northern California Group Psychotherapy Society, a former President of the Israeli Association of Group Therapy, and a former member of the Board of the International Association of Group Psychotherapy and Group Processes.

Gerhard Wilke, MA Cantab, DipFHE, is a group analyst and organizational consultant in private practice in London. He is an associate of the Ashridge Business School, a teacher on the MA Course in Group Analysis at The Institute of Group Analysis and Birkbeck College, London, a former member of the Board of the International Association for Group Psychotherapy and Group Processes, and a former member of the Executive Committee of The Group Analytic Society (London).

Gerda Winther, MA, is a clinical psychologist in private practice in Copenhagen. Formerly an associate professor, chief psychologist and co-director of a psychiatric university hospital, Past President of the Group Analytic Society (London), a former chair of the Institute of Group Analysis, Copenhagen, she is also a former member of the Board of the International Association for Group Psychotherapy and Group Processes.

David Wood, MB, BS, FRCPsych, MIGA, is a consultant child and adolescent psychiatrist, group analyst, and family therapist. He specializes in the inpatient treatment of young people suffering from anorexia nervosa. He is Clinical Director of the Ellern Mede Service for Eating Disorders in North London.

FOREWORD

Trauma and Organizations is the first book in a sub-series of The New International Library of Group Analysis concerning the study of organizations of various kinds.[1] Although the preparation of this book has been a collaborative project, it also reflects an intellectual and personal journey of my own.

During the 1970s and 1980s, I was preoccupied with the study of personal and social trauma and the social unconscious in terms of an open systems perspective. Much of this work is discussed and/or reflected in my (Hopper, 2003a) *The Social Unconscious: Selected Papers*. In a preliminary way, I argued that the experience of failed dependency on leaders and leadership was, in essence, traumatic, in terms of strain, cumulative and/or catastrophic processes, leading to feelings of profound helplessness and the fear of annihilation. Traumatized people were likely to defend themselves against such painful affects through various interpersonal processes and manoeuvres that were manifest in the structure of their groups. I discussed these structures in terms of group regression, using the concepts of aggregation and massification in order to describe two socio-cultural formations that are like phases of development that become "positions", similar to the paranoid–schizoid and depressive positions in the development of persons. I wondered if these formations and processes could be understood in terms of a fourth basic assumption in the unconscious life of groups.

In my (Hopper, 1997) Foulkes Lecture "Traumatic experience in the unconscious life of groups: a fourth basic assumption", I argued that whereas Bion's theory of three basic assumptions offered many insights into the dynamics of groups, it was possible, by acknowledging the aetiological importance of the traumatic experience of failed dependency, to conceptualize a fourth basic assumption in the unconscious life of groups and group-like social systems. I called this fourth basic assumption "Incohesion: Aggregation/Massification" or "(ba) I:A/M", and illustrated some of the hypotheses in my theory of incohesion with clinical data from group analysis with traumatized patients. In my (Hopper, 2003b) book *Traumatic Experience in the Unconscious Life of Groups*, I presented a more elaborate and detailed version of my theory of incohesion, and illustrated this with further clinical data from psychoanalysis and group analysis, including data from a group of child survivors of the Shoah. However, in this book, I did not present examples of traumatized organizations, at least, not in a single chapter showing how the theory of incohesion was relevant to the study of them.

In fact, I had been consulting to organizations since the 1970s, and to organizations in which traumatic experience was ubiquitous since the 1980s. I had come to think about these organizations as "traumatized organizations", but with the same reservations that I had about using the term "traumatized groups". I was uncertain whether to regard them as "broken", "wounded", "disintegrated", "non-functional", etc., because each word had its own theoretical implications, and was based on certain assumptions about the nature of social systems.[2] These organizations ranged in kind and size from an Embassy of a Western government in London to an international and publicly owned manufacturing firm, to a film production company, to a psychiatric hospital, to a clinic offering psychotherapy for the learning disabled, etc. They were located in many different countries, including Argentina, Australia, Hong Kong, Israel, Mexico, Northern Ireland, the UK, the USA, etc. I have worked with personnel in various echelons of these organizations, ranging, for example, from the management executive committees of boards of directors and boards of trustees to the members of teams of social workers and counsellors in local authorities, the former having a great deal of autonomy and responsibility for their own work and the work of others, and the latter having a limited scope for the interpretation of their roles, etc.

In (Hopper, 1975) my open-systems perspective, I tried to be aware of the binocular/multi-vision focus, gestalt, and frame of reference of my observations. I tried never to lose overall sight of the spiral of concentric systems and sub-systems that guided my perception of personal and social realities: organism, person, relationship, group, committee, organization, society, and globe. Thus, in any particular consultation, I sometimes focused on the challenges faced by the incumbent of a particular role, sometimes on the structure and function of the role itself, sometimes on the structure of the organization in which the role was embedded, sometimes on the wider contextual society in which the organization as a whole was located. For example, in working with the management of an organization that was regarded by its wider community as having failed to respond adequately to a deadly, disastrous fire that had engulfed a particular plant/factory, I focused: sometimes on a particular manager who was regarded as having failed in his exercise of authority in taking appropriate safety precautions; and sometimes on the dynamics of the community who had recently experienced a rapid influx of immigrants who had become the objects of envy and "resentment" by the core members of the community, and vice versa. Similarly, in working with a small institute for training psychoanalytical psychotherapists that had become so ridden with conflict that it was no longer able to continue its committee work, I focused: sometimes on a particular senior therapist who had analysed, supervised, and mentored several of the younger members of the institute, but who had been found guilty of sexual boundary breaking with one of his patients; sometimes on two of his former patients who had become his colleagues, and who were accused of similar transgressions; and sometimes on the wider contextual society in which biological psychiatry was in the ascendance and psychoanalysis in the descendance, to the point that, unfortunately, in this community, psychoanalysis had come to be regarded as a useless—if not actually a fraudulent—form of treatment.[3]

In these consultations, I was influenced by the early work of Gabbard (1989) on personal and social splitting. In so far as I focused on the personnel as incumbents of particular roles within these organizations, I consulted to both the personnel and their organizations. Actually, in so far as I always tried to understand the dynamics of these organizations in the context of the foundation matrices of the societies in which they were located, it could also be said that I was consulting to the society-as-a-whole. This was painfully obvious in Northern Ireland and in Israel. Such a broad perspective is not as grandiose as at first it might seem: after all, the incumbents of these roles within an organization go home at night and live their lives within communities within which their organizations are embedded; whether or not they are citizens of their organizations, these role incumbents are citizens of their wider societies (Hopper, 2000). Moreover, shareholders of publicly owned organizations have a right to seek access to information that is generated from the consultancy process.

The managers of these organizations often reported themselves and their employees as feeling "traumatized" and as being traumatized. By traumatized, they usually meant that they had trouble coping with a variety of painful affects, ranging, for example: from chronic and diffuse anxieties, to acute, immobilizing panics; from the vague sense of having lost confidence in their abilities to make decisions, to the fear that the teams under their management were suffering from a collapse of morale; and from a sense that their work was characterized by incompetence and even negligence, to the fear that some of their actions had been perverse and traumatizing to other people, etc. Many of these difficulties could be understood in terms of the vicissitudes of traumatic experience of failed dependency on management, whether or not management really had failed to meet any reasonable expectations of them (Galford & Seibold, 2003). If things went wrong, it was always the fault of "management"! Even the death of a senior manager was experienced as his own fault, perhaps in the same way that children cope with the death of a parent, setting in train a series of problems based on the inability and refusal to mourn, partly because such deaths are perceived as the result of unconscious but wishful assassinations (Hyde & Thomas, 2003). Although this was hardly of the same magnitude as the experience of failed dependency of, for example, the inmates of a concentration camp, or of children who were sexually abused, such processes in the world of work were disconcerting, disorientating, and profoundly painful, and tended to reawaken all previous experiences of trauma. In fact, I began to think that any consultation to the management of an organization whose personnel defined their problems in terms of failed dependency should be regarded as a consultation to a *trauma-tized* organization, and vice versa. Thus, all the members of such an organization as well as the organization-as-a-whole were likely to benefit from the explication of incohesion.

Yet, the study of traumatized organizations was faced with a number of difficult problems. We needed a model, or an "ideal type", of complex organizations that allowed for the measurement of effective and efficient performance on the basis of which variations or departures from it might be assessed and described. The theory of basic assumptions was not formulated in tandem with, and complementary to, a theory of the work group, which had usually been treated as a residual category. It was not helpful to think in terms of the "pathology" of an organization, because we had no notion of the normality and abnormality of an organization as a social system. The discussion of systemic regression required the specification of particular dimensions of regression and progression; organizations did not have "natural" lines of development, and, therefore, their lines of regression and progression could not be assumed *a priori*. The concept of the dynamic matrix of groups could not be extended to organizations without qualification, and, in any case, the concept of the dynamic matrix of groups itself needed to be developed.

It seemed to me that, although traumatic experience was rarely mentioned in the standard texts in the psychoanalytical study of organizations, people who were traumatized in the world of work were likely to defend themselves against painful affects through various interpersonal processes and manoeuvres that became manifest in the informal structures of their organizations.[4] Such organizations became like families in which incest had taken place and/or in which children had developed an eating disorder, oscillating between patterns of alienation and patterns of enmeshment.[5] Such organizations tended to lose their formal structures and to become large groups or like large groups. As such, they became characterized by the dynamics of basic assumptions, especially the dynamics of the fourth basic assumption of Incohesion.

In my consultations to traumatized organizations, I worked in dyads and in small groups, but I also worked in large groups in which I tried to include as many members of the organization as possible, from all sections and echelons of it (Kreeger, 1975; Schneider &

Weinberg, 2003). I was always surprised by how much was revealed in large groups about the unconscious life of an organization. Large group work is like a mirror in which management seldom likes what it sees, much of which it already knows. This is one of the reasons why management is so reluctant to allow large groups to be used in the consultation process (Stiers & Dluhy, 2008). Large group work requires endless negotiations with management in order to locate the right room and the right time and the right chairs, etc., and is always under constant threat of being stopped or trivialized by being turned into plenary meetings.

The study of parallel processes, projective and introjective identifications, and equivalence is essential in consultations to organizations in the media and the arts, especially when the material on exhibition includes narratives of trauma that provoke anxieties that cannot be processed and are, therefore, enacted (Gurian, 1995). In this connection one of my most interesting consultations was to Hugh Hudson, the director of *Greystoke: The Legend of Tarzan, Lord of the Apes*, concerning the script and its production, partly in Cameroon in the midst of the colonial legacy of considerable poverty and pantheistic religious traditions. The unconscious life of making a film of this kind is accurately described by Fowles (1969) in *The French Lieutenant's Woman*, which was later made into a film, and by Truffaut (1973) in *Day for Night*. It is often impossible to draw a clear line between a script, its production, and "real" life.

Consultations to traumatized organizations are always disturbing to the consultant. It is essential for him to maintain an attitude of revelation rather than salvation (Lawrence, 2000, pp. 173–178). He is obliged to discover what is true but hidden, more than to proffer advice and solutions to ill-defined problems, although this is always a matter of negotiation, balance, and emphasis. The consultant must be able to work with his own countertransference to the organization and its management who employed him. His countertransference is a source of information about the system, and not just an impediment to the work, in exactly the same way that the countertransference is an important source of information about patients in clinical sessions.

I continue to consult to traumatized organizations in many different societies. I have also begun to organize workshops on the theme of "Trouble at t' Mill", from which I learn as much as I teach: for example, at conferences and symposia of the International Association for

Group Psychotherapy and Group Processes (IAGP), the Group Analytic Society (GAS), and the American Group Psychotherapy Association (AGPA). In 2001, I initiated and convened an informal international study group of group analysts, psychoanalysts, and organizational consultants who were interested in the topic of trauma and organizations. We met in my rooms in London several times per year for five years. I also consulted to some of the members of this study group, several of whom also consulted to the management of various organizations throughout the world.

The early drafts of most of the chapters in *Trauma and Organizations* were presented to this international and interdisciplinary study group. In a way, we became one another's co-authors.[6] In fact, for me, this book is a version of the chapter on traumatized organizations that I was not yet ready to write in *Traumatic Experience in the Unconscious Life of Groups*, and a prelude of the chapter that I might yet write for a revised edition of it. Fortunately, I will be able to draw on the ideas and findings that are presented here.

Trauma and Organizations begins with an up to date outline of my theory of the basic assumption of Incohesion: Aggregation/Massification or (ba) I:A/M in the unconscious life of groups and group-like social systems. This theory informs the empirical studies of traumatized organizations and reports of consultations to them that comprise this book. The challenge is to find ways of supporting the recovery of work group functioning and, in general, supporting the forces of progression and growth, rather than regression and stagnation.

Trauma and Organizations is divided into two parts: in the first, the chapters focus on the structure and processes of organizations as systems, and in the second part, the chapters focus on leaders and leadership, with respect to both the work groups and the basic assumption groups of the organizations studied, as well as various other figurations in them. Of course, the "leader" of a basic assumption group or other kind of figuration does not mean the same thing as the "leader" of work group processes: the former is more a matter of being a central person or personifier who has become sucked into a particular role, and the latter is more a matter of trying to fulfil the requirements of the tasks of co-ordination and management.

Part I, "Processes and systems", begins with "A study of institutional change: the experience of trauma and the role of rumour in a case of paranoiagenesis", in which Howard Kibel analyses the responses to trauma that originate in the context of an organization, including the development of paranoiagenesis, the consequences of which are themselves traumatic. As an attack on truth, rumour alters the processes of communication on which an effective and efficient organization depends. He explains that under such conditions, personal identity and organizational identity become narcissistically merged, and it becomes virtually impossible to maintain effective and efficient work group processes.

In Chapter Two, "Traumatic processes in a psychiatric hospital: unconscious destructiveness of leadership change", Bent Rosenbaum and Gerda Winther describe the processes through which a generative administrative couple, which is typical of modern complex organizations, was transformed into a perverse and destructive couple whose collusive actions were traumatizing to both patients and the personnel of the organization. The traumatogenic processes originated within the societal context of the organization, but were eventually recapitulated throughout its many echelons, affecting both patients and staff. It is often impossible to break these vicious circles, partly because the life of a traumatized organization so closely reflects the life of a traumatized society.

In Chapter Three, "Trauma as cause and effect of perverse organizational process", Susan Long describes how failed dependency in an organization leads to the regressed turning away from the recognition of truth and from the honouring of commitments, which, in turn, lead to the collapse of trust and the ability and willingness to meet more informal agreements on which organizational activities are based. In this sense, perverse processes in organizations are not exciting, but destructive and stultifying, and even banal.

In Chapter Four, "Baked beans and mashed potato: incohesion: aggregation/massification in organizations treating adolescents with eating disorders", David Wood illustrates the connections between the unconscious life of highly traumatized patients with severe eating disorders and the interpersonal structures that emerge in the clinics in which they are cared for and treated. Family patterns of isolation and incestuous enmeshment are repeated within the patterns of life within wards and the clinic as a whole. Wood illustrates how the personnel of the clinic can easily be caught in the externalization of the psychic lives of the traumatized in ways that prevent and limit the efficacy of therapeutic activities.

In Chapter Five, "A study of trauma and scapegoating in the context of incohesion: an example from the oil industry", Ellen McCoy illustrates how trauma leads to complex processes of scapegoating in order to maintain states of massification as protections against the forces of aggregation that follow from the perception that management has failed to control and prevent turbulence at the boundaries of the organization and its environments. The sacrifice of individual personnel and the corruption of ethics on which this depends create the conditions for further failures to manage turbulence. The maintenance of massification depends on extremely aggressive processes, which are often sexualized in a way that makes women especially vulnerable to them. Such vicious circles can lead to the demise of the organization.

In Chapter Six, "The survival and development of a traumatized clinic for psychotherapy for people with intellectual disabilities", the team of Alan Corbett, Tamsin Cottis, and Elizabeth Lloyd show how the recapitulation within organizational structures and processes of the internal lives of the severely traumatized learning disabled and the societal devaluation of them can lead to perverse, corrupt activities on the part of "management". This is recursively traumatizing for both staff and patients. However, such processes can be modified through determined leadership and open discussion, which is inevitably painful and disturbing to all who are involved in this.

Part II, "Leaders and leadership" opens with Chapter Seven, "Personal trauma and collective disorder: the example of organizational psychodynamics in psychiatry", in which Robert Hinshelwood reviews the extent and depth of the anxieties experienced by the staff of organizations who, on behalf of both their patients and the contextual society, provide care and treatment for the mentally ill. He explains how strain and cumulative trauma characterize their professional lives, and how this is reflected recursively in the structures and processes of the organizations in which their experience is situated, which, in turn, exacerbate the anxieties of those who live within them.

In Chapter Eight, "Disorganized responses to refusal and spoiling in traumatized organizations", Christopher Scanlon and John Adlam, using eating disorders as a paradigm, examine the manifestations of the anxieties of the homeless and of the staff of organizations entrusted with the care of them, within the context of the society which itself is characterized by a myriad of traumatogenic processes. They explain how these anxieties and traumatogenic processes are encapsulated within organizations for the homeless, which, in turn, become encapsulations for the society. Unconsciously, these social–psychic retreats are used as both sanctuaries and rubbish dumps, the contents of which offer many insights into the dynamics of those who organize these locations.

In Chapter Nine, "Trauma and leadership succession: congregational leadership transition in the context of socio-cultural changes", Louis Reed explains that the anxieties associated with traumatic loss continue to influence the leadership of an organization long after the loss occurred, especially if it has not been mourned, and the anxieties associated with the loss have not been resolved, or at least understood. The idealization of the old and the denigration of the new become an obstacle to the dynamic administration of the succession of organizational leadership in a way that takes account of the changing demands of both the organization itself and its wider environments. Even within the church, the effects of trauma are transgenerational. The search for authoritarian massification leadership seems to be eternal, partly because the dependency needs of church congregations are so strong and the leadership of churches so human.

In Chapter Ten, "Leaders and groups in traumatized and traumatizing organizations: a matter of everyday survival", Gerhard Wilke, based on his comparative international and empirical research, explains that within the context of the turbulence and chaos of modern society, work within organizations no longer functions as a container for anxieties. The management of large, complex organizations is faced with the central and often primary tasks of ensuring the survival of the organization. This includes the survival of management. So much time and effort are devoted to this that one wonders what resources are left for the realization of the mission of organizations in modern society.

In Chapter Eleven, "Organizations in traumatized societies: the Israeli case", Orit Nuttman-Shwartz and Haim Weinberg show how the traumatogenic processes of the wider society are constantly recapitulated within their organizations, especially when the dynamic matrices of these organizations are associated with ideologies that are central to the foundation matrix, and with the management and containment of painful anxieties within the wider society. They also examine the pressures on leaders to personify basic assumption processes. They ask under what circumstances are work-group processes likely to prevail, and whether leaders of work groups will emerge, and whether their succession is ensured.

In Chapter Twelve, "Two perspectives on a trauma in a training group: the systems-centred approach and the theory of incohesion", Susan Gantt and Earl Hopper describe a traumatic event and its aftermath within a training course, based on reports from participants, including Gantt and Hopper, who were invited to observe retrospectively their experience of the event. These traumatogenic processes are described and analysed from the point of view of the theory of living human systems and systems-centred practice, as developed by Yvonne Agazarian, and from the point of view of Hopper's theory of the basic assumption of Incohesion: Aggregation/Massification. Noting the differences between these two points of view, it is suggested that systems-centred practice can and should be developed for consultation to organizations, especially those that have been traumatized.

In Chapter Thirteen, "Building individual resilience and organizational hardiness: addressing post-trauma worker's block", Jeffrey Kleinberg, based on his work with a variety of organizations in the aftermath of the 9/11 terrorist tragedies in the USA, explains that some organizations and their personnel are more capable than others of surviving traumatogenic challenges to their very existence. However, organizational hardiness and resilience are the products of the decisions and actions of the personnel and management of an organization, and they can be developed and fostered. Hopefulness in an organization is an essential element of work-group processes, and not merely a matter of manic defences associated with basic assumption group processes.

It is altogether right that *Trauma and Organizations* should end with a study of hardiness, resilience, and hope. Many traumatized organizations do not recover, or at least do not recover very efficiently, from the experience of failed dependency. Some organizations are even doomed to repeat the vicissitudes of traumatic experience that seem to have been encoded in their own conception and inauguration, and, thus, that have made them especially vulnerable to later traumatic events.[7] However, still other organizations are able to make creative use of traumatic experience. They are able to rally, grow, and prosper, perhaps taking new forms and developing new goals and missions. I hope that this book contributes to our efforts to understand variations in individual, group, and organizational survival of traumatic experience.[8]

Notes

1. For example, I am working with Victor Schermer, Cecil Rice, and others on a Special Issue of *The International Journal of Group Psychotherapy* about trauma and organizations, which we hope to develop into a book, and with Haim Weinberg and others on a volume about the social unconscious and dynamic matrices of organizations.

2. In personal communication, Kenneth Eisold has shared these reservations. See also the "Introduction" to Hopper and Weinberg (2011), in which the problems of using these analogies and homologies are discussed in terms of the implications of regarding social systems as organisms, persons, machines, etc.

3. The work of Gabbard and Lester (1995) was especially helpful to me. However, I learnt that in traumatized organizations boundary breaking in the form of sexual harassment and seduction is commonplace, as seen, for example, in the behaviour of senior male managers towards their female secretaries and assistants, of male university lecturers towards their female students, of male physicians towards nurses, of male therapists towards their patients and supervisees, etc. These exploitative activities are not merely a matter of living a sophisticated libertine way of life, but both a source of traumatic experience and a product of it. Of course, nowadays, the perpetrators and the victims of such abuse might be male or female. It was on the basis of this work that I wrote the "Introduction" to *Compromise* by John Woods (2007), a play concerning boundary violations in psychotherapy training organizations in London.

4. For example, consider the excellent and comprehensive text written and edited by Yiannis Gabriel (1999) with contributions from colleagues.

5. This set of observations is entirely consistent with those of Hormann and Vivian (2005) and Vivian and Hormann (2002), who have shown that the patterns of interaction within traumatized families can also be seen in large, complex organizations that have been traumatized, and, similarly, with the observations of Kahn (2003), who has focused on care-giving organizations, such as schools.

6. Although their participation in the study group was invaluable, Ann Allen, John Hook, and Melvyn Rose decided not to write chapters for the book. On occasion, Wil Pennycook-Greaves and Christer Sandahl participated in our discussions.

7. Marina Mojović (2011) has coined the term 'conception trauma', which may even contribute to birth trauma in both people and metaphorically their groupings.

8. I had planned to write an Introduction and an Epilogue for this book with my friend and colleague Gordon Lawrence, one of the founders in Britain of the psychoanalytical and group analytical study of organizations (for example, see Lawrence (1979)). Unfortunately, Gordon is ill, and it is impossible for us to complete this task together. We have been meeting regularly for several years for dinner and discussion, trying to specify the parameters of what might be regarded as the group analytic study of organizations, drawing from the work of Freud, Klein, and Winnicott, as well as Bion and Foulkes, and from the literature associated with the group relations/Tavistock tradition as well as that associated with the group analytic tradition. I have benefited from his generously shared knowledge and insights. I hope that we will resume our discussions soon. We are still trying to conceptualize the dynamic matrix of an organization as distinct from that of a group.

References

Fowles, J. (1969). *The French Lieutenant's Woman*. London: Jonathan Cape.

Gabbard, G. O. (1989). Splitting in hospital treatment. *American Journal of Psychiatry, 146*(4): 944–989.

Gabbard, G. O., & Lester, E. P. (1995). *Boundaries and Boundary Violations in Psychoanalysis*. New York: Basic Books.

Gabriel, Y. (1999). *Organizations in Depth*. London: Sage.

Galford, R., & Seibold, A. (2003). *The Trusted Leader*. New York: Free Press.

Gurian, E. (Ed.) (1995). *Institutional Trauma*. Washington, DC: American Association of Museums.

Hopper, E. (1975). A sociological view of large groups. In: L. Kreeger (Ed.), *The Large Group: Dynamics and Therapy*. London: Constable (reprinted London: Karnac, 1994, and in E. Hopper (2003) *The Social Unconscious: Selected Papers*. London: Jessica Kingsley.

Hopper, E. (1997). 21st S. H. Foulkes Annual Lecture, 'Traumatic experience in the unconscious life of groups: a fourth basic assumption'. *Group Analysis, 30*(4): 439–471.

Hopper, E. (2000). From objects and subjects to citizens: group analysis and the study of maturity. *Group Analysis, 33*(1): 29–34.

Hopper, E. (2003a). *The Social Unconscious: Selected Papers*. London: Jessica Kingsley.

Hopper, E. (2003b). *Traumatic Experience in the Unconscious Life of Groups: The Fourth Basic Assumption: Incohesion: Aggregation/Massification or (ba) I:A/M*. London: Jessica Kingsley.

Hopper, E., & Weinberg, H. (Eds.) (2011). *The Social Unconscious in Persons, Groups and Societies: Volume I: Mainly Theory*. London: Karnac.

Hormann, S., & Vivian, P. (2005). Toward an understanding of traumatized organizations and how to intervene in them. *Traumatology, 11*(3): 159–169.

Hyde, P., & Thomas, A. (2003). When a leader dies. *Human Relations, 56*(8): 1005–1024.

Khan, W. A. (2003). The revelation of organizational trauma. *The Journal of Applied Behavioral Science, 39*, 4, 364–380.

Kreeger, L. (Ed.). (1975). *The Large Group: Dynamics and Therapy*. London: Constable (reprinted London: Karnac, 1994).

Lawrence, W. G. (Ed.) (1979). *Exploring Individual and Organizational Boundaries*. Chichester: John Wiley.

Lawrence, W. G. (2000). *Tongued With Fire: Groups in Experience*. London: Karnac.

Mojović, M. (2011). Personal communication.

Schneider, S., & Weinberg, H. (Eds). (2003). *The Large Group Re-Visited*. London: Jessica Kingsley.

Stiers, M., & Dluhy, M. (2008). The large group and the organizational unconsciousness. *Group, 34*: 251–260.

Truffaut, F. (1973). *Day for Night*. Film.

Vivian, P., & Hormann, S. (2002). Trauma and healing in organizations. *O.D. Practitioner, 34*(4): 52–57.

Woods, J. (2007). The Play by John Woods. In: *Compromise: A Play About Psychotherapy*. London: Open Gate Press.

The theory of Incohesion: Aggregation/Massification as the fourth basic assumption in the unconscious life of groups and group-like social systems

Earl Hopper

Although I (Hopper, 2003) have developed my theory of the basic assumption of Incohesion: Aggregation/Massification or (ba) I:A/M in *Traumatic Experience in the Unconscious Life of Groups*, and have clarified and refined this theory in more recent publications (for example, Hopper, 2005a, 2009, 2010), I believe that this summary is the most lucid statement of it. The key text is *Experiences in Groups* (Bion, 1961), and further discussion and applications of Bion's ideas about groups can be found in, for example, "Bion's contribution to thinking about groups" (Menzies-Lyth, 1981), and *Tongued with Fire: Groups in Experience* (Lawrence, 2000), which include extensive bibliography.

The term "group" indicates a social system that is a group, and not some other kind of social system. Although all groups are social systems, not all social systems are groups. A group is not, for example, a committee, but a committee is a group. Similarly, a group is not a family, but a family is a group, and is sometimes called a "family group". Neither is a group an organization, a society, or a village, etc. It is sometimes useful to refer to an "actual group" in order to indicate that a particular social system is, in fact, a group and not some other kind of social system.

Actual groups might be understood in terms of their work group dynamics and/or their basic assumption group dynamics, which is a matter of the frame of reference and the gestalt of the observer of them. However, generalizations about work groups are rare, primarily because there are so many different kinds of work group, and they evince such a vast range of variation in parameters, such as size and complexity. None the less, it is widely agreed that the effectiveness and efficiency of work groups are manifest in their social cohesion, which is expressed in the integration (as opposed to the disintegration) of their interaction systems, the solidarity (as opposed to the insolidarity) of their normative systems, and in the coherence (as opposed to the incoherence) of their communication systems, and in many other dimensions of their organization, such as styles of thinking and feeling, and various aspects of leadership, followership, and bystandership.[1] Although the dynamics of work groups can be studied psychoanalytically (Armstrong, 2005), a more complete understanding of them is best served by the social sciences.

Although the work group might use the mentality of basic assumption processes in the service of its work, the basic assumption group is, in essence, both pathological and pathogenic. The pathology and pathogenesis of the basic assumption group are expressed unconsciously in terms of the dynamics of various so-called "basic assumptions". Using a Kleinian model of the mind, Bion (1961) conceptualized three basic assumptions associated with specific kinds of anxieties, processes, and roles: Dependency, associated with envy, idealization, and the roles of omnipotence and grandiosity, on the one hand, and with the roles of passive compliance and low self-esteem, on the other; Fight/Flight, associated with envy, denigration, and roles of attack, on the one hand, and retreat, on the other; Pairing, associated with the use of sexuality as a manic defence against depressive position anxieties and the roles of romantic coupling, on the one hand, and their messianic progeny, on the other. I would suggest that there are two variants of the basic assumption of Pairing: one concerns the conception and birth of the new and desirable; the other, which I (Hopper, 2003) have termed "perverse pairing", concerns the use of pain under the guise of pleasure leading to stasis and an absence of fertility and creativity.

Many Kleinian students of basic assumption theory have argued that it is impossible to conceptualize more than these three basic assumptions, because the Kleinian model of the mind, from which the theory of these three basic assumptions is derived, does not permit the conceptualization of a fourth. However, using an alternative model of the mind, I have conceptualized a fourth basic assumption in the unconscious life of groups. This model of the mind is associated with the work of many of the founding members of the Group of Independent Psychoanalysts of the British Psychoanalytical Society, such as Fairbairn, Balint, and Winnicott, and is shared by many sociologists and group analysts. Its central tenet is that, although it is important to study envy, it is more important to study helplessness, shame, and traumatic experiences within the context of interpersonal relationships, which are at the centre of the human condition. In this model, envy does not arise from the death instinct, but is a defensive or protective development against the fear of annihilation, and is directed towards spoiling the resources of people who are perceived as potentially helpful but who do not or will not actually help. In other words, envy might be more of a protective defence than it is a primary impulse.[2]

The basic assumption of Incohesion: Aggregation/Massification or (ba) I:A/M

Derived from this model of the mind, in which traumatic experience within the context of the relational matrix is privileged over envy and the putative death instinct, my theory of the fourth basic assumption provides a bridge between the Bionian study of "group relations" and Foulkesian "group analysis", and, in a way, between psychoanalysis and sociology. I call this fourth basic assumption "Incohesion: Aggregation/Massification' or, in the tradition of the literature concerning basic assumptions, "(ba) I:A/M". Although each of the three basic assumptions conceptualized by Bion is, in a sense, a source of incohesion in groups, this fourth basic assumption pertains specifically to the dynamics of incohesion. It indicates that the very survival of the group is in question.

The bi-polar forms of Incohesion are Aggregation and Massification "Aggregation" and "Massification" refer to the processes through which and by which the group becomes either an aggregate or a mass. The terms "aggregate" and "mass" are taken from early sociology and logy. The underlying basic assumption is that the group is not group, but is either an aggregate or a mass. Although a mass o be more cohesive than an aggregate, in fact these two bi-polar of incohesion are equally incohesive. They are transitory and pable of sustaining co-operative work.

An aggregate is neither a group nor merely a collection of people no have absolutely no consciousness of themselves as being members of a particular social system. An aggregate is a very simple social formation that is barely a social system at all. The members of it hardly relate to one another. They are often silent for long periods of time, and engage in various forms of non-communication in general: for example, gaze-avoidance. Among the metaphors for an aggregate are a collection of billiard balls or a handful of gravel. However, these metaphors are not quite right, because they utilize inorganic objects, and it is important to recognize that an aggregate involves a degree of libidinous interpersonal attachment. A better metaphor would be a bowl of whitebait, or a flock of ostriches, flamingos, or penguins, the flock having survival value. If sub-grouping does occur, it takes the form of contra-grouping rather than differentiation, specialization, and co-operation.

A "mass" also refers to a social system that is not quite a group. However, whereas an aggregate is characterized by too much individuality, a mass is characterized by too little. Whereas an aggregate refers, for example, to a collection of people who are window shopping while strolling down a street, or who are walking through a tube station in order to catch many different trains, or heading for the exit, a mass refers, for example, to a highly charged political demonstration or rally in a confined location. In the former situations, people rarely touch one another, but in the latter they are so physically close that in any other situation they would be experienced as violating one another's sense of personal space, and might even be accused of frotteurism. Whereas in an aggregate people avoid one another's gazes, in a mass they are mesmerized through staring into one another's eyes or focusing on an object that they hold in common. Whereas the silence of an aggregate is one of diffidence, non-recognition, and non-communication, the silence of a mass is rooted in a shared sense of awe and wonder in which people feel that they do not need words or even gestures in order to communicate. In fact, a mass of people prefers slogans and jargon to careful exposition, but most of all they prefer the silence of "true communication". Among the metaphors for a mass are a piece of basalt, a nice piece of chopped fish, or a *quenelle de brochette* (in which the fish from which it has been made can no longer be recognized as a fish, let alone as several fishes), a chunk of faeces, or a handful of wet sponges squeezed together. The metaphor of a herd of walruses is also useful.[3] Of course, during states of massification, neither sub-grouping nor contra-grouping is likely to occur, virtually by definition.

It is well known that Turquet (1975, p. 103) referred to the state of aggregation in terms of "dissaroy", which was his neologism for social, cultural, and political chaotic disorder, and that Lawrence, Bain, and Gould (1996, p. 29) referred to it in terms of "me-ness". Similarly, Turquet (1975) referred to the state of massification in terms of "oneness", and Lawrence and his colleagues (1996) in terms of "we-ness". Although these neologisms are appealing, in fact most social scientists would favour the use of the terms "aggregate" and "mass", and, therefore, aggregation and massification. This is not merely a matter of semantics. In fact, these technical terms cover the confluences of interaction, normation, communication, and styles of thinking and feeling that characterise these polarized states, and go beyond the distinction that Bion made between narcissism and socialism.

Group trauma and the unconscious life of the group

Incohesion is caused by trauma and traumatogenic processes. Before outlining the main steps of these processes, I will stress that personal traumas are different from, but overlapping with, group trauma. Group trauma could occur in several interrelated ways: for example,

- through management failures on the part of the group analyst, or by other events that break the boundaries of holding and containment, causing the members of the group to feel profoundly helpless and unsafe;
- the members of the group regress to an early phase of life in which certain kinds of traumatic experience are virtually universal and ubiquitous;
- the members of the group share a history of specific kinds of trauma;

- processes of equivalence occur through which traumatic events and processes within the contextual foundation matrix of the group are imported and then enacted.

Group trauma provokes social and cultural regression and the collapse of boundaries between people and their groupings. Therefore, it is only in these circumstances that the language and concepts of personal trauma are really apposite for the study of group trauma. This is also why I try not to refer to the life of a group but to the "life" of a group, conscious or otherwise.[4]

Failed dependency and the vicissitudes of feeling of profound helplessness and the fear of annihilation[5]

The first step in the process through which trauma causes incohesion is that, through various combinations of strain, cumulative and/or catastrophic experience of failed dependency on parental figures is likely to provoke feelings of profound helplessness and the fear of annihilation. The phenomenology of the fear of annihilation involves psychic paralysis and the death of psychic vitality, characterized by fission and fragmentation, and then fusion and confusion of what is left of the self with what can be found in the object. Fusion and confusion are defences against fission and fragmentation, and vice versa: the fear of falling apart and of petrification is associated with fission and fragmentation; the fear of suffocation and of being swallowed up is associated with fusion and confusion, but the former offers protection against the latter, and vice versa.

Each psychic pole is also associated with both its own characteristic psychotic anxieties and its own characteristic modes of defence against them. Ultimately, disassociation and *especially* encapsulation occur as defences or protection against the fear of annihilation, which is characterized by psychic motion but not by psychic movement or psychic development.

These bi-polar intrapsychic constellations are associated with two types of personal organization: one, the "contact shunning" or "crustacean", and two, the "merger-hungry" or "amoeboid". These two types of personal organization have often been delineated in similar terms: for example, the crustacean type as a schizoid reaction against the fear of engulfment, and the amoeboid type as a clinging reaction against the fear of abandonment (e.g., Rosenfeld, 1965).

Traumatized people tend to oscillate between these bi-polar intra-psychic constellations, and crustacean and amoeboid character disorders are very common among people who have been traumatized. Such disorders are apparent among people with gender dysphoria and in more narcissistic homosexuals, whose characteristic "not-me" psychic postures oscillate with fusionary identifications as a way of protecting themselves from psychotic anxieties. Such disorders are also associated with perversions, which are often characterized by early traumatic experience.

The traumatogenic and interpersonal origins of the basic assumption of incohesion

Thus, the basic assumption of Incohesion: Aggregation/Massification or (ba) I:A/M derives from the fear of annihilation and its two characteristic forms of personal organization. The second step in the process through which trauma gives rise to incohesion is that, with respect to those states of mind characterized by fission and fragmentation in oscillation with fusion and confusion, traumatized people tend to use projective and introjective identifications involving the repetition compulsion and traumatophilia (that is, the love and craving for traumatic experience) in the service of the expulsion of their horrific states of mind, and in their attempts to attack and control their most hated objects. These processes are also used in the service of communication of experience that is not available through conscious narrative. In fact, traumatized people feel unconsciously compelled to tell the stories of their traumatic experience.

When they are unable to tell their stories, perhaps because they have no one to listen to them, or when they are unable to tell their stories in a particular way, perhaps according to ritualized procedures, traumatized people attempt unconsciously to communicate through enactments, which might be studied from various points of view in connection with various forms of psycho-pathology. Enactments are of particular interest to forensic psychotherapists, because they involve a failure of the symbolic process.[6] Within the context of a group, enactments also involve processes of resonance, amplification, and mirroring. Thus, such enactments precipitate the emergence of the basic assumption of Incohesion.

Patterns of enacting the intrapsychic dynamics of traumatic experiences

With respect to the bipolar forms of incohesion, the group is likely, in the first instance, to become an "aggregate" through a process of "aggregation", in response to the fear of annihilation as manifest in the psychic processes of fission and fragmentation. However, as a defence against the anxieties associated with aggregation, the group is likely to become a mass through a process of massification. This is partly in response to the fear of annihilation as manifest in the psychic processes of fusion and confusion of what is left of the self with another. The process of massification also involves the "hysterical" idealization of the situation and the leader, and identification with him and the group itself, as well as with its individual members, leading to feelings of pseudo-morale and illusions of well-being. However, the first group-based defence against the anxieties associated with massification is a shift back towards aggregation, thus precipitating the same anxieties that provoked the first defensive shift from aggregation towards massification.

Thus, a group-like social system in which the fear of annihilation is prevalent is likely to be characterized by oscillation between aggregation and massification. However, such oscillations are rarely total and complete, and, at any one time, vestiges of aggregation can be seen in states of massification, and vestiges of massification in states of aggregation. Moreover, each polar state can become located simultaneously in different parts of a social system, and even in different geographical locations.

Oscillations between aggregation and massification are not only a matter of the externalization of intrapsychic and interpsychic processes. Such oscillations are also a product of the dynamics of these two socio-cultural states, involving, for example, nomogenic responses to the anomogenic forces of aggregation, and differentiation and specialization in response to the anomogenization and homogenization that are typical of massification (Hopper, 1981).

Sub-grouping characterizes the first phases of the shift from aggregation to massification, in the same way that contra-grouping characterizes the first phase of a shift from massification back to aggregation. Sub-groups and contra-groups can become more clearly demarcated in the service of attempts to purify the system-as-a-whole; their boundaries become more and more rigid and impermeable, and silence and secrecy prevail.

Intrapsychic encapsulations are the basis of various kinds of subgroups and contra-groups. These groupings are the basis of various kinds of social–psychic retreat.

The emergent roles and their personifications by crustaceans and amoeboids

During oscillations between aggregation and massification, many typical roles emerge. The role of whistle-blower is typical of states of massification, as is the role of jester or fool. The role of stable-cleaner, characterized by a sense of mistrust, in-fighting, and refusal to co-operate is typical of states of aggregation, as is the role of the endearing but ineffectual peacemaker. More generally, "lone wolf" roles are typical of aggregation and "cheerleader" roles are typical of massification.

Whereas Individual Members (Turquet, 1975) and Citizens (de Maré, 1991; Hopper, 2000) are likely to fill the leadership roles that are properties of the structure of work groups, Singletons and Isolates (Turquet, 1975) are likely to fill aggregation roles, and Membership Individuals (Turquet, 1975) massification roles. In other words, traumatized people with crustacean character structures are likely to become lone wolves, and those with amoeboid character structures are likely to become cheerleaders. As Foulkes would have put it, the former are likely to *personify* aggregation processes, and the latter, massification processes. As Bion would have put it, such people have *valences* for these roles. And as Kernberg, following Redl, would have put it, such people are exceedingly vulnerable to "role suction", because specific roles offer them skins of identity. However, traumatized people are also likely to create the roles in question. Thus, this process is recursive, and the basis of the relations between personal systems and group systems.

Alford (2001) has provided a profoundly incisive analysis of whistle-blowers, to which I would add moral masochism in the form of altruistic surrender (Freud, A., 1922). I would also suggest that it is only a matter of time before someone is sucked into the role of whistle-blower.[7] Whistle-blowers are often scapegoated in the search for people to blame for aggregation, involving the splintering of relationships and the state of mind associated with this, and the violation of the sense of perfect conformity and purity and the state of mind associated with this.

The role of jester allows its incumbents to speak the truth, as they see it, sometimes outrageously, often with humour and irony. The incumbents of this role often have an attractive, adolescent quality, which carries a degree of self-protection for them, which tends to blunt the acuity of their message.

The myth of Hercules is entirely apposite to a description of the role of stable cleaner: there is so much to do in order to ensure the survival of the organization! The female incumbents of the role of stable cleaner often become the housekeepers and cleaning ladies of the organization, roles that they have rejected within the realms of their own domesticity. The male incumbents are more like workaholics who sacrifice themselves to the "firm" and to an older male mentor. Stable cleaners are not always reliable, and might suddenly take revenge on their mentors and the organizations as a whole.

The role of peacemaker tends to suck in those who become the voice of platitude and homilies. The peacemaker idealizes the need for compromise, but denigrates the recognition of the importance of taking tough decisions that are necessary for survival.

These roles and their incumbents have been described by Shakespeare with brilliance and acuity. Briefly: *Julius Caesar* is an examination of a traumatized society and its traumatized governmental organizations. I suppose that Brutus is the main personifier of the whistle-blowing role, although others in the group of assassins and saviours should be considered. With respect to the "fool", any of the plays in which Falstaff appears is relevant, but the fool aspect of the role of Caliban is also important. With respect to the peacemaker, consider Gonzalo in *The Tempest*, and Menenius in *Coriolanus*. So much horror follows the refusal to face reality (Hopper, 2003)!

Aggressive feelings and aggression

Aggressive feelings and aggression are especially important in the dynamics of incohesion. Both crustacean (contact-shunning characters) and amoeboid (merger-hungry characters) are likely to personify the processes of aggression associated with incohesion. They have great difficulty in acknowledging and experiencing aggressive feelings, not only in themselves but also in others. However, when crustaceans become angry, they become cold and over-contained; when amoeboids become angry, they become intrusive and engulfing, based on their tendencies towards vacuole incorporation.

The crustacean personification of the group's rampant aggressive feelings in states of aggregation is fairly easy to understand. It reflects a sense of one against all, and all against one, each and every one.

In contrast, the amoeboid personification of the group's aggressive feelings in states of massification is much more difficult to understand. It is important to recognize the forms of aggression that are typical of massification processes. One form of aggression involves the actual maintenance of massification processes: the manipulation of moral norms and moral judgements in such a way as to control the processes through which certain people and their sub-groups and contra-groups are labelled as deviant, immoral, and corrupt, which leads to their marginalization and peripheralization. Also important are anonymization, rumour-mongering, and character assassination, if not actual assassination. Of course, processes of scapegoating and more general attacks on all those who are defined as "Others" or as "Not Me" support massification processes. In fact, the fatal purification of the system of all that is different, strange, and foreign is central to the study of traumatized social systems. Terrorism involves the use of violence in the service of purification.

Threats to personal and group identity

(ba) I:A/M is an acronym for the first three letters of the words Incohesion: Aggregation/Massification. However, I:A/M can also be read as "I am!",[8] which is an assertion of personal identity when identity is felt to be threatened. As in the dynamics of exhibitionism, an assertion of identity is not as convincing as an expression of identity based on authentic feeling and belief. An assertion of identity is based on grandiosity and fantasies of omnipotence and omniscience, which come into being when dependency fails, that is, when our parents and our leaders fail us and disappoint us. Such affects and ideas are associated with traumatic experience.

The dynamics of the assertion "I am!" are closely related to the assertion "I am not!", as Winnicott (1955) realized in his discussion of the development of identity as a function of what he called "unit status", in terms of becoming aware of what is "not me", that is, of what one is not within a particular group context. It is in this sense that one develops a sense of being both a subject and an object simultaneously, a self and another, both from the point of view of oneself as a subject and from the point of view of another person as an "other". None the less, regression to this phase of development involves the experience that one's identity is threatened and, thus, is associated with either too much me-ness and too much not-meness, on the one hand, or with too much we-ness and us-ness, on the other.

Under conditions of optimal cohesion, the willingness and ability of the members of a group to refer to their sense of "we-ness" and "us-ness" indicate that a social system exists, as do notions of collective identity and of membership. We-ness and us-ness also develop in tandem with a sense of you-ness and other-ness. In this, there is a shared recognition of a boundary concerning who is inside and who is outside, or who should be included and who excluded from a particular social system (Stacey, 2005).

In contrast, the assertions "We are!" and "We are not!" suggest that the existence of the group is under threat, because otherwise there would be no need for the members of the group to assert their identity as members of it. "We are!" and "We are not!" might be statements by the members of a group during states of massification, but such statements are not possible during states of aggregation, because people lack a sense of we-ness and us-ness. The reason why these processes can be conceptualized in terms of a so-called "basic assumption" is that people who have regressed because their groups are under threat enact their fantasy that they are not a group but an aggregate, or a mass, both of which are states of collective being that offer protection from extreme anxieties.

Applications

The basic assumption of Incohesion occurs in traumatized societies.[9] Social traumas range from strain trauma, such as stagflation, to catastrophic trauma, such as economic and natural disasters. Massification breeds nationalism and fascism, which are always associated with racialism of various kinds. Fascism can be understood as a set of properties of interaction and normation systems. Despite their inequalities of economic and status power, all members of massified systems become equal with respect to their commitment to shared core values and norms. Fundamentalism can be understood as a set of properties of the communication system. Fundamentalism involves the transformation of words into objects, based on the ritualization of language (Klimova, 2011).

Although the protection of socio-cultural diversity is essential for the long-term survival of the society as a whole, encapsulated contraformations are, in essence, enclaves and ghettos, which might be sanctuaries for those within them, but might also be sources of suffocation (Mojović, 2011). Although life within enclaves and ghettos might be culturally rich and nourishing, these social–psychic retreats might also be rubbish dumps that reflect processes of splitting and projection that lead to the depletion and distortion of the "cultural capital" of the society as a whole.

The basic assumptions of traumatized societies are likely to be perpetuated across the generations, recapitulated by macro-social systems and by their component micro-social systems, and vice versa. Based on projective and introjective identifications and other forms of interaction and communication between parents and children, teachers and students, etc., these processes occur within the foundation matrices of contextual social systems. In order for people to break these vicious circles and cycles of equivalence, adequate and authentic mourning and reparation are necessary. Yet, people rarely have or take opportunities for such work. Actually, unauthentic, ritualized mourning can make matters worse. Circles of perversion, in the sense of turning away from the truth, involve chosen traumatic events and the perpetuation of sadomasochistic experience (Long, 2008, and in Chapter Three of this volume). After all, if the golden rule of civilized societies and mature people is to do unto others as you wish them to do unto you, then the leaden rule of traumatized and regressed societies is to do unto others as you have been done by.

Of special interest are those spontaneous communities that emerge after disasters of various kinds, such as floods and earthquakes. Although they are highly transitory, tending to become structured and institutionalized very quickly, they evince the defining parameters of large groups. Under certain circumstances, the members of these groups are extremely altruistic (Solnit, 2009), but I wonder whether this is an expression of massification as a defence against aggregation, and, thus, an example of how people make use of the basic assumption of Incohesion in the service of survival. Knowledge of (ba) I:A/M should inform the work of government agencies and local and community authorities in their interventions in the aftermath of natural disasters.

The fourth basic assumption of Incohesion is typical of traumatized organizations, and perhaps especially of organizations within traumatized societies. It is especially typical of prisons, mental hospitals, and, perhaps, even our professional societies and training institutes in which the capacity to suffer mental anguish is virtually a criterion for admission. Large, complex organizations are especially vulnerable to aggregation and massification, because they are, in essence, composed of units of various kinds, both with respect to their membership populations and with respect to sets of roles. This involves the paradox of complexity in which aggregation is characterized by excessive differentiation and specialization of work combined with the greater need for co-ordination of it. Knowledge of (ba) I:A/M should inform the work of consultants to traumatized organizations.

The basic assumption of incohesion is also typical of large groups, in which the trauma of regression is ubiquitous and often overwhelming. Large groups are especially vulnerable to aggregation, and, therefore, massification is also typical of them. However, although we work in and with large groups in conferences, large groups rarely occur in "social situ", with certain exceptions, such as certain kinds of audience, meeting, and rally. They can be constructed within organizations in order to facilitate the consultation process, in which case they tend to function as mirrors for the organization as a whole, and, thus, as an important source of information about the organization as a whole.

With respect to small groups in the context of traumatized organizations and organizations associated with trauma, the unconscious life of committees tends to be characterized by constant oscillations between aggregation and massification, which is why it is so difficult to accomplish their work agendas over a reasonable period of time. The members of such committees have difficulty in co-operating with one another, and in holding a sense of common purpose. Similarly, committees can become massified, as seen in the tendency of their members to agree with one another all the time, and to intrude into one another's work. Although patience in the chairmanship of such committees is certainly a virtue, it is often necessary to acknowledge the anxieties that threaten to overwhelm the members of them, and offer the space for discussion of the personal dimensions of the work.

The basic assumption of Incohesion also occurs in small groups that meet in order to study themselves or for the purpose of providing psychotherapy for their members, especially for the treatment of traumatized patients. In these treatment groups, all attempts by patients to express their individualities must be treated with care, because "individuality" might actually indicate schizoid isolation and an inability and refusal to co-operate with others, or be a step towards volunteering to become a scapegoat. The emotional life of treatment groups characterized by incohesion is likely to be either very cold or laden with affect. Intense demands are made on the group analyst and his use of countertransference processes (Hopper, 2005b). It is especially difficult to help clinical groups of forensic patients, who are often caught in the throes of enacting and perpetuating traumatic experience (Welldon, 2009). None the less, the personification of this basic assumption must not be met with containment and holding forever, but subjected to understanding and interpretation.

Yet, the basic assumption of Incohesion: Aggregation/Massification or (ba) I:A/M does not constitute a closed system. Incessant and eternal oscillations between aggregation and massification are not inevitable. People and their groupings can be resilient and can manifest mature hope. This depends on the development of citizenship and the recognition of the rights of others. It also depends on our making identifications with people who will be alive after we have died. These are the key elements of the transcendent imagination. I believe that pure and applied psychoanalysis and group analysis might be of help in the realization of this "project", in the existentialist sense of the term.

Notes

1. The nature of social cohesion depends on the type of social system in question. For example, the main source of the cohesion of a societal social system is the integration of the patterns of interaction of its work group, whereas the main source of the cohesion of an actual group is the coherence of the patterns of communication of its work group. The reason why the cohesion of an actual group depends primarily on the coherence of its communication system is that so many of an actual group's essential functions are fulfilled by people and organizations within its social context. For example, an actual group does not have to provide for the economic needs of its members, because these needs are met through activities in its wider social context.

2. This is not merely a piece of esoteric meta-psychology. In his Introduction to *Traumatic Experience in the Unconscious Life of Groups*, Lionel Kreeger suggested that, in essence, I had repunctuated Turquet's work, and, in so doing, changed its meaning. In so far as it was Kreeger (1975) who extensively shaped Turquet's notes into the now famous "Threats to identity in the large group" in *The Large Group: Dynamics and Therapy*, Kreeger's comment was really a suggestion that I had repunctuated his version of Turquet's argument. I think that apart from using the sociological concepts "aggregate" and "mass", rather than Turquet's neolisms of "dissaroy" and "oneness", and apart from making several clarifications of his argument, my main departure from Turquet's theory was to emphasize the importance of trauma and the relational matrix. This slight turn of the kaleidoscope of psychoanalytical theory permitted the conceptualization of the fourth basic assumption of incohesion, which really should be regarded as the first of the four, because it is prior to Dependency. In other words, unless trauma is privileged over envy, it is impossible to conceptualize a basic assumption that is prior to Dependency, which is based on envy and idealization, which, in the Kleinian model, are assumed to be primary.

3. It is hardly surprising that when I lectured on this topic in Dublin, several women in the audience suggested that whereas a bowl of boiled potatoes is the perfect icon for aggregation, a bowl of mashed potatoes is perfect for massification. Potatoes are a potent symbol of traumatic experience in

Ireland (and in some other countries, too), involving starvation, on the one hand, and emigration and loss, on the other. During the discussion, an argument ensued about the best way to make mashed potatoes. I remember thinking that, in much the same way that a shift towards aggregation provides transitory relief from the pain of massification, a simple bowl of boiled potatoes would have settled the argument.

4. It is important to remember that although in the study of social systems it is sometimes useful to think in terms of organismic and "personistic" *analogies*, it is rarely useful to think in terms of organismic and personistic *homologies*. Social systems are *like* organisms and persons, but they are *not* organisms and persons. This distinction is especially relevant to the study of social systems that are changing, and when they are characterized by political conflict. (Incidentally, the same points can be made with respect to the use of "mechanistic" analogies and homologies, although they have the opposite implications.) Although it is not entirely apposite to this outline of my theory of incohesion, I and Weinberg (2011) have discussed this issue in greater depth in the Introduction to *The Social Unconscious in Persons, Groups and Societies: Volume I: Mainly Theory*. Also, since writing this particular outline, I have read Weinberg's (2006) discussion of regression in groups, which provides a useful review of the literature on regression in social systems and some clinical illustrations of this.

5. I have learnt from Gordon Lawrence that more or less at the same time that I began to use the notion of failed dependency, Eric Miller (1993) also began to use this term, although we were working independently of each other. Gordon preferred to use his own notion, "thwarted dependency". This is typical of innovation in the community of intellectuals of London. Of course, we were all influenced by Winnicott's ideas about development from dependency to independent unit status.

6. Consider the masturbatory movements of traumatized patients in hospital settings, such as in the films that we have seen of Romanian orphans painfully and incessantly banging their heads against their cots, or the rhythm, cadence, and repetitions of "trauma poetry", for example, in Kipling's narratives of war, influenced by life in English boarding schools, or in Coleridge's *The Rime of the Ancient Mariner*, the hero of which was compelled to find a wedding guest to whom he could tell his story. It was hardly accidental that Coleridge knew something about addiction to opium: the use of addictive substances is ritualized, involving unconscious masturbation, often with other people, involving a tense balance between isolation and merger.

7. Actually, the perceived threat that the role of whistle-blower will soon be filled leads to the process of hiring a consultant from outside the organization. In this context, the first task of the consultant is to be wary of processes of manipulation and seduction through which the existing management attempt to protect themselves from the shrill voices of those who are at the margins of power.

8. It is ironic and of more than passing interest that, as Martin Buber (1923) noted in *I and Thou*, when, as reported in the Old Testament, Moses asked God his name and what he wished to be called, God replied "I am". This highly condensed dialogue occurred during a period of massive social trauma, at the beginning of the attempts by Moses to lead the Jewish people out of slavery. However, "I am" was also used in the New Testament when Jesus referred to himself in terms of his personifying a number of essential qualities, for example, "I am the light". This, too, was a time of trauma.

    As discussed in *The Times* by the Right Reverend Geoffrey Rowell (2010), Bishop of Gibraltar in Europe, the poet Samuel Taylor Coleridge argued that

    > If you begin with 'it is'—that everything is reducible to the material—you have no place for the experience of being a human person. If you begin with 'I am', with the experience of being a person, then that reality is as fundamental as the nature investigated and explored by the science of material things. So, too, if God is no more than nature then there is no source of transforming grace, of forgiveness . . . (p. 37)

    Rowell continues, "The tension of explanation between 'It is' and 'I am' continues to challenge us in our own world, and in our own lives . . . The language of 'I am' cannot be reduced to the language of 'It is'".

    I do not wish here to open up my argument to a consideration of the spiritual aspects of identity, but I would argue that when personal and group identities are severely threatened, the boundaries between the realms of the socio-cultural, the psychic, and the somatic tend to be dissolved, and there is a very strong tendency to both doubt and explore one's relationship with both our neighbours and with God.

9. The Panel Report by Ira Brenner (2006) provides a useful but limited discussion of societal regression from a psychoanalytical point of view, most of which involves the implicit assumption that traumatized societies begin to regress, taking on the structure and functions of large groups. Some of these ideas can also be found in the work of Hannah

Arendt (2007). Of course, the work on this topic by Vamik Volkan (e.g. 2009) has become obligatory reading.

References

Alford, C. F. (2001). *Whistleblowers: Broken Lives and Organizational Power.* Ithaca, NY: Cornell University Press.

Arendt, H. (2007). *The Jewish Writings,* J. Kohn & R. Feldman (Eds.). New York: Schocken Books.

Armstrong, D. (2005). *Organization in the Mind: Psychoanalysis, Group Relations and Organizational Consultancy.* London: Karnac.

Bion, W. R. (1961). *Experiences in Groups and Other Papers.* London: Tavistock.

Brenner, I. (2006). Terror and societal regression: a panel report. *Journal of the American Psychoanalytical Association, 54*(3): 977–988.

Buber, M. (1923). *I and Thou,* R. Gregor Smith (Trans.). New York: Charles Scribner's Sons, 1958, p. 26.

De Mare, P. (1991). *Koinonia.* London: Karnac.

Freud, A. (1922). Beating fantasies and daydreams. In: *The Writings of Anna Freud: Volume I* (pp. 137–157). New York: International Universities Press, 1974.

Hopper, E. (1981). *Social Mobility: A Study of Social Control and Insatiability.* Oxford: Blackwell.

Hopper, E. (2000). From objects and subjects to citizens: group analysis and the study of maturity. *Group Analysis, 33*(1): 29–34.

Hopper, E. (2003). *Traumatic Experience in the Unconscious Life of Groups.* London: Jessica Kingsley.

Hopper, E. (2005a). Response to Vamik Volkan's Plenary Lecture, 'Large group identity, large group regression and massive violence'. *Group Analytic Contexts, 30:* 27–40.

Hopper, E. (2005b). Countertransference in the context of the fourth basic assumption in the unconscious life of groups. *International Journal of Group Psychotherapy, 55*(1): 87–114.

Hopper, E. (2009). The theory of the basic assumption of Incohesion: Aggregation/Massification of (ba) I:A/M. *British Journal of Psychotherapy, 25*(2): 214–229.

Hopper, E. (2010). Ein Abriss meiner Theorie der Grundannahme der Incohesion: Aggregation/Massification oder (ba) I:A/M. *Die analytische Großgruppe. Festschrift zu Ehren von Josef Shaked, 4:* 55–76.

Hopper, E., & Weinberg, H. (Eds.) (2011). *The Social Unconscious in Persons, Groups and Societies: Volume I: Mainly Theory*. London: Karnac.

Klimova, H. (2011). The false collective self. In: E. Hopper & H. Weinberg (Eds.), *The Social Unconscious in Persons, Groups and Societies, Vol 1: Mainly Theory* (pp. 187–208). London: Karnac.

Kreeger, L. (Ed.) (1975). *The Large Group Dynamics and Therapy*. London: Constable (reprinted London, Karnac, 1994).

Lawrence, W. G. (2000). *Tongued with Fire: Groups in Experience*. London: Karnac.

Lawrence, W. G., Bain, A., & Gould, L. J. (1996). The fifth basic assumption. *Free Associations*, 6(37): 28–55. Reprinted in 2000 in *Tongued with Fire: Groups in Experience*. London: Karnac.

Long, S. (2008). *The Perverse Organization and its Deadly Sins*. London: Karnac.

Menzies-Lyth, I. E. P. (1981). Bion's contribution to thinking about groups. In: J. Grotstein (Ed.), *Do I Dare Disturb the Universe?* (pp. 661–666). Beverley Hills, CA: Caesura Press.

Miller, E. (1993). *From Dependency to Autonomy*. London: Free Association Books.

Mojović, M. (2011). Manifestations of psychic retreats in social systems. In: E. Hopper & H. Weinberg (Eds.), *The Social Unconscious in Persons, Groups and Societies, Volume 1: Mainly Theory* (pp. 209–234). London: Karnac.

Rosenfeld, H. A. (1965). *Psychotic States: A Psychoanalytical Approach*. London: Maresfield Reprints.

Rowell, G. (2010). Credo: Verses that lead us towards a greater understanding. *The Times*, 20 March.

Solnit, R. (2009). *A Paradise Built in Hell: The Extraordinary Communities That Arise in Disaster*. London: Viking.

Stacey, R. (2005). Organizational identity: the paradox of continuity and potential transformation at the same time. *Group Analysis*, 38(4): 477–494.

Turquet, P. (1975). Threats to identity in the large group. In: L. Kreeger (Ed.), *The Large Group: Dynamics and Therapy* (pp. 87–144). London: Constable (reprinted London, Karnac, 1994).

Volkan, V. (2009). The next chapter: consequences of societal trauma. In: P. Gobodo-Madikizela & C. van der Merve (Eds.), *Memory, Narrative and Forgiveness: Perspectives of the Unfinished Journeys of the Past* (pp. 1–26). Cambridge: Cambridge Scholars Publishing.

Weinberg, H. (2006). Regression in the group revisited. *Group*, 30(1): 1–17.

Welldon, E. V. (2009). Transference and countertransference in group analysis with gender dysphoric patients. In: G. Ambrosio (Ed.), *Transvestism, Transsexualism in the Psychoanalytical Dimension* (pp. 81–106). London: Karnac.

Winnicott, D. W. (1955). Group influences and the maladjusted child: the school aspect. In: C. Winnicott, R. Shepherd, & M. Davies (Eds.), *Deprivation and Delinquency* (189–199). London: Tavistock, 1974.

PART I

PROCESSES AND SYSTEMS

A study in institutional change: the experience of trauma and the role of rumour in a case of paranoiagenesis[1]

Howard D. Kibel

Introduction

T he clinical material for this study comes from change that occurred in a major psychiatric teaching hospital in the early 1990s. The process began in a subtle manner. For a long time, the principal clinicians at this hospital were in denial about what was happening. Specifically, they knew that change was occurring, but minimized or even ignored its significance. Once the change had occurred, they reacted in a manner that was uncharacteristic of them. They demonstrated paranoid reactions that were transmitted through rumour.

Paranoiagenesis has been described by Kernberg (1993). He applied psychoanalytic concepts to the study of organizations. He noted that in organizations that are not structurally sound, specifically if its stated tasks cannot be accomplished, paranoid-like states occur. He noted that members evidence "markedly paranoid features in their institutional dealings that contrast with their normal personality characteristics outside organizational life" (p. 48). In the case studied here, interactions had paranoid features, but frankly paranoid rumours occurred. The organization studied here was in a state of social flux in so far as its fundamental identity was changing. Specifically, it was being transformed from an academic institution that promoted scholarship into one where fiscal considerations dominated decision making.

The rumours to be described centred around one clinician who became a "gadfly", one who embodied the rebellious attitudes of all by becoming overtly resistive to the change. He personified the resistance of all the senior clinicians to the change that was encroaching upon their perceived roles as academicians.

Rumours capture the imagination. They serve as psychological spaces into which people can project a host of fantasies, from ones of rescue to those of destruction. They draw the members together, serve to reinforce cohesion in the face of divisive forces, and serve as mediums for working out troubling emotions and fantasies about the environment. In this case, they embodied threatening affects and provided the members with a vehicle for expression. They gave the senior clinicians a temporary reprieve from the reality that was soon to come upon them, which was that the academic institution, as they knew it, would soon be gone. Frankly paranoid rumours, as occurred here, occur only in the extreme, but it is in the extreme that information about more subtle processes can be gleaned.

The function of rumours

The phenomenology of rumour has been studied extensively by sociologists. They have noted that rumour occurs under conditions of uncertainty and serves to reduce anxiety that is associated with insecurity. It is a collective phenomenon that allows for coping with the external environment during periods of social flux. Whenever there is a possibility of major change, or when it actually happens, people's sense of security is threatened. Specifically, each individual begins to lose track of where he or she fits in the social context, fearing that his/her place in the large group is in jeopardy. Rumour functions as improvised news whenever there is uncertainty or ambiguity as to the implications of social change. It creates a sense of order, rescuing each person from ambiguity by constructing a seemingly meaningful interpretation of events (Shibutani, 1966). Thus, it constitutes a process of *social sensemaking* (Bordia & Difonzo, 2004).

Rumour has been distinguished from gossip in that it has been said to transcend the individual and even time. Thus, rumour can spread beyond the confines of the immediate social group and remain in the culture for some time. Gossip is said to focus on the private life of individuals, whereas rumour focuses on the larger sphere of human events (Ambrosini, 1983). Yet, often a rumour that assumes importance in the fantasy life of a group can focus on an individual. He/she becomes the object of projection and embodies attributes that the group fears in itself, needs to deny, or even envies. In this case, the person who was the focus of the rumour served as a container of fantasy.

The analogy to scapegoating is evident. Scheidlinger (1982) noted that scapegoating constitutes a group defence against unacceptable emotions. It can serve as a means of dealing with threats to the group's narcissistic balance. Through the process of projective identification, internally threatening fantasies and associated affects are denied and then projected into, or merely on to, someone who is seen for the moment as not central to the group's experience of itself. Yet, in fact, the scapegoat is sometimes essential to the group, giving it a false sense of cohesion, particularly when its essence is threatened. This is a form of defensive massification, in the sense used by Hopper (2003), who has described this form of pseudo-mutuality.

Rumour might have little regard for reality or might embody some aspect of it that can be construed to fit the social situation. Its content is unauthenticated and its source might be obscure. But, it takes on a life of its own because it serves the group well, on the one hand, by bridging the gap between a state of isolation that occurs when uncertainty abounds and, on the other, whenever the group's former identity has been upended. This is the gap between a new reality and what had existed prior to the state of social flux. It can be both adaptive, in that it protects the group from insecurity, and has defensive attributes by allowing the members to be blind to change.

Adaptation to social change is necessary in order to prepare members of a group or organization for the tasks ahead. This generally includes modification of each person's role and function in the larger entity. Rumours that serve to avoid facing reality allow the group to remain in a state of denial and for its members to believe that their former sense of self-in-the-group is solid. Members can lull themselves into the belief that all is stable when, in fact, instability looms on the horizon.

Rumour is evocative and is part of the spectrum of human fantasy. It is related to mythology, which has been commented on in the psychoanalytic literature. Freud (1921c) noted that myths become receptacles of both identification and projection, as people identify with the myth whenever they hear it. Bion (1959) viewed myths as central to the formation of basic assumption mentality. They create a sense that the group is an integrated whole; that is, that on an unconscious level there is group cohesion (Dunphy, 1974). The mechanisms of projection, introjection, and identification that have been associated with mythology can also be found in rumour (Ambrosini, 1983).

Identification with the institution

The psychiatric hospital in question was unique. It was fairly large and located in a bucolic setting. It constituted one half of a prominent psychiatric department. Consequently, it was dubbed a "division" of the department and of the main hospital, which was located elsewhere in an urban setting. The other half of the department was on the same site of that large general hospital. The prestige of the other half was associated with its famous name. The chairman of the department was a nationally recognized psychiatrist. However, the medical director of this division was even more renowned, having international fame. The chairman and the medical director were close associates. Together, they had recruited first-rate academicians who were referred to as the *senior faculty*. Their membership became stable over time, since most were granted tenure by the university of which this department was a part. In contrast, junior faculty came and went; they were more temporary. Being a member of that senior group was quite prestigious; it immediately gave one an aura of legitimacy in wider academic circles, even those abroad. In short, this institution was the pinnacle of academia.

Members of the senior staff felt identified with this division. Stacey (2005) has referred to organizational identity as emanating from a set of norms and values that develop in an organization, which characterize the interactions between its members, and is sustained by particular patterns of discourse. Ongoing patterns of relating, interacting, discussion, and decision making constitute the culture of the institution. There is almost an ideological quality to the members' thought.

Groups that develop an organizational identity "give rise to the 'we' identities of their members, providing them with a powerful sense of identity or self" (ibid., p. 486). An atmosphere of stability, even permanency, enables organizational identity to be self-sustaining. Likewise, Turquet (1975), and later Armstrong (2005), postulated that membership in an organization creates what they dubbed to be an "organization-in-the-mind". This is the emotional experience of the organization as a whole that registers in each member's mind, both consciously and unconsciously. An organization-in-the-mind affects one's relationship to the organization, to fellow members, and one's own role in it. The latter includes assumptions that each one makes about his or her task, position in the organization, and relative power to affect its functioning, as well as the aims and goals of the institution. Postulating an unconscious effect on the individual implies that the identification is both formidable and penetrates deep into the psyche of its members.

Kohut (1976) had postulated the existence of a group self as a way of explaining the cohesiveness that he observed in the psychoanalytic community. Yet, in a footnote (pp. 419–420), he made a distinction between the group self, as a structure that dips into the deepest reaches of the psyche, and group identity, which he viewed to be a surface, more transient, configuration. Karterud and Stone (2003) expanded on the concept of the group self. They state that "People come to together in order to achieve something, and the group self is the conscious and unconscious structure that embodies the project" (p. 10). They note that certain individuals identify profoundly with the ambitions and ideals of the project, to such an extent that "they can have difficulties in differentiating between their personal self and their part of the group self . . . [so that] . . . An insult to the group will then be perceived as an insult to the personal self" (p. 10). In this way, they conceptualize the group self as something that has a much more profound effect on behaviour, thereby making it akin to the concept of organizational or institutional identity that is used here.

In this institution, the stability of the senior faculty allowed for a sense of inclusion, while junior faculty had a less influential role. The latter felt partially alienated, but were filled with admiration for the seniors. During major lectures at the hospital, senior faculty sat at the front of the auditorium while junior faculty sat at the back, rarely asking questions. Throughout the institution there were subtle signs of denigration of "outsiders". For example, although the administration took the stance that psychiatrists who referred patients into the hospital should be regularly included in the treatment, they never were. In fact, they were often discussed in a disdainful manner. Events at the institution were scheduled without regard to potential conflicts with those events sponsored by the local psychiatric society. On one occasion when this practice was questioned, the response was that "they [the local psychiatrists] should schedule their functions around us". It appeared as if the members of this institution were somewhat aware of its narcissism. Yet, in the professional community, it was seen as blatantly arrogant.

Once, an eminent, senior psychoanalyst gave a lecture on a theory that was not in concert with the dominant ideology of the institution. He prefaced his talk with a joke that embodied the notion of disdain for another point of view. The response to that joke was enthusiastic, but there was irony in this laughter. The senior faculty was dimly aware of its own narcissism. As individuals, each faculty member would disown institutional arrogance. Rather, it was consciously embodied in the chairman of the department and the medical director of this division. The joke was well received because it reflected the unconscious, rebellious attitudes of all against the two leaders, whom they held in awe, simultaneously admiring and fearing them. The laughter was an expression of appreciation for this eminent clinician who had the courage to stand up to and challenge the ideology of the institution.

None of this is to suggest that the institution was lacking in excellence; it had that. Neither is this to suggest that the chairman and medical director were not respected. In fact, they were genuinely admired. Rather, this is to suggest that fame and prestige inevitably induce narcissistic reactions in all who are associated with it. Notoriety stimulates latent exhibitionistic wishes that are ubiquitous. Defences against fantasies of humiliation occur. A narcissistically cathected organization affects the actual self-concept of its members. The way the institution is seen by others also has a profound effect on its members. Praise, power, and envy that emanate from prestige, along with actual success in the academic world at large, all combine to accentuate normal narcissistic tendencies which are inherent to the human condition.

This argument raises a question about the narcissism that is often attributed to famous people, such as film stars and politicians. Do these fields attract narcissistic individuals, or does the experience of success and fame induce narcissistic reactions? The latter is not considered often enough, and neither is some combination of the two.

Kernberg (1975) has noted that normally there is tension between the actual self, on the one hand, and the ideal self and internalized ideal object, on the other. In pathological narcissism, an inflated self concept occurs when the actual self is confused with this duo of the ideal self and internalized ideal object. Failure of the inflated self concept, or confrontation between the disparity between the actual self and that duo of the ideal self and internalized ideal object, causes decompensation in the patient. The result is a predominance of primitive defensive mechanisms, such as splitting, denial, projective identification, and even paranoia. By the same token, in many people, failure following upon the heels of enormous success can cause reactions similar to those found in narcissistic decompensation, and might be considered as protection against the pain of the inevitable narcissistic injury that is associated with severe set-back.

The contention here is that when organizational identity becomes infused with narcissism by virtue of the institution's notoriety, success, and proven excellence, *narcissistic equivalents* can be found throughout the institution, particularly affecting those most identified with its culture and ideology. In this case, when the early signs of change became evident, they were denied (and split-off). Later, when the social system of the hospital was shaken by major change that rocked a foundation that was rooted in scholarship, projective identification and paranoid ideation found its expression through rumour. Rumour, as will be shown, served as a container for paranoia, while giving evidence of the experience of institutional transformation as traumatic.

Identifying with an institution where one has spent many years is natural; it is even a normal and healthy aspect of humanity. It enables one to become devoted to the work of that institution, its functions, its goals, and endeavour to enhance its reputation. Under certain circumstances that are not too uncommon, the organization-in-the-mind, as a part of the self, can assume too much importance, whereby it overwhelms personal aspects of identity and co-opts private parts of the self, causing excessive merger and fusing with it. At such times, the individual can have difficulty distinguishing between his or her own sense of self and his or her organizational identity, thereby making the person excessively vulnerable to what happens to the institution. This is not an all-or-none phenomenon. In the extreme, the notion presented here helps to explain why people will sacrifice their lives for their country or a cause. In moderate form, it helps us to understand why disruption of organizational identity can be experienced as traumatic.

Background to the main events

For nearly twenty years, this psychiatric hospital (and the entire psychiatric department) had an explicit mission, which was openly stated by the department chairman. The faculty was told that he valued academic activity: teaching and publication of peer-reviewed articles, to be precise. Partly because of external circumstance,[2] this became a "publish or perish" institution. Scholarship and research had been equally valued, but, during recent years, research had assumed primacy. Clinical care benefited from such academic activity. The presence of a very large training programme was given priority; for the faculty, it was a requirement for all to teach.

This formula had been quite successful. Moreover, this division of the department proved to be a profitable enterprise that helped to support that half of the psychiatric department which was located on the site of the main hospital. Unfortunately, external pressures forced the main hospital to economize. Memoranda were issued by the Chief Executive Officer of the entire hospital, whose office was in the main hospital; these were seen by the senior faculty at this psychiatric division, but were ignored. In retrospect, avoidance was at work. That was easy, since the chairman of the psychiatric department did an effective job of protecting his domain from the encroachment by that administrator. The shelter provided by his stature was not to last long.

The entire hospital was closely affiliated with a major medical school. The affiliation was so close that the two were virtually fused. In previous years, the Dean of the medical school was the pivotal person whose policies held sway. The power lay with him, not with the administration of the hospital. All members of the faculty were technically employed by the medical school and felt an allegiance to it. But, in recent years, the balance of power had shifted, as insurance companies reduced their reimbursement rates to hospitals. Moreover, the main medical hospital, whose reputation was prestigious, had antiquated facilities. A new, modern hospital was needed on the main campus in order for it to remain competitive with other hospitals in the region.

Two years prior to the events that will be described, the long-standing chairman of the psychiatric department was offered the position of Dean of the medical school. By that time, it had become clear to all that power had shifted from the Dean to the Chief Executive Officer of the hospital. This now former chairman appeared to have been "pushed upstairs", so to speak, by being given a prestigious position, but one that lacked influence. For two years, the vice-chairman of the psychiatric department served as interim chairman until a new chairman could be recruited and assume his duties.

On one occasion during the tenure of the interim chairman, a new policy was instituted at this division of the hospital. It was a guideline regarding the pace of the discharge of patients to the community. This was to counteract a long-standing pattern of increased discharges and reduced bed occupancy during certain times of the year.[3] The message was clear: do not let the hospital's census fall. But, in the past, the census had often waxed and waned. After all, this division, as noted, was quite profitable. The new policy was the beginning of a financial squeeze that would be put on this countrified division. Yet, nobody seemed to recognize this. Denial was in effect.

During the second year of the interim chairman's reign, the educational budget for this hospital division was cut in half, resulting in the loss of two half-time positions. (Within a few years, the training programmes would be all but eliminated.) This occurred without any acknowledgement from the leadership that the mission of the department was changing. In retrospect, it was apparent that the reduction in the education budget constituted a message that scholarship and teaching were no longer a priority. As a consequence, fledgling researchers would no longer be supported. Yet, research that had already become self-supporting continued to be valued (as it brought money to the department). These changes were mistakenly viewed by all as consequences of the financial constraints imposed by insurance companies. But, more was involved. The mission of the department was changing. No longer was a premium placed on education, teaching, research, and scholarship; rather, financial profit was becoming the *raison d'être* for the very existence of this division. None of this was stated explicitly and the faculty never spoke about it. They avoided the reality that was becoming evident. It was known that a new chairman would soon be selected, but how his management of the department would affect the faculty was never discussed. The anticipation of this appointment was filled with unspoken anxiety.

The year of change

The new departmental chairman arrived at the beginning of the next academic year. This was also the beginning of the last year that the internationally renowned medical director of the division would serve in that position. It was commonly known that because of an alleged institutional regulation, he would have to give up his administrative position because of age.

The new chairman held meetings with members of the faculty, as a group and individually. He spoke of a changing environment for the delivery of clinical care. However, he talked about this as if it were coming from social forces that were beyond anyone's control, specifically, the insurance industry and the federal government. At one particular meeting with the entire faculty of this hospital division, he announced that the workload of the junior faculty (and a few senior faculty members) would be increased by one-third. This was accepted by all with resignation, given the assumption that larger forces were at play. The response of the clinical staff was almost "patriotic", in the sense that the attitude of all was that the time had come to pull together to work so that this division (of the department) could survive in an unfriendly environment.

Shortly thereafter, minor budgetary changes were made. For example, the rent for those who lived on the campus of the division was slightly increased. These changes did not appear to be significant. However, a pattern of multiple changes to improve the department's financial position soon became evident. There were discussions about consolidating the support services of this division with that of the main hospital in order to be economically efficient. For example, it was said that their respective laundry services might be merged. One senior member of the faculty became exceedingly concerned about these changes. He recognized a pattern of economizing that suggested that this division would be squeezed for every dollar that it could provide to the main hospital, which was due to be rebuilt. He believed that the Chief Executive Officer of the hospital was encouraging the new chairman of the department to move forward with economic changes that would help to put the entire hospital in a very favourable economic position. This would make the bonds that would be sold to finance the construction of a new medical hospital more attractive to investors.

Why this senior faculty member saw the situation this way when others were less convinced was not clear. Perhaps it had to do with his unique role in the hospital. Up until the preceding year, when the educational budget was slashed, he had spent half his time in education, a role that enabled him to examine group processes on its various units. Perhaps it was because he had known the internationally renowned medical director many years before the latter had achieved fame. Perhaps it had to do with some unidentified aspect of his personality.[4] In any case, whenever he shared his concerns with other senior faculty on a private basis, they reluctantly agreed with his assessment. This experience of consensual validation reinforced his conclusion and helped him decide that he must act to stem the tide that he saw was being propelled by the new chairman. He realized that if the faculty did not act soon, the institution as he had known it would be transformed from one of academic excellence into a profit-making machine.

After consulting with colleagues who were in academia elsewhere, he charted a course of action. He drafted a letter to the new chairman of the department, which would come from the senior faculty at this division. Its contents acknowledged that further changes in this division were in the offing in order to preserve the hospital as a whole and advised that the faculty should work with the chairman to ensure that these changes would go smoothly, so as not to disrupt clinical care. The tone of the letter was mild. It was double-spaced and the word "DRAFT" was placed in the upper right-hand corner of the letter. There were spaces below for faculty members to sign. This format was chosen to signal, as sometimes happens in academic circles, that the letter would be unofficial. Yet, delivering this letter to the chairman would clearly be an act of protest.

This senior faculty member showed the letter to a few close colleagues within the institution, who made some helpful suggestions for its modification. Yet, those close associates believed that this letter would provoke the medical director's wrath. Despite that, the author of this letter was determined to move forward and present it to the faculty. He did so at the monthly medical staff meeting, one where the entire medical faculty would be present.

Fortuitously, at this divisional medical staff meeting, the medical director announced a new department-wide policy. Part of each faculty member's income had been derived from private practice that was conducted at the facility. The arrangement had been quite generous to the faculty, as only a small portion of the funds collected was retained by the department. The medical director announced at this meeting that an additional 5% of the funds collected from private practice would be retained by the department. The reaction of the medical faculty was one of outrage.

The senior faculty member who had drafted the aforementioned letter to the chairman saw this as opportune. He was convinced that, given the reaction of the medical faculty to this new policy, his colleagues would rally round him and sign the letter. He presented the letter after making a brief speech in which he noted that this new policy on private practice monies was part of a trend that would surely get worse over time. Yet, much to his amazement, nobody signed the letter!

Later that day, this senior faculty member passed the medical director in the hall. The latter greeted him with a warm smile. This convinced the senior faculty member that his colleagues' warning that he would become the object of the medical director's wrath was unwarranted. In retrospect, their fantasy of how the medical director would receive the request, at that meeting, for faculty to sign the letter was part of the developing paranoia within the institution.

Shortly thereafter, two other senior faculty members approached the author of the letter to confess feeling ashamed that they did not sign it, believing that open support for him might harm them politically and adversely affect their future in the hospital. Yet, they agreed with his assessment that the situation in the institution would get worse.

This senior faculty member was undeterred by the failure of his initial effort. Therefore, he decided to organize a Committee of Salaried Faculty. This was an effort to cast a wider net by including a few senior social workers and the smaller cadre of psychologists in the division, who were also considered to be faculty. A mild, but carefully worded memorandum was sent to all members of the faculty on the campus, notifying them of an organizing meeting for this proposed committee. Only some junior faculty came to the meeting. They were of one voice. They admired the initiative of this senior faculty member, but said that they could not act openly since they did not have "tenure", as this senior faculty member did. In short, they feared that open action could cause them to be fired.

After that, this senior faculty member concluded that his effort to stem the tide of change was futile. He believed that the situation would get worse over time, that the new chairman would institute more stringent measures, that his workload would be further increased, that his income would diminish, and that the academic atmosphere of the institution would be destroyed. (His only mistake was to underestimate the rapidity and severity of the changes that would follow.) Therefore, he decided that ultimately he would leave the institution and seek employment elsewhere.

Events moved more rapidly than he had anticipated. A telephone call to a psychiatric department of a nearby medical college was greeted with enthusiasm. The chairman of that department and his two intimate colleagues there were eager to have this senior faculty member join them. He was offered a good position, with a promotion to full professor with tenure. During his negotiations with the second medical college, he kept the medical director informed of his actions. This was done out of courtesy, respect for the medical director, and their long association, dating back to his days in training.

Once the arrangement with the second medical college's department of psychiatry was finalized in an official letter that offered him the position, he prepared his letter of resignation from this department. He was giving the department more than three months notice, as the above events had consumed nearly three-fourths of the academic year. He informed the medical director and, on one particular day, spent much time in the hallways of the hospital meeting his colleagues so as to inform them personally. By now, he had been with the institution for sixteen years and had strong personal attachments to fellow senior faculty members.

The response to the news of his departure by his colleagues varied. Some said that his departure would be a great loss to the institution, since he was highly valued. Some said that he was fortunate to be leaving in time, since they anticipated that the conditions of work would continue to deteriorate. However, the overwhelming majority shared with him the rumours that had been circulating about him throughout the institution.

Some believed that he was being forced out. Nothing could have been further from the truth. In fact, the medical director, whom he had kept apprised of his plans, had non-verbally communicated support for him. (He was not the type to have openly acknowledged such support.[5]) Some believed that the non-medical administrator of the division was creating a special file on his activities during his years at the institution to (somehow, in a non-specified manner) use against him. (That too was not true. That administrator was not the sort of person to do anything surreptitiously. Moreover, he had continued to be friendly to this senior faculty member. Ironically, within one year, this non-medical administrator was abruptly fired by the new chairman of the department.) Some believed that the hospital had hired a lawyer whose sole task was to remove this senior faculty member's tenure, thereby making him vulnerable to dismissal. (Again, this was complete fiction.)

These rumours were totally without foundation. Further developments at this hospital confirmed to the author that they had no basis in fact. Yet, these fictions had vitality. They reflected the fear that the faculty members had of pending change, change that would destroy the institution as they had known it. Their very professional identity as members of a prestigious, world-renowned academic place of excellence was threatened. Indeed, in subsequent years it lost that reputation. They were obviously threatened by the changes that had already occurred and those that they feared were on the horizon. Rather than accepting the inevitable, they imagined that this senior faculty member was the only person who was being assailed. This gave them a false, albeit temporary, sense of relief. Ironically, he was not being forced out as rumoured; they, in a sense, were being forced out of an academic life that they had come to know, identify with, and feel comfortable in. The view that this senior faculty member was the object of harassment constituted projection.

Unrealistic power was attributed to the non-medical administrator of this division. He had come to embody the persecutor. However, in reality, he was a mild-mannered person who had little effect over what had transpired and what would follow. By seeing him as the threat, the faculty members could lull themselves into believing that those with real power, such as the Chief Executive Officer and the new chairman, were less of a threat. The former was far removed from them, as they had virtually no contact with him; they needed to ally with the latter in order to maintain their (false) sense of job security. Believing that the resigning senior faculty member was threatened with loss of tenure allowed them to feel as if their own status was secure; he was in danger, not them. Yet, deep-down, they knew that he was, in fact, one of them.

As in scapegoating, the rumours served to psychologically separate this particular senior faculty member from the rest. He could be seen, by virtue of his openly rebellious actions, as outside the core group of senior faculty. To continue to view him as part of that group would imply that if he were vulnerable, so were they. The rumours allowed them to deny the fragility of their status as members of an academic elite. They allowed them to deny the evidence that their organizational identity would be upended. That identity was rooted in the foundation of their overall professional identity, since they had joined this institution to be part of an exceptional academia. This was too traumatic to contemplate. At the same time, these rumours allowed the group to be captivated by the idea that he, and only he, was the object of attack. Denial and projective identification are the foundations of paranoia, which was intrinsic to those rumours.

Discussion and conclusions

The *organization-in-the-mind* penetrates deep layers of the psyche. It has a profound effect on the way individuals relate to the institution. In this case, they identified with the aims and goals of the psychiatric department that had been explicitly stated by the previous chairman. Specifically, the members of the senior faculty were told that they were required to teach and publish either research or scholarly papers. Participation in the academic community at large was highly valued and encouraged. Thus, invitations to lecture and teach elsewhere in the USA and abroad were recognized in departmental newsletters. Time away from the hospital to undertake such endeavours had been generously granted. All this was virtually cast aside during the period of change described above. Without saying so, the aims and goals of the institution were radically altered from promoting scholarship to making money that would support the general hospital on the urban campus. The identification of the senior faculty with the hospital's former aims and goals was trashed. This was traumatic for this faculty, who had come to this hospital many years ago with the explicit understanding that they were entering academia, an institution that pursued fame in that arena. The trauma was compounded by the changes not being articulated. The new administration acted as if nothing major had changed; only minor adjustments to the economic reality of the social times were said to have been instituted. Unspoken change is more painful than a transformation that is articulated, as the latter gives one time to adjust.

The rumours that had developed about this clinician served a defensive function for members of the entire senior faculty. Upon him was projected their opposition to unspoken change, their own rebellious yearnings, their desire to do combat with the new chairman, to somehow destroy him (even if in fantasy), and restore the institution to its former state. Collective projection gives a group a false sense of cohesion, producing, as Hopper (2003) claimed, a state of massification. Contagion of affect, which emanated from the very real threat to annihilate the *organization-in-the-mind* of the members of the senior faculty, fostered the development of paranoid-tinged rumours. Pseudo-cohesion gave them a false sense of security. If, in fact, the senior faculty could have consciously recognized what was afoot, they might have turned on one another in order to grasp the remnants of what once was, or have taken flight impulsively out of anxiety.

Next to this senior faculty member, who openly expressed opposition to the new leadership, the others felt inwardly ashamed that they could not take a stand, could not rebel, or even slow the pace of change. Transformation of the division was inevitable; in fact, it was happening all around them. The institution with which they felt strongly identified was beginning to disappear, shattering their organizational identity. The department's eminence would soon vanish. The institution as an object of a narcissistic identification was crumbling; the potential for the others to experience the pain of mourning for what had been and could never be again was imminent. Projection and paranoia, which the rumours embodied, represented a desperate attempt to ostracize the rebellious clinician. Excluding him, in fantasy, gave the senior faculty as a group the illusion that they were immune from the dangers of social flux. At the same time, feelings of humiliation over their own passivity were assuaged.

Along with psychologically ostracizing this one man, they might have envied him. He appeared to have the unspoken sanction of the medical director, who would soon step down from that position. Aggression towards an object of envy is often sown into the fabric of paranoid projections, producing a kind of scapegoating in fantasy. Thus, the comments that were made to this man when he announced his pending departure contained statements of admiration (envy) along with revelations about the rumours (paranoia) that had been circulating throughout the hospital.

Kernberg (1993) had noted how, in dysfunctional organizations, the relationship of the employees to supervisors is characterized by fear, suspicion, and resentment, hyperalertness and caution, a search for subtle and hidden meanings in the communications and behaviour of others, and an effort to establish alliances with peers to defend against perceived common dangers. That is what happened here. Kernberg stated that so-called *paranoiagenesis* comes about through "the activation of regressive group processes under conditions of insti-tutional malfunctioning and the latent predisposition to paranoid regression that is a universal characteristic of individual psychology" (p. 49). However, elsewhere (Kernberg, 2003) and in a different context he stated,

> the surprising universal nature . . . [of these paranoid potentials] . . . point to a persistent, unmetabolized core of primitive aggression, primitive object relations and primitive defensive operations as an important, perhaps even essential part of the psychological make-up of the individual . . . [that is] . . . characteristic of normal identity and ego integration that function in ordinary life situations. (p. 688)

When social conditions are ripe, this paranoid potential that resides in everyone becomes activated and focused on some aspect of social reality.

Kernberg stated (1993) that organizational dysfunction can be the result of faulty leadership or the conditions in which the organization finds itself because of external or internal factors. Leadership can be pathological, such as when a leader is malignantly narcissistic, incom-petent, or restrained, hampered, or defeated by political processes. The conditions that prevent an organization from functioning prop-erly can include faulty structure, especially when authority and accountability are mismatched. There can also be a dysfunctional administrative hierarchy or inadequate resources to carry out the assigned task.

Kernberg's theory of paranoiagenesis can be applied to traumatized organizations. Organizations can be said to have been traumatized whenever there is a sudden and radical change in personnel and/or whenever there is a sudden change in its mission, that is, in the purpose towards which its components are orientated. The latter is especially traumatic if the change of purpose is not articulated, as occurred here. In this case, the organizational identity of each member of the senior faculty was threatened. They had signed on, so to speak, to be part of a department that was devoted to scholarship, research, and teaching; that is, to be part of an academic institution of excellence. Now, they found themselves in one whose purpose was purely fiscal.

In part, the purpose of this study has been to amend Kernberg's theory. Armstrong (2005) has identified four conditions of what he states is the experience of the organization as an object of cathexis. They are its contextual embedment, its enterprise (an identity dimension), its task, and its structure. Kernberg's writings have focused somewhat on the first, but primarily have addressed the latter two. This study addresses the second one, the assumptions about the institution that cause one to identify with it. This study has shown that paranoid reactions can develop in normal individuals during periods of social flux[6] and when aspects of their personal identity (in this case, a vocational aspect) are disrupted. Paranoia occurs whenever narcissistic identification with an organization, that is, people's organizational identity, is battered, so that something similar to narcissistic decompensation occurs. Although on the scale of human endeavours the change that occurred here would not rise to the level of what is usually called trauma, for each individual the experience was, indeed, traumatic.

Notes

1. The author wishes to thank both the editor of this volume and Leonard Horwitz, PhD, for their invaluable comments and editorial suggestions, which were helpful in the preparation of this chapter.

2. Whereas most psychiatric departments of universities have developed a system for those who are unable to advance in academic rank, this department was forbidden to do so by its parent university.
3. Because this was a hospital with a large training programme, the trainees tended to discharge more of their patients shortly before rotating from one unit to another.
4. My perspective on this is limited, since I was too close to these events to claim to be objective.
5. The medical director subsequently gave this departing faculty member an enthusiastic, sterling recommendation to that nearby medical college.
6. This should not be surprising. The election in the USA of the first African-American President is a dramatic representation of social change in the fabric of the nation. Thus, paranoid reactions have been emerging in an array of political discourse.

References

Ambrosini, P. (1983). Clinical assessment of group and defensive aspects of rumor. *International Journal of Group Psychotherapy*, 33, 69–83.

Armstrong, D. (2005). *Organization in the mind: psychoanalysis, group relations, and organizational consultancy*. London: Karnac Books.

Bion, W. R. (1959). *Experiences in Groups*. London: Tavistock.

Bordia, P., & Difonzo, N. (2004). Problem solving in social interactions on the Internet: rumor as social cognition. *Social Psychology Quarterly, 67*: 33–49.

Dunphy, D. C. (1974). Phases, roles, and myths in self-analytic groups. In: G. S. Gibbard, J. J. Hartman, & R. D. Mann (Eds.), *Analysis of Groups: Contributions to Theory, Research, and Practice* (pp. 300–314). San Francisco, CA: Jossey-Bass.

Freud, S. (1921c). *Group Psychology and the Analysis of the Ego. S.E., 18*: 67–143). London: Hogarth.

Hopper, E. (2003). *Traumatic Experience in the Unconscious Life of Groups*. London: Jessica Kingsley.

Karterud, S., & Stone, W. N. (2003). The group self: a neglected aspect of group psychotherapy. *Group Analysis, 36*: 7–22.

Kernberg, O. F. (1975). *Borderline Conditions and Pathological Narcissism*. New York: Jason Aronson.

Kernberg, O. F. (1993). Paranoiagenesis in organizations. In: H. I. Kaplan & B. J. Sadock (Eds.), *Comprehensive Group Psychotherapy* (pp. 47–57). Baltimore, MD: Williams & Wilkins.

Kernberg, O. F. (2003). Sanctioned social violence: a psychoanalytic view, Part I. *International Journal of Psychoanalysis, 84*: 683–698.

Kohut, H. (1976). Creativeness, charisma, group psychology: reflections on the self-analysis of Freud. In: J. E. Gedo & G. H. Pollock (Eds.), *Freud: The Fusion of Science and Humanism* (pp. 379–425). New York: International Universities Press.

Scheidlinger, S. (1982). Presidential address: on scapegoating in group psychotherapy. *International Journal of Group Psychother*apy, *32*: 131–143.

Shibutani, T. (1966). *Improvised News: A Sociological Study of Rumor.* Indianapolis, IN: Bobbs-Merrill.

Stacey, R. (2005). Organizational identity: the paradox of continuity and potential transformation at the same time. *Group Analysis, 38*: 477–494.

Turquet, P. (1975). Threats to identity in the large group. In: L. Kreeger (Ed.), *The Large Group: Dynamics and Therapy* (pp. 87–144). London: Constable.

CHAPTER TWO

Traumatogenic processes in a psychiatric hospital: unconscious destructiveness of leadership change[1]

Bent Rosenbaum and Gerda Winther

Background

Before 2000, the leadership of Danish hospital departments, including departments of psychiatry, was exercised by the so-called "Administrative Leadership Couple", usually a doctor and a nurse whose qualities and skills as leaders varied a great deal, and who had not necessarily received managerial training. The purpose of this type of leadership constellation was to ensure professional management of the two main functions of a psychiatric institution: to perform medical/psychiatric investigations and diagnostic procedures followed by prescription of different kinds of treatment to patients; and to undertake the daily, twenty-four-hour, inpatient-milieu treatment, planning, and care. Furthermore, this leadership constellation was tacitly assumed to establish a balance of power between the two most influential groups in the hospital system: doctors, with their culture of conducting medical investigations and addressing the patients' conditions in terms of diagnosis and treatment, and nursing staff, with their culture of bodily and mental care, seeing the whole person in his or her mental ways of functioning in their social context.

During the 1990s (the decade of the brain), treatment modalities changed from the prevailing paradigm rooted in 1970s' focus on a comprehensive psychotherapeutic and psychosocial model to a new paradigm founded on a model of medically orientated care that placed less, if any, focus on dynamic milieu therapy. This change went hand in hand with a trend in which psychiatric hospitals discharged all patients who were not severely ill, and admitted only those who suffered from acute exacerbation of their psychotic symptoms (either psychoses manifesting themselves for the first time or relapsing as part of a long-term illness course), severe depressions, or were suicidal, and/or patients who were severely self-destructive. This left the hospital with a population of severely disturbed in- and outpatients for whom the medical viewpoint and treatment would tend to dominate at the expense of the broader humanistic view of the psychodynamic psychiatry.

This change of focus was perceived by many staff members as one that implied that their work was neither valued nor promoted. In spite of all its advantages, the medical expertise (i.e., knowledge about the brain and biological treatment methods, and a model of the socially dysfunctional brain) involved no transfer of expert knowledge to the non-medical staff. At that time, the skills to be applied by the staff in the training of the patients' social and cognitive deficits (social skills training, psycho-education) had not yet been developed sufficiently for the benefit of inpatients in general. The same period saw a growth in size and number at the societal level of the consumers' movement (patients' and relatives' organizations) in Denmark. Public awareness of conditions in the wards came into focus and found its way to the front page.

Against this background, governmental efforts were proposed in the mid 1990s to help the most severely ill, to help the homeless people with psychotic disorders, and to improve the treatment of cases of first-episode psychosis. Furthermore, a move in leadership structures was initiated, a move towards managerial systems where the leaders of a hospital or a department were seen more as managers than as experts in the field of treatment. This was opposed by many psychiatrists, who felt that their medical expertise was in danger of being set aside and that the academic standard of psychiatry was facing a decline.

A case example

Uphill and downhill

We shall describe and discuss the traumatic outcomes of the efforts to guide a large psychiatric hospital (220 beds) out of the period of stagnation of the 1980s and the 1990s. The new idea that underpinned this change was to engage a more dynamic leadership in milieu-therapy at the hospital units. It was hoped that this would provide the drive and inspiration that such a transition required.

The initial moves in this transition seemed to be successful. The change attracted new staff and generated new ideas for the construction of psychodynamically based treatment models. The leadership not only tried to promote integrated treatment models, it also brought new ideas of leadership into the organization. At the request of regional politicians and on the recommendation of a well-known management consultancy company, a psychologist and group analyst was brought into the leadership, which had hitherto consisted only of the leading psychiatrist and the leading psychiatric nurse. A leadership troika was created.

This new constellation was quite unknown in any psychiatric hospital organization in Denmark. It was also unusual because the third person was a psychodynamically orientated psychologist with expertise in the dynamics of groups and organizations. This was, therefore, to a certain extent perceived as a provocation by both the medical and the nursing establishment. The process and the new structure of the administration became a thorn in the flesh of those who played a key role in the political and professional systems.

What initially seemed to be successful changes initiated a series of traumatogenic processes. A few months followed that were characterized by chronic attacks on the successes that had been achieved by the incorporation of this new administrative and management structure. Then developed what can only be described as a "chronic crisis", which led to a period of "acute crisis" that involved the breakdown of the vitality and morale of the organization, which became unable to exercise its formal mandate.

The structure of the mental health hospital

At the time of our case, mental health hospitals in Denmark had three executive levels above the staff level. These levels were active in the sense that activities—whether they concerned financial affairs, staff–patient ratio, or rules and regulations—were likely to have direct consequences for the daily treatment of patients.

The four levels of the National Health System (NHS) are as follows:

1. The County Council executive level (political level):
    This level sets the financial framework for the hospital sector. It executes the politicians' "visions" for psychiatry.
2. The hospital executive level (general hospital level):
    This level sets the financial framework, the budget, for the psychiatric service at the hospital. Through its economic power, this level might interfere in the standard of treatment (staff–patient ratio) and the treatment modalities offered to patients in treatment. In principle, the hospital executive level should collaborate positively with the department's executive level, but if personal mismatches and power relations take over, then collaboration might become an unproductive, monological, one-way process.
3. The psychiatric department executive level (the level of the psychiatric leadership team (the troika described above)):
    This level sets the overall framework for treatment: organization, treatment philosophy, education, research, and public relations outreach. In principle, taking on the role of leadership, the department's executive level collaborates with staff officials and staff advisory boards. However, again, mismatches might turn collaboration into monologues and attempts at dominance; devaluation and neglect might lead to open or tacit oppositional attitudes in staff and between staff and the leadership team.
4. The level of the psychiatric hospital staff.
    At this level, the ground level, the unit leaders' and the individual staff members' skills and levels of competence set the standard for the treatment of patients and for the well-being and the well-functioning of the staff as a whole. Democracy and group dynamic thinking at this level should, in principle, support voices (creative and/or critical ideas) being heard and relevant issues being discussed. This work-group atmosphere is, of course, always threatened by possible basic assumptions about which leaders at levels three and four should be aware.

Phases in the rise and fall of a dynamic leadership

We shall now describe the phases in the rise and fall of the leadership, that is specifically the ability (or lack of ability) of the leadership to formulate and implement its visions or ideas. Of course, such a description implies a reduction and a condensation of facts and events in order to portray the phases of destabilization and catastrophic change. Moreover, in daily life, these phases will not be as linear as outlined below. At this point of our case description, however, the outlining of interdependent phases might serve as a starting point. These phases will be discussed from a theoretical perspective towards the end of this chapter.

Phase 1: Conservatism and institutional "still life"—nothing is going to be changed

This phase, in a way, belongs to the period that precedes the time of the trauma, but it remains important considering the incipient nature of time in the development of a trauma. The first phase harbours, or nests, the possibility of trauma. The institution could best be described as a very large and traditional psychiatric ward, characterized by conservatism and dominated by the medical establishment and its patriarch-like ethics. Interestingly enough, in the 1960s, three decades before the first phase, this very same hospital was psychodynamically the most progressive psychiatric hospital in the country, with an open mind to patients' rights, group activity, staff involvement, and engagement in activities in collaboration with the patients. At the time of the "still life phase", the institution suffered from a fatal lack of economic support from the County Mental Health System, both for the treatment of the hospital's inpatients and for its outpatients at the community mental health centres. Complaints from patients and relatives had been numerous and some had been described in the newspapers. The politicians realized that something had to be done.

Phase 2: Reform/revolution—phase of destabilization of old fixed patterns and incipient hope for another future

This phase of transformation also precedes the phases during which destructive traumatization became discernible. A general investigation of all levels and functions of the hospital was instituted from above (the county level) and carried out by a team of consultants from outside the hospital. It was supported by some of the leaders and staff who for a long time had wanted change and sought inspiration. As a result of the investigation, a new department leadership was established who based their leadership on psychodynamic and group-minded principles. This meant that all staff (including doctors) went through group-analytically informed teaching courses and milieu-therapy programmes (with small- and large-group experiences). A unique feature of this development was that it was supported by the new leaders of the County Mental Health System and the Hospital Executive Director (whose positive attitude towards psychiatry seemingly had been dormant). They supported the spirit of "we can make it".

In accordance with their psychodynamic understanding of the institution, the new department leadership attempted to be mindful of external and internal critical voices, adopting a listening attitude, while at the same time *both* persevering *and* persisting in the course they were pursuing.

Hope for a new and better future was disseminated to the staff, and the hospital became an attractive place of work for both nurses and doctors interested in psychodynamic psychiatry (Gabbard, 1994).[2] However, during this radical process of change, anti-group forces (Nitsun, 1996) also emerged. Some doctors felt that this psychodynamic model was an "ideological" attack on the medical model and their own discourse and power. Establishing a psychodynamic treatment philosophy became provocative in itself, not least because it took place in an era following the "decade of the brain", where cognitive therapy and the concept of the best evidence-based treatment modalities obtained a firm foothold at the psychiatric institutions with regard to the choice of treatment methods.

*Phase 3: Betrayal of the overall progressive psychodynamic ideas—
a phase of destabilization with traumatic shock and disillusion*

Some years were spent on the build-up phase. Then the leaders of the psychiatric department entered a phase in which they felt that they were not being adequately supported by the Mental Health System and the Hospital Executive Director. As a reaction to this, one leader, the administrative doctor of the psychiatric department, left the hospital, not feeling trusted and not trusting his colleagues and the leadership team any more. This came as a shock to the department, because this leader had the organizational talent and had been extremely active in organizing the process of change towards the psychodynamically based treatment methods. There was not much talk about it; the effect of the loss of an organizer was simply denied. This inadequate containment of the damage suffered could be seen as the forerunner of the traumatic experience of failed dependency (Hopper, 2003a), the feeling that nothing can protect me or us any longer.

In the wake of the breakdown of the leadership team, a senior psychiatrist saw his chances of being promoted and, thus, becoming a partner in the coming leadership. By doing so, he unconsciously contributed to the interruption of the newly established development of psychodynamic milieu-therapy. This process was at first silent and covert, later more open.

Phase 4: Final attack on the psychodynamically orientated leadership—third phase of destabilization: post trauma shock

A modern, authoritarian, but very dominating director took over the leadership of the General Hospital (Level 2, as described above); in this capacity he was also responsible for choosing the new leadership of the psychiatric hospital (Level 3, as described above). He fired the leadership team proponents of the psychodynamic ideas (the psychologist and the substitute doctor in the psychiatric troika leadership team), and, thus (without knowing it), executed the death sentence on the treatment philosophy of psychodynamic psychiatry, which had begun to bear fruit (portrayed in Phase 2 above, and in the spiral model (see Figure 1, below)). In doing so, he forged an alliance with the nurse of the former leadership team, whose grounding in psychodynamic orientation was seemingly superficial, and, furthermore, he instituted the psychiatrist, who, in spite of protests from colleagues, was willing. Submissively, and in collaboration with the nurse, the psychiatrist followed a new dictatorial way of leading the department of psychiatry. The new leadership couple (supplanting the team of psychodynamically orientated leaders) was formed, and, in the dynamics of this leadership, the two persons seemed to be united in common envy and denial of the ideas of the former leadership. In reality, that is, in their concrete actions, which many times amounted to not-having-any-plans-and-resisting-any-development, this leader-ship couple was responsible for the burying of the dynamic ideas that had previously brought change to the department. The couple was unable to understand the "obvious" and "evident" that was in front of their noses concerning the cohesion of the organization and the quality of the treatment. Slowly, this lack of understanding was trans-formed into a state dominated by either denial or their search for narcissistic mirroring (just like in the adventure of Snow White, where the queen stepmother could see only one true edition of the world's beauty, which was the one incarnated in herself). We regard the changes during this phase as being guided by a kind of "perverse pairing" (Hopper, 2003a) and a perverse state of mind (Long, 2008), a concept that Long, in her book, attributes also to institutional struc-tures, and, she argues, might have to be present for institutional trans-formations to turn into traumatic ones.

Phase 5: Protest against instalment of marionette leadership

Extensive and renewed protests were levelled against the new leader-ship couple. Three-quarters of the staff and practically all specialists signed the protest against the decision of the hospital directorship and, thus, against the department's new leadership couple. While being a sign of power, this protest was, at the same time, a sign of despair. The arguments and protests from doctors and the staff were not "heard", and the protests against the new leadership therefore exhausted the protestors.

Phase 6: Protest neglected by silence

The new leadership couple was not able to sense any "truth", and it responded to its perception of the unpleasant and chaotic atmosphere with denial and feelings of victimization and persecution. Leadership was supplanted by management of purely institutional matters rather than patient-centred and staff-centred management. The new leaders acted as officials who, in order to stay in power, were willing to silence the staff's progressive ideas in so far as these ideas implied criticism of the executive level of the psychiatric hospital. Malignant mirroring processes and splitting found their way into the institution. Critics among the staff were simply defined as not relevant and even non-existing. This also took place at peer level, and it affected the treatment of patients. Management consultants were brought in to bring the staff to silence. The implication of this, and the subsequent mismanagement of the organization at the units, meant that experienced and qualified people fled and found other jobs, which was easy for them because of the qualifications they had acquired through the above-mentioned psychodynamic training programmes.

Phase 7: The process of incohesion—fourth phase of destabilization

All staff groups in the psychiatric department harboured mixed feelings of aggression and emptiness towards the new leadership couple. These mixed feelings were expressed as indifference ("why should we care, nobody listens anyway"), hostility, and withdrawal from possible developmental activities ("why should we do anything to make this institution better, since we do not know whether anybody will respond to our efforts").

The staff's aggression slowly became more latent than manifest. A state of aggregation (Hopper, 2003a) emerged: people wished to avoid the recognition of agency and responsibility.

Phase 8: Malignant/negative mirroring—new phase of stagnation, incohesion, aggregation; anti-forces take over

In this phase, signs of crustacean and intelligent-lout behaviour surfaced. The couple lived in isolation and exerted its power by dictates or by statements such as "It can't be done otherwise—no counter-arguments will be listened to". The leaders mirrored their weaknesses in each other, but saw these images as something they had to hide as much as possible or to get rid of by projections. The weakness was denied by adoption of "we have to look forward, not backward" attitudes: "There is no need for analysing the past, and you (staff) are making everything worse by attempting to do so"; "The failures of the institution are not our fault, but come exclusively from above, and we have no share in this—you (staff) are the bad guys if you don't understand that", etc. Thus, the leadership couple tended to communicate using euphemisms and bureaucratic language, and the staff responded with profound silence with no resonance and with a deep sense of isolation, that is, with elements of aggregation (Hopper, 2003a).

The phase development can be summarized in a spiral model (Figure 1).

Discussion

Reversibility and irreversibility of descructive processes

The phases and subsequent progression from one step to another was seemingly irreversible and, thus, constituted a malignant "one-way" spiral.

From a group analytic and organizational point of view, it is interesting and important to grasp the possibility of reversal of processes so that things do not stiffen and appear functionally dead: that is, with the fourth basic assumption (Hopper, 2003a) as an outcome. Progression and creativity in groups and organizations require a certain

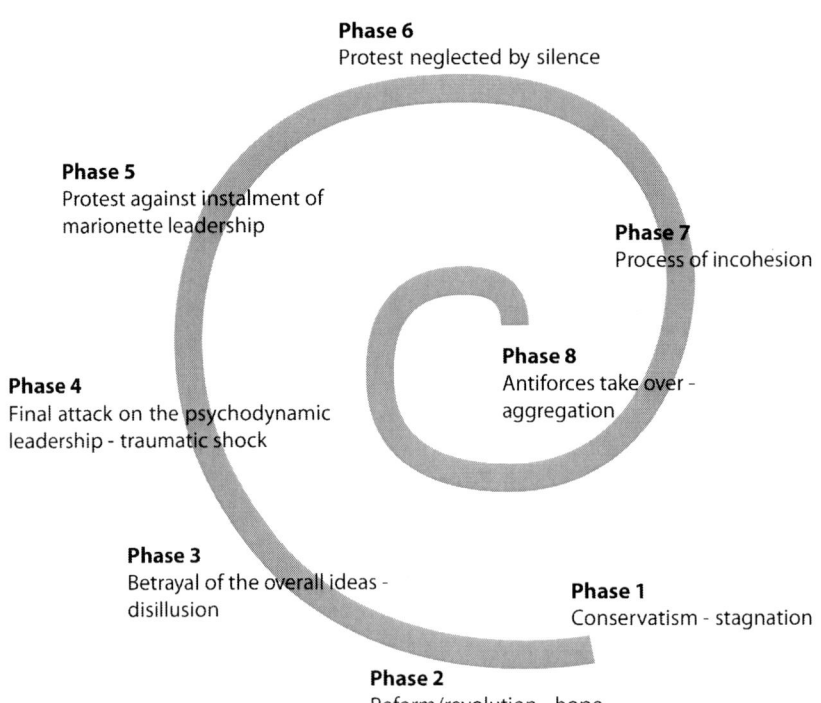

Phase 6
Protest neglected by silence

Phase 5
Protest against instalment of
marionette leadership

Phase 7
Process of incohesion

Phase 4
Final attack on the psychodynamic
leadership - traumatic shock

Phase 8
Antiforces take over -
aggregation

Phase 3
Betrayal of the overall ideas -
disillusion

Phase 1
Conservatism - stagnation

Phase 2
Reform/revolution - hope

Figure 1.   Spiral model of phase development.

element of instability, characterized by the dynamics of Eros *vs.* Thanatos, new moves/ideas *vs.* repetition, the uncertainty of intuition *vs.* doing the already-known, etc. In principle, interpersonal and organizational processes in each phase vibrate between opposite poles of ideas, dividing subjects and objects, leaders and staff, administrators and clinicians, who might be attracted and repelled by different poles (Figure 2).

Problems arise when these poles are seen in isolation: that is, if they become points of orientation that nothing can alter and if they form no dialectic relationship with other poles. More problems arise when poles of orientation are blurred in terms of content, and when an obvious rationale is lacking, notably if the move towards a goal is at the same time being portrayed as rational.

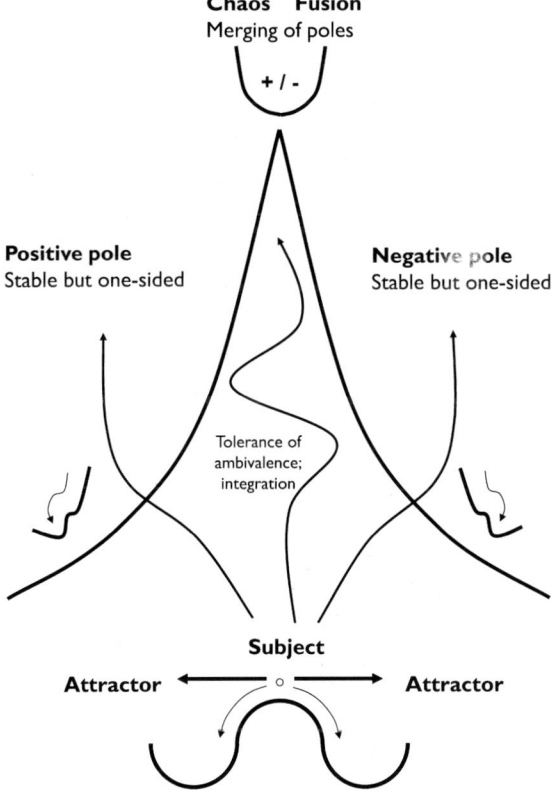

Figure 2. The opposite poles in interpersonal and organizational processes.

Each step follows the other because a change in the organization was pursued without making it clear why the old structure of the organization and treatments should be abolished and what the new paths of progress should consist of. Guidelines for reaching an aim were lacking, and a chaotic pattern therefore emerged because forces were pulling in opposite directions.

Other generalizations

We believe that generalizations can be drawn from our experience and that the turns of the negative spiral model (see Figure 1) support these generalizations. The steps illustrated in our case model give rise to a series of destructive changes where one conflictual situation develops into a new, worse, conflictual situation. We believe that with slight modifications these steps and stages might be seen in other kinds of organizations as well.

At the heart of our argument that these are general steps lies our understanding of change and trauma as two dynamically linked concepts. Changes in the form of rupture, discontinuities, emotional deadlock, chronic resistances, and contradictions are, logically speaking, a precondition for trauma, even if not all ruptures, discontinuities, deadlocks, etc., lead to severe trauma. The link between trauma and change is asymmetrical. Not all changes can be conceived as traumatic, although they might harbour a potentiality for such a development.

Ironically and sadly, but maybe also logically necessary, the roots of the traumatic transformations within the hospital organization that we have described had been planted in the soil of an apparent success. Speculation could be raised as to whether organizational success and organizational failure will invariably exist side by side in a highly complex organization of a large psychiatric institution, where many decisive micro-transformations go on simultaneously and in parallel. We believe that this is possible as long as the processes balancing these parallel transformations are kept within certain frameworks. Sometimes, one part of a large organization works and functions successfully while other parts do not. In these cases, it might sometimes look as if the different parts are indifferent to each other's dynamics, but this is only true from a superficial point of view. Rather, one could see how the spill-over effect of the successful part of the organization becomes a kind of motor for the other parts. At other times, the successfulness of one part gives rise to envy, jealousy, or arrogance. In both cases, leadership determines how the opposite directions of success and failure are tackled and how they subsequently develop into a new situation.

There are stages during which an administrative leadership might intuitively sense the presence of processes of imbalance within the leadership itself and among the staff as a whole. Through creativity, courage, and internal power, the leadership might undertake manoeuvres for the purpose of counterbalancing a variety of structural conflicts and of revealing possibilities for development in the imminent "chaos". However, if, for various reasons, the leadership team does not succeed, then a traumatic situation might evolve into a severe post trauma organizational process in which traumatogenic processes become crystallized.

The non-linearity of trauma

The process of traumatization seldom, if ever, evolves in a linear way. The process of traumatization is often both multi-factorial and multi-causal. Moreover, the very structure of traumatization is not in accordance with linearity. Very early in his theoretical reflection, Freud proposed a dynamic mechanism that he called *Nachträglichkeit* (see Laplanche & Pontalis, 1973, p. 110). In accordance with this concept, an actual traumatic development is grounded in an unconscious, retroactively exerted tacit knowledge with consequences for future thoughts and actions. The concept of *Nachträglichkeit* involves many considerations when analysis of institutional traumas is propounded. Even devastating organizational developments might not be instantly foreseeable, and they might draw on and acquire nourishment from previous conflicts that were neglected or repressed and not given full meaning when they first occurred. The concept of *Nachträglichkeit* is an important tool in the analysis of organizational trauma, among other things because it brings the inchoate aspects of time into the understanding of organizational development. For good and for bad, it also contributes to the complexity of the analysis.

In the process of traumatization, the staff often sense both the present conflicts and the previous ones, even if they are not fully conscious of them. They embody the conflicts, so to speak. Daily routines, discussions about treatment and patients, and even the concrete ways of expressing oneself toward each other and towards the patients are coloured by these conflicts. This influence might manifest itself in instability, fatigue, stress, lack of joy, unproductive quarrelling, guilt feelings, wild and unrealistic interventions, and other signs of projective thinking processes that undermine the daily work routines. It might be difficult for the staff groups and for individual members of the group to react to conflicts in a timely way. The staff might explicitly try to communicate to the leaders that the situation is far from optimal. However, these attempts at communication are impeded by the non-linearity of the trauma. It becomes impossible for the staff to formulate logically how "situation x" could have led to "situation y".

Characteristics of good and bad leadership couples

The creatively balanced couple

The leadership couple can be viewed as a sort of marriage, and, thus, be analysed in a way that is similar to the analysis of harmonious and disharmonious marriages. The best marriages are the ones in which the partners are able to accept and use each other's differences constructively and creatively, including mirroring each other positively. This could be described as productive pairing. In a leadership couple, this kind of pairing fulfils wishes "from below", that is, from staff who are in daily interaction with patients and who perform best when they can rely on support "from above". Clearly, we are using the parent–child relationship as a paradigmatic description. Productive pairing manifests itself as a capacity for

- promoting security;
- exerting changes which imply the creation of new ideas and modes of collaboration;
- containing the pain which is often the consequence of new structures.

The staff feed on and develop this leadership nourishment (the good organizational breast and brain) and challenges (the demands for a genital development of the mind).

The "good" or "good enough" leadership team in the psychiatric hospital organization implies instillation of a great, although not unrealistic, amount of hope for the organization and its members. Tacitly, the idea is expressed that a happy combination of a mother and father is presiding benevolently over the welfare of its children. Naturally, this is a double-edged sword, because it also promotes the illusion or myth that development (i.e., pursuing a thirst for knowledge and skills) is secured as long as the couple, the parental object, stays intact.

Kernberg (1980) has listed some important characteristics of the mature leader, which, in our view, are also characteristic of the good leadership couple/team:

- intelligence;
- capacity for deeper interpersonal relations;
- healthy narcissism;
- a certain portion of healthy paranoia.

We would add the following characteristics:

- creativity;
- capacity to handle conflicts by listening and understanding, and to mediate the understanding before concluding;
- the capacity to contain the anti-group forces that will always, to a larger or smaller degree, be part of institutional life, and to be able to voice one's own vulnerability.

Our observations have led us to believe that the essential core of mature leadership is the triad:

- the *capacity to contain emotional pain*—which is almost always part of transformational processes, and, connected to separation and vulnerability, such pain is almost always manifest in group processes;
- the *capacity to think*—which involves promoting thoughts and ideas, as well as having a sense of the right timing for argumentation, and a precise intuition of perspectives for raising new questions and challenges;
- the *containment of hope*—which involves feelings of affiliation with others, feelings of building up something "different" "new", and "necessary", and, to some extent, feelings of healing a wound.[3]

Mature leadership needs the functioning and linkage of all these three capacities.

Malignant and unbalanced couple

These three functions of the triad and the parental object are vulnerable and fragile elements in the dynamic of the organization. Their stability and the leadership team's ability to maintain this stability at times of unforeseen obstacles and hardship depends both on the team itself and on the developmental process of the organization as a whole. This development takes time and requires a sense of timing. Attempts at speeding up the process or inappropriately slowing it down might be damaging. It might lead to an *as if* constitution of the basic processes and the process of development might, therefore, have very little chance of surviving stress, disappointment, or lack of success. Failure in one of the triad functions, or in their linkage, could rob the leadership of its capacity for positive mirroring and its capacity to be creative and to model creativity. Instead, a negative or malignant mirroring process might begin. Pathological patterns, rigid, monological, sadistic, etc., might become dominant. Zinkin (1983) points out that malignant mirroring is like cancer: its destructiveness lies in its unbounded consumption of its host.[4]

Malignant mirroring might be defined as a mirroring process whose outcome leads to destruction of the good object (good ideas or retention of progressive staff) and, thus, of the subject's ability to develop. Collusive, negative, and/or malignant pairing in the leadership couple often makes use of malignant mirroring and this leads to small or major catastrophes at the institution. Although a "small catastrophe" might seem to be a contradiction in terms, actually, it is not, because small shocks have major reverberations that might last for a very long time. In any case, it is possible to see the beginning of regressive traits in leadership management, and manifestations of pathological features of the leaders might be prominent.

Leaders might possess a combination of pathological traits (Kernberg, 1980). We would add that a leadership couple might also have traits that are likely to cause deleterious projective effects "downwards" in the organizational system. We shall mention a few of these traits.

Leaderships with schizoid and narcissistic traits

Our observations concern the combination and conflict of two types of personalities: the ones with schizoid and narcissistic features.

These traits are alike in some ways and they differ in others. They are alike in so far as they represent traits of the "lonely rider", and they each involve a fear of the intrusion by others. A narcissistic leader might sometimes employ pseudo-democratic manoeuvres, which could leave the staff with the impression that no one really runs the place, an impression that is also predominant when leaders take on schizoid administrative attitudes.

They differ in the sense that leaders with schizoid personality traits hide in their offices behind closed doors, and when they meet others, the meeting is highly ritualistic; often, they scorn staff leaders and keep them at arm's length, which is actually very aggressive. They do not understand that the staff need warmth, support, and care; at least, they do not understand how to exude these qualities and do not really care as long as they can keep the fantasy alive that they stay in power for good reasons, although they are isolated.

Leaders who have narcissistic personality traits might also be unable to evaluate themselves and others in depth, which brings about a lack of capacity for empathy and for sophisticated discrimination of other people. But the narcissists will make themselves visible in public performances to ensure that they are liked and admired. Moreover, their envy of others will be denied internally by these public appearances and will instead be turned into grandiosity, which might manifest itself in many different ways.

Pressure of different sorts, disappointment, deprivation, and other stressors affecting the organization might lead to severe imbalance in the dynamics of the leadership couple. These aspects might imply the dissolution of formerly trustworthy attachment morphology, linking each leader to the other in their tasks. They might also imply secret reorientations towards the possibility of finding other collaborating partners, which will create a triangular set of roles (Willi, 1982) involving a "third" who is imagined as being able to save each one's individual position, and sustain their narcissism. Such a triangular set might be created at the expense not only of the other, but also of the organization as a whole. Imbalance in the dynamics of the leadership couple might evolve when one envies the other, disbelieves in the other's capacity, feels bypassed, subjugated to, or controlled by, the other, feels isolated, misunderstood, or rejected.

This mistrust in the other is often initiated by different types of pressures or demands on the leadership couple from "above" in the NHS structure (economy, ideology, and power). Mistrust might begin, for example, when the leaders submit opportunistically to the political pressure with a view to implementing, unrealistically, a bigger "production", a change in the structures of the organization, or budget cuts. By not arguing on behalf of reality, or by not defending the quality of the staff's work, but by trying instead to convince the public that these reductions or cuts will not reduce the level and contents of the service, the staff feel distrusted and cannot themselves mobilize trust in the leadership couple. Thus, a projective space of mistrust is set in motion.

Basic assumptions about incohesion

The leadership couple is a very important part of the contextual institution, and, as such, is consciously and unconsciously influenced by group processes at any given time. Of course, the couple is also influencing these processes in turn.

Kernberg (1978) suggested that institutions like large psychiatric hospitals easily function according to Bion's three basic assumption groups (Bion, 1961): dependency, fight/flight, and pairing. These assumptions constitute the basis for group reactions that potentially always exist, but are activated particularly when task structures start breaking down, which, in turn, further enhances these processes. In addition, Turquet (1974), Lawrence, Bain, and Gould (1996), and Hopper (1989, 1997, 2003a) have all attempted to conceptualize a fourth basic assumption.

For our specific purpose, we will here focus on what Hopper calls the basic assumption of Incohesion: Aggregation/Massification, or (ba) I:A/M. He proposes that

> when people have been traumatised and have experienced the fear of annihilation, and, subsequently, have encapsulated intrapsychic oscillations between fission and fragmentation, and fusion and confusion, then, on the basis of various kinds of externalisation, especially projective and introjective, their groups are likely to evince processes

of incohesion. In the first instance this is characterised by aggregation in response to fission and fragmentation, and then by massification in response to fusion and confusion, and, in turn, by oscillation between massification and aggregation. (Hopper, 1997, p. 451)[5]

. . . An aggregate is characterised by a minimal degree of mutual attraction or involvement. The group state of aggregation is barely a group. An aggregate is an incohesive social formation with dynamics of its own. In contrast, a mass is characterised by maximal degree of mutual attraction and involvement. A mass seems to be cohesive, but is, actually, as incohesive as an aggregate. (ibid.)

Hopper also emphasizes, and this is important in our case, that incohesion in the form of aggregation is likely to follow *failed dependency*. The staff, who first idealize and, thus, become dependent on the leadership couple, might—if the couple is removed, or otherwise fails—react with a variety of social and cultural formations that could be described as aggregation.

The basic assumption formations are often used in the service of the work group, but at times of leadership instability and pressures on the task structure, the basic assumption formations will emerge in aggravated forms and will interfere with the work group's activity. In situations characterized by failing leadership, the basic assumption I: A/M will become manifest; a space of malignant—distorted, destructive—projections will dominate the relationship between staff and leaders, and will, thus, affect the work atmosphere of the whole institution, and it will also influence the patients.

The personification of basic assumption processes is critical during times of severe stress and violation of expectations:

. . . the roles associated with processes of incohesion: aggregation/ massification are likely to be personified by traumatised, contact-shunning, crustacean characters and traumatised merger-hungry amoeboid characters, the former being sucked into the roles that are typical of aggregation and the latter of massification. (Hopper, 2003a)

In our example from the psychiatric hospital, we have presented dynamics of the steps in the change of the basic morphology and investigated the transformation from a good leadership couple characterized by creative pairing to a malignant and perverse one characterized by envy, aggression, and destruction.

Summary

From a psychoanalytical and group analytical point of view, the concept of trauma seldom allows one to pinpoint the exact starting moment. Trauma is always a process and it takes place at several levels, and rarely so at the same time at these levels. In our case, we saw how incohesion, as one outcome of the traumatic processes in the institution, occurred at the level of:

- *interpersonal* interactions (within the institutional leader group);
- *inter-group* interactions (e.g., different outsider groups affecting the development of the psychodynamic department);
- *intra-group* interactions (e.g., how individuals and staff groups helped or were counterproductive in the development, terminating in a state of fourth basic assumption);
- *transgenerational* interactions (how the history of the department influenced the development either positively or negatively).

We have illustrated how building up an organizational structure based on principles of psychodynamic psychiatry, and accepting heterogeneity in the unity (the basic principle of the work of the unconscious) underwent traumatic processes that subsequently, stepwise or moving in a negative spiral, pushed the organizational form from a predominantly cohesive structure toward an incohesive one characterized by aggregation. This had severe implications for staff, such as less engagement, a staff flight from the hospital, numbness and loss of creativity in the patient treatment and care, dissatisfaction, and feelings of giving up.

Notes

1. We owe our gratitude to the scientific working group who gathered for many years in Earl Hopper's rooms, and who, in the period of 2003–2006, regularly gave feedback to our project in a critical, constructive way.
2. The reference is given to the first edition of Gabbard's book; revised editions were published by Gabbard in 2000 and 2005). The first book on psychodynamic psychiatry appeared as early as the 1940s.
3. Pines (1998) and Hopper (2003b) emphasize the healing aspect of mature hope as one concerned with working through trauma. Whether this can

be said to function in our case can be questioned. A critical voice might, in fact, assert that in our case, which in a relatively short time attempted to build up a psychodynamic unit, built up an illusionary hope, and, thus, the setting up of a process through which increased dependency leads to failure and disappointment. Hope may, thus, also be seen in the forms of illusionary, regressed, or infantile hope, and these forms avoid the trauma by neglect, denial, repression, and foreclosure.

4. An illustrative example of malignant (perverse) coupling is that of the main actors in the novel by Choderlos de Laclos (1782), *Les Liaisons Dangereuses*, Vicomte de Valmont and Marquise de Merteuil. They seem to be united in their common envy of innocence and the capacity to love, but, as a consequence of that, they destroy everything good around them and, thus, undermine the fertile ground for their own relationship.

5. In an interesting footnote concerning the originality of theories of the fourth basic assumption, Hopper (2003a, p. 51, fn 5) mentions an unpublished paper from 1938 by John Rickman called "Uniformity and diversity in groups", in which Rickman analyses optimal cohesion and contrasts heterogeneity–diversity–unity with homogeneity–uniformity–fragmentation. He points to helplessness and frustrated desires and ambitions as prime movers towards states of incohesion. The two opposite states do not exist as either/or, but as poles in between which the pendulum might swing. Neither Bion nor Turquet refer to this paper.

References

Bion, W. R. (1961). *Experiences in Groups and Other Papers*. London: Tavistock, 1985.

De Laclos, C. (1786). *Les Liasons Dangereuses*. Paris: Gallimard-Jeunesse, 2008.

Gabbard, G. O. (1994). *Psychodynamic Psychiatry in Clinical Practice* (4th edn). Washington, DC: American Psychiatric Association.

Hopper, E. (1989). Aggregation/massification and fission (fragmentation)/fusion: a fourth basic assumption? Unpublished paper presented to the VIII International Conference of IAGP, Amsterdam, August.

Hopper, E. (1997). 21st S. H. Foulkes annual lecture: Traumatic experience in the unconscious life of groups: a fourth basic assumption. *Group Analysis*, 30(4): 439–470.

Hopper, E. (2003a). *Traumatic Experience in the Unconscious Life of Groups: The Fourth Basic Assumption: Incohesion: Aggregation/Massification or (ba) I:A/M*. London: Jessica Kingsley.

Hopper, E. (2003b). On the nature of hope in psychoanalysis and group analysis. In: *The Social Unconscious: Selected Papers*. London: Jessica Kingsley.

Kernberg, O. (1978). Leadership and organisational functioning: organisational regression. *International Journal of Group Psychotherapy*, 28(1): 3–25.

Kernberg, O. F. (1980). Regressive effects of pathology in leaders. In: *Internal World and External Reality* (pp. 253–276). New York: Jason Aronson.

Laplanche, J., & Pontalis, J. B. (1973). *The Language of Psycho-Analysis*. The International Psycho-Analytical Library Vol 94. London: Hogarth Press.

Lawrence, W. G., Bain, A., & Gould, L. (1996). The fifth basic assumption. *Free Associations*, 6: 28–55.

Long, S. (2008). *The Perverse Organisation and Its Deadly Sins*. London: Karnac.

Nitsun, M. (1996). *The Antigroup*. London: Routledge.

Pines, M. (1998). Reflections on mirroring. In: *Circular Reflections* (pp. 17–41). London: Jessica Kingsley.

Turquet, P. M. (1974). Leadership: the individual and the group. In: A. D. Colman & M. H. Geller (Eds.), *Group Relations Reader 2* (pp. 71–87). Washington, DC: Rice Institute.

Willi, J. (1982). *Couples in Collusion*. New York: Jason Aronson.

Zinkin, L. (1983). Malignant mirroring. *Group Analysis*, 16, 113–125.

CHAPTER THREE

Trauma as cause and effect of perverse organizational process

Susan Long

I n this chapter, I will argue that trauma and perversion are related recursively at the systemic level of organizations. Trauma and perversions are, of course, related at the individual level of persons, but it is generally overlooked that they are also related at the systemic level. It is important to maintain the distinction between the systemic level and the individual level of analysis.

Over the past half century or so, the increasing culture of individualism, market competition, and consumerism have led to the experience of what Miller (1993; Miller & Khaleelee, 1985) and Hopper (1989a,b, 2003) have termed "failed dependency", leading to a loss of trust in public institutions and large private corporations. The culture of individualism and privatization has changed the nature of the relation between persons and the institution. The patient, the university student, the citizen have been rendered equivalent to the shopper under the banner of "customer" (Long, 1999), or, more generally, the consumer. For those with economic power, this might be experienced as a freedom. For those without such power, the experience is more likely to be one of abandonment.

All organizational life is affected by these changes. The rhetoric of customer extends to a range of organizational stakeholders and to the internal relations between different organizational role holders. In larger corporations, jobs are rarely for life and organizational loyalty is primarily based on an emotional connection to the immediate work group rather than to the corporation as a whole. In addition, the 2008–2009 global financial crisis has left many with a mistrust of the global financial system: a privately based set of institutions that were bailed out by public monies.

It is within this context that dynamics of perversion within organizations within both the public and private sectors have arisen:

1. While in the rhetoric of capitalism the dynamics of individualism, competition, privatization and increased consumerism are claimed to be beneficial, in fact they often conflict with the desire that organizations be both dependable producers of high quality goods and services, and also supportive employers. While the employee strives for better wages and working conditions, the same person in the role of consumer strives for more goods and services at a lower price. Although the internal conflict between these roles is hidden and denied beneath a narcissistic culture (Lasch, 1979), the postmodern psyche is split between consumer and producer (Long, 2008), and the experience of each set of roles and functions is saturated with competition and envy.

2. When organizational leaders are preoccupied with their own narcissism and its demands for gratification, the probability of failed dependency is likely to increase. In the public sphere, it is as if the moral yardstick and compassionate baby of the welfare state were thrown out with the bathwater of the state's inefficiency. In the private sphere, the growth of the corporate form has led to groups of senior executives being able to take business and financial risks with little personal consequence (Bakan, 2005). If the catchword has now become "profit only", then the corporation is likely to function in a predatory, and perhaps even sadistic, fashion.

Finding a way out of the cycle of perversity–trauma–perversity can only be achieved through a deeper understanding of the process. The role of the consultant from outside the perverse organization is extremely important. Bringing in a neutral outside consultant is tantamount to creating the space of the "third" as a contribution towards resolving the psychotic confusions that often characterize a traumatized mother–infant dyad and disturbed couples in general.

Perverse organization

Perversion might be found in small acts of bullying, unseen acts of "turning a blind eye", the fetishism of consumer lust, the voyeurism of celebrity, the unthinking denial of one's involvement in the suffering of the third world, or the causes of global warming. A big and repulsive word, "perversion", is usually reserved for those who are overtly cruel, and who take their pleasure at the expense of the other in the context of the disavowal of responsibility for this: the paedophile, for example. However, the underlying dynamics of perversion are also played out in the workplaces where we spend much of our daily lives. We must understand these unconscious dynamics both in work and in play, not just in individuals but in the social fabric that surrounds them, because the function of these dynamics is similar in both the system of the Individual and in the system of the Organization. Only then can we make informed choices in our actions, and try to limit the consequences of them.

Although the psychiatric definition of perversion has its own precise meaning, to be perverse is commonly understood as "persistent in error; different from what is reasonable or required; wayward; peevish; perverted, wicked; against the weight of evidence" (*Oxford English Dictionary*).[1] This fits well with a description of an organization behaving perversely through the damaging activities of those in roles with authority for its actions. I have examined many such organizations, for example: Enron and Long Term Capital Management in the USA, Parmalat in Italy, and Heath International Holdings in Australia (Long, 2008). The senior managements of these and other organizations are often described as corrupt. This has led to criminal charges in some cases. At times, such managers and owners are consciously aware of their own deceits. But, too often, other dynamics can be found. Their deceit is masked by their self-delusion, expressed through perverse pride, greed, and arrogance. Often an omnipotent and omniscient belief is retained that the leaders can bring about an upturn in the fortunes of the organization despite overwhelming indications that this is not possible. Yet, the perverse dynamics that brought about the various problems and collapses I describe were not achieved without broader systemic assistance—from the financial industry, for example—or even societal collusion, mostly at a less than conscious level. Perverse system dynamics are not the result of perverse individuals as such, but consist of a collective unconscious collusion involving denial and the instrumental use of others. These dynamics usually sit alongside normal and ethical behaviours in the organization and often involve a gradual slide across the boundary between the "everyday acceptable" and the perverse.

In order to discern the dynamics of the perverse organization, I had first to understand these dynamics as they occur in the individual. Perversion in the individual is understood more specifically in terms of sexual abnormality and/or pleasure gained from harm to others; waywardness nowadays predominantly defined in psychiatric terms. This has some problems, since there are still many debates about whether perversion is a treatable illness or a moral deficiency, and its aetiology and prognosis have often led those with indications of perversion to find themselves in penal rather than medical institutions. Moreover, what is considered to be perverse has changed with the changing attitudes of society and differs across cultures. None the less, there are broad indications that help to define perverse dynamics.

Many psychoanalytic schools of thought consider perversion as a specific set of symptoms, primarily including sadism.[2] In my discussion, to behave perversely is not limited to overt sexual perversion, even if its roots lie in sexuality, and I will refer, within the psychoanalytic tradition, to a state of mind that can be considered to be perverse. There are five major indicators of this state of mind.[3]

1. The perverse state of mind is not simply a deviation from normative morality. It has to do with individual pleasure at the expense of a more general good, often to the extent of not recognizing the existence of others or their rights. Stoller (1975) refers to perversion as an "erotic form of hatred". This seems a hatred of all otherness.

2. The perverse state of mind acknowledges reality, but, at the same time, denies it. This leads to a state of fixed ideation and phantasy to protect against the pain of seeing and not seeing at the same time. This is the psychological defence of denial and lies at the basis of castration anxiety and the fear of difference

(Chasseguet-Smirgel, 1984). The perverse state of mind turns a blind eye.

3. The perverse state of mind engages others as accomplices in the perversion. While this is a critical aspect of organized perversity, it is also present in the dynamic of the perverse individual. First, there is nearly always a system that "turns a blind eye", and second, the objectification and humiliation of the other in many perversions aims to create an abused and used subjectivity; not a simple instrument, but a complex instrumentality (Benvenuto 2006). The other is needed.

4. The perverse state of mind is likely to flourish where instrumental relations have dominance in the society. This is because instrumentality ignores the rights of others to independent existence. This is in itself abusive.

5. Perversion begets traumatic experience, and traumatic experience begets perversion. This cycle is hard to break. Corruption breeds corruption because of the complicity of the accomplices and their subsequent denial and self-deception.

These five indicators can be used to look at broader social states of mind. The mind of an individual, after all, is shaped and constrained by the social conditions in which it is formed and expressed, many of which s/he is not consciously aware of (Hopper, 2003a). An organization is more than a set of interacting individuals. It has its own systemic qualities arising from the individuals and their interactions over time. In fact, the system, in terms of its history, pre-dates the individuals who enter it and (most often) who become acclimatized or encultured.

In practice, the system and the individuals within it co-develop or co-evolve and do this through the "actions" of people in roles. The role is the organizational unit that is filled by the person and also shaped by the system (Newton, Long, & Sievers, 2006). In one role, a person might think, feel, decide, and act quite differently from when he/she is in another role—police detective or father, for example. Such is the pressure of the system, its needs and requirements! When in a role, a person is subject to its responsibilities and accountabilities, its rewards and its authority, all derived from the purpose and tasks of the broader system—police force or family, in the case of the example.

Moreover, a large complex organization might have many sub-cultures, each of which might have a predominant state of mind for various lengths of time. Each might contain roles that support or are in conflict with the broader organizational culture. A predominant state of mind in the organization or a sub-culture might be, for example, entrepreneurial, conservative, risk-taking, aggressive, philanthropic, defensive, or family friendly. The list is only restricted by the list of adjectives serving to describe collective behaviour.

True, and quite reasonably, all the facts cannot be known by all the players, sometimes not even by all the senior players. Humility, co-operation, and communication are required. Fidelity to understanding one's role, not only as a set of tasks, but as a container for important thoughts, feelings, hunches, and information about the organization is needed. Also, it is important to understand how others think and feel in their roles. To do this is a fundamental of good teamwork (Long, 2002). The complexity of an organization demands that no one role is privileged; each plays a part in the whole.

It is possible to understand the presence of perverse states of mind in any of these sub-systems. In fact, in very simple terms, the five indicators of perversion are found in cultures of selfishness, denial, systemic collusion, and instrumentality. The leaders and managers involved might think they are being tough; know what they are doing and do not need to consult widely; are really the experts; have the vision, even if things are not going quite right just now; trust in others (often buddies) without going through normal double checks; believe they are doing good on behalf of others who do not know what is good for them. Importantly, organizational perversion is collective—a mass delusion that many buy into as part of the culture, not really knowing all the facts. This is often a central element in states of massification (Hopper, 2003b).

The effects of the perverse dynamics can be traumatic on a wide scale. We have come to trust institutions and organizations, not deeply or in a personal way, but pragmatically because, mostly, they are all we have for transacting our lives in today's global world. They have our impersonal trust and we have only the law, not a personal relation, to uphold this trust. But that trust becomes the basis for security in terms of one's income, housing, and capacity to provide for loved ones; when broken, the experience is traumatic.

If we are to examine cases of organizational perversity, we must see them in the context of those broader social dynamics underlying the breakdown of institutional trust. In the past half-century, we have moved increasingly from a general culture of dependency to a culture of individualism and consumerism (Miller, 1993). The relationship between citizens and the large social institutions has changed. This is evidenced, for example, in the concept of "user pays", in the privatization of public utilities, and in the increased need for private health cover and superannuation.

The case that I discuss in this chapter is not that of a large corporation. It is the case of a small graduate programme in a university. None the less, according to anecdotal evidence, similar dynamics to those involved in this case have been played out across the wider university sector. The participants had their trust in the organization severely battered. Many suffered stress, anxiety, and depression. The story is illustrative of many similar stories where the dynamics of denial, envy, greed, sloth, and instrumentality have been played out alongside more creative dynamics. My data comes from discussions with the staff and students involved. I have made minor changes to disguise the players, but present the actual facts of the case as I observed or had them reported to me.

The case of the graduate programme

The programme was designed for mature people in industry and government, many of whom did not have tertiary academic qualifications but had gained their positions through "on-the-job" experience. Its focus was to provide them with a range of ideas and tools to support their development in their work roles. From the beginning, a learning community with ideals of adult education was formed, within which the students developed both personally and professionally. This community became an important part of the student experience where ideas, tribulations, problems, and learning were shared.

The programme founder/director was an energetic, entrepreneurial man, charismatic in his teaching style, but also thoughtful and strongly dedicated to an ideal of supporting his students collectively and personally and aiding them to learn independently from their experience. He was quick to adopt new ideas and schemas and to challenge his students with these. However, not being an angel, he was not always easy to work with, and, at times, made enemies in the context of disputes that are both typical of and inevitable in organizational life. His success in gaining students might well have provided a basis for envy among some of his protagonists.

A small project-based programme with intensive workshops, this programme did not fit easily into the usual university format. Reading was only prescribed when the student needed it in relation to some project. Assessment was rarely through written essays or scholarly work. But, for the most part, the students were hard working and dedicated. They were involved in action learning projects that were judged by the outcomes produced in the work practice of the student and through an intensive oral presentation. Its place in the organizational structure changed over the years. Due to its "boutique" nature, the programme found places in hidden corners, nested by "champions" found by its director among university academics and managers, some of whom were its graduates. None of these seemed the natural place for the programme, but graduates worked in all sectors of industry.

The programme was well attended, though deliberately small for pedagogical reasons, including its learning philosophy, small classes, and direct experiential learning. Various in-house forms occurred through the years, where companies paid for employees to be trained. By all accounts, including those of the enthusiastic alumni, it was a success.

In the early 2000s, it was joined by a "sister" programme that moved from another university, together with its director. At that time, a sympathetic vice chancellor welcomed it. Together, the two programmes were able to form a significant, if small, part of an applied science faculty, and a professional doctorate was developed. This, with a PhD programme, provided a further research programme for graduates of the two Masters programmes; all three formed the basis of a small centre with over 150 students, a core staff of four, several associate staff, a research and consultancy programme, public lectures and workshops, and was host to several prominent international scholars and researchers on a visiting basis. This group saw themselves as part of the spearhead of the vision required of graduate tertiary education programmes in Australia. They were totally reliant on their own income, not on government money, were running innovative programmes, were linked to industry through research and consultancy, and were a leading edge in their field, with professors taking up leading roles in local and international associations. What more might an innovative university want?

The simple answer, of course, is money. The group moved from having to provide 40% of its income to the central university coffers in 2003 to a demanded 70% *before* wages by 2009. This was catastrophic. Each year (2004–2008) the requests for larger overheads and central contribution had been met by increased staff activities in consultancy and research, plus cost cutting wherever possible. In late 2008, one professor retired from a full-time professorial position in order to work sessionally with the research students. There were plans also for this professor, being a writer and journal editor, to take up a mentoring role for graduates in terms of publishing their research, This looked likely to save some salary and allow a younger member to join the staff group, in line with the group's succession planning. Still, the 70%, consisting of overheads and "contribution", loomed menacingly in the 2009 budget plans.

The contextual "political" scene must also be considered. The group was in a sympathetic and supportive school, but, by 2008, it was itself in trouble. Financial cuts had to be made in several areas and demands from the central administration were not being lowered. Also, there had been changes at the top. A new vice chancellor had been appointed and, more recently, a new pro vice chancellor and head of a newly restructured faculty where the school sat. This senior team had no real knowledge of the group and its work. If it was seen at all, it was regarded as part of small "cottage industry" type programmes that, in the view of this leadership, had no real place in the university. The new vice chancellor visited many parts of the university, but not this small post-graduate area. The restructuring of faculties also meant that the location of programmes was revisited.

The head of group negotiated a deal with the head of the school where the programmes were located. This was around the time of the global downturn in late 2008, when the financial situation looked very bad. The two remaining professors agreed to leave full-time employment and take redundancy payments, thereby saving senior salaries, but would continue to teach sessionally in the programmes. This would allow the budget to include the 70% university overheads and contribution payments. The students would be getting the same programme, with the same staff. This would mean that succession plans for staffing would be brought significantly forward and the two more junior staff members would have to take on administrative and leadership roles. But each of the three senior staff who left agreed to give support when and how they could, while still teaching in the programmes. The senior lecturer, after wrestling with her uncertainties and anxieties, agreed to take up the leadership.

All plans were upturned overnight! On the day prior to a major public holiday, after the agreement with the head of school was signed and the associate professors took redundancies, the programme was moved to a predominantly undergraduate school with no consultation.[4] The new head of faculty did not consult staff or students, nor did the vice chancellor. At that time, in the role of adjunct professor, the retired professor was speaking with the head of another faculty of the university where it might have been appropriate to locate the programmes. But the decision was made and, when he enquired about this, he was told that the move as decided was final.

Following the move, the senior lecturer, unable to manage three programmes alone, stayed with just one; this was the second programme that had come from the other university a few years prior and was her primary field. The first programme moved to being managed by a staff member from the new school. Huge changes took place without consultation with students or staff members who had previously taught in the programme. These changes brought the programme somewhat in line with other programmes in the school, but meant it lost its uniqueness. For instance, changes were made to the assessment of student work. Staffing was reduced and the climate of the class was different; experiential aspects of the original programme, such as reflection space and time to work on group dynamics, were dropped. The changes broke agreements that had been made with students when they entered the programme. This proved to be a mistake with consequences for the school, as students from the industry programme complained and their organization threatened to litigate. In further negotiations, the university agreed its responsibility to the students, and, despite the students' disappointment that the type of education they had enrolled for was no longer available, in the service of finishing their degrees, they were willing to negotiate new conditions.

The whole episode involved is, of course, a breach of trust. Many students spend years saving and preparing themselves to enter the programme. It is regarded by them as fulfilling a time to make changes in their mid-career lives.

The programme has ostensibly been made more "academic". But it appears that a formulaic approach is being taken to mask the fact that the staff members from the new school just do not have extensive experience with post-graduate programmes of this kind and do not know how to run this programme. The programme is to be renamed and become central to the school. In fact, the school has obtained the programme through a kind of theft and has done none of the hard work that is necessary in getting a programme approved through regular channels. It has simply taken it over.

Processes of perversion and trauma

How might the process here be seen as perverse? The individual academics involved are not necessarily perverse. It can be argued that they suffer from the effects of the current university system and have had little chance to adapt to the passing of the older system located in the dependency culture of government funding. In the current climate, academic staff has to do more with less, and small class sizes are rarely possible, proving a severe barrier to experiential learning. Industrial relations changes have resulted in lowered job stability. Some of the academics feel themselves to be quite helpless in the process and are trying to do their best with what has landed in their laps. The person having to take up the management of the Masters programme within the new school is working hard to hold it on course in its new setting and still to meet the requirements of the school overall. Others appear somewhat triumphant in getting the programme without its founder. Also, the situation should not be seen as split, with one side totally "good" and the other "bad". The group as a whole had managed a succession plan for the future, but the first programme had been, for too many years, reliant primarily on its founder, leaving it vulnerable to takeover when he left.

The culture of the new school is extremely hierarchical, bureaucratic, and rule bound, probably as a defence against differentiation and possible envy. Office space, for instance, is strictly regulated, with more senior people having offices with windows and other staff members having no natural light. Even when an office space was found with a window, this could not be assigned to a lecturer (low in the hierarchy) and was designated as a room for a printer. This culture made it more difficult for the programme to become part of the new school and yet retain its integrity.

The senior management members of the university are not necessarily perverse. They are subject to nationwide views about how a competitive university should be and rely heavily on income from the government and the fees of international undergraduates to achieve this. They are part of a vast bureaucratic system of higher education where regulatory and quality audit systems have vastly increased the number of administrative staff in the past thirty years, changing the ratios of administrative to academic staff. They are subject to satisfying large compliance demands. Moreover, in their own university, they have a system where no one role is in the position to see every part of its complexity. It is a large university that has grown over the years from an original "working man's college" to a multi-campus institution with many programmes at many levels. During such changes, there have been few opportunities for healthy adaptation, including mourning the past.

So, is there perversity involved? Is the fate of this Masters programme simply one of a programme out of step with the current academic climate and victim of economic constraints? Consider the context.

The goals of university education include excellence in research and teaching. At a first glance, it might seem rational, even helpful, that a small postgraduate programme should be rationalized to fit into the culture of a school where, on the surface, it appears to belong. However, as I indicated at the beginning of this chapter, elements of perverse process as often occur in an otherwise "healthy" system. Originality, links to industry, world-class research, global links, and financial sustainability are all regarded as important within the university. The group described here, with its three programmes, achieved all these aims, so it appears irrational to have dismantled the group. However, it is necessary to examine the dynamics more closely.

1.   The new school appears to have achieved an aim to gain a desirable programme through the redesign of an existing programme purloined from another group who had developed it and whose leader had, within an agreement with a head of school, resigned

from his full-time position in order to sustain it financially. In this redesign, agreements with students were broken, such that an employer who was paying for a group to go through the programme threatened litigation for breach of contract. In all of this, the school seems to be operating from a "narcissistic" position in which the narcissism seems to rest in the idea that some few made decisions on behalf of others on the basis of incorrect or minimal evidence and information. In fact, information about the programme's specific nature and requirements and about its specialized market was never sought. This is not a question of the formal authority to do this, but a question of the interests involved and the duty to students. In addition, the head of research within the new school made no attempts to understand the nature of the research doctorate that was moved there with the Masters programme. It was as if he thought he already knew, or he did not care. No contact was made with regard to its structures and processes, and students were left uncertain about which school they were enrolled in up to eight months after the move.

2.   When the vice chancellor was questioned about non-consultation with staff and students from the programne, he denied that this was as claimed, and stated that consultation had occurred. Whether the vice chancellor believed this was the case and was in denial, or whether consultation with other senior managers was regarded as representing consultation with teaching staff and students, was not determined. Further discussion did not occur. The vice chancellor did indicate that the move was done in the best interests of the students, as it was feared that, in the absence of the senior staff members, the programme would collapse. But, in the absence of consultation with teaching staff, it is hard to see how this could be ascertained. In fact, arrangements had been made to support the more junior staff through a succession plan where senior staff would gradually withdraw. In any case, it appears that the system as represented by its senior management—whose members did make the decision to move the programme and renege on agreements with the previous head of school is denying the lack of consultation and initially denied its responsibility to agreements made with students.

3.   There is a denial of a conflict between the aims of the university and its actions, because the stated aims are always subjugated to

the needs of the administration, whether these are financial or "keeping up appearances". By keeping up appearances, I refer to the tendency of university administrations to seem to know what is best for programmes in the absence of really being able to know much about those conducted in their institutions. The problem is, of course, sheer size, the distance of the administration from the grass roots, the rise of managerialism, and the impersonality of current higher education systems. Much higher education now seems to be credentialism rather than education. So, denial of the inherent conflict between the educational enterprise and its managerialist management philosophy is built into the process. It is a painful trap to be caught in, but then, so many of the stated aims and actions in organizations are in conflict. When the conflict is denied and, therefore, the realities involved cannot be examined, the grounds for perverse process are laid.

4. We can look at this situation in terms of the accomplices and bystanders. The new school had for many years been unsuccessful in running Masters programmes within the broad field of the programmes in this case study. A graduate school had been formed, so the predominantly undergraduate school had no graduate programmes in the area, despite wanting one and having the authority to run Masters programmes. At a time when the programne was vulnerable to a takeover, the university senior management stepped in and supported that takeover. Under most circumstances, a process of consultation with staff and students would take place and arguments would be put forward as to the most appropriate "home" for a programme. None of this occurred.

All of this happened within a climate of instrumentalism. The two Masters programmes and the professional doctorate that together had a high profile within their markets were seen as "products" to be moved within the organization without regard to the people involved—staff, students, and employers. Although one of the employers was able to challenge the changes made to the assessment procedures and other issues, those students in the general programme and their employers have had little comeback. Discussion with the students reveals that many feel a deep loss for the type of education

in which they had initially enrolled. They are left with simple credentialism.

One student described the process as having stamped on his heart
and dreams.

I wrote a poem on the basis of what he told me. It gives something
of the feelings in this case.

The University

I want to tell a story
And it's very hard to tell it
About a man who found his soul
Then found he had to sell it.

And it wasn't to the Devil
Though YOU may question that,
It was to an institution!
I can tell you for a fact

When he went there, he was welcomed
With arms that opened wide
And that smiling congregation
Called his name to come inside.

In this fine institution
In a small place in the crowd
He found a place where he could fit
Of which he was quite proud

Though he didn't like their complex words
Like 'epistemological toxicology'
'Ontological paradox'
Or other such phraseology

Yet as a man of simple words
(Plain English was his fashion)
He brought that worthy institute
His deep enduring passion

For learning from the things he did.
He hoped that he'd be taught
Some helpful tools to craft his work
And influence his thought.

And how it seemed he had come home
To warm containing nest
Where learning was exciting;
With its riches he was blessed.

But I met him on a ravaged plain
Where storms had blown aside
The structures that he'd come to love
Foundations of his pride.

'She's reached into my chest' he cried
'And wrestled with my heart
She's pulled it from its place of rest
And torn its strands apart.

And while she bled away my joy
Till I no more could feel
She threw my soul upon the floor
And ground it with her heel.'

I stood . . . and though I felt aghast
I turned my head away
For shame and fear and horror
Of the part that I might play

Unwittingly!—add to his pain.
In that slow advancing dance
Of the thoughtless carapace
That doesn't cast a glance

At the human desolation
That it leaves there in the wake
Of its bureaucratic dictates
And its endless, needless hate.

Oh, I understand that change must come
And all of us endure
Some change is for the better
Brings us health and love and cure.

But to do it with no thought about
Agreements once in place.
To do it with no single shred
Of humility or grace

To wrench away the meaning
That we once had held so dear
Is to clothe us in the shadows
And breed anger from our fear.

Within an organization, the perverse process of breaking trust, denial, narcissistic self-interest, and collusion with accomplices leads to demoralization, depression, and/or anger. This leads to loss of creativity and organizational effectiveness. Small, perverse dynamics give way to further perverse dynamics as a gradual slide leads to tacit acceptance of perverse practice. And, having seen what has occurred, others find themselves either joining the denial and instrumentalism or fearing that they might be its targets at a later time, depending on their sense of power in the system.

The pressures of competitive capitalism in the current university environment are experienced institutionally as a lack of care for the educative process. Financial considerations are perceived to be more important than educational merit, leading to a mistrust of the institution. The students who paid hard-earned money for the programmne and enjoyed the self-respect that came with applying themselves to study, despite the fact that many had no previous tertiary qualification or had not studied formally for many years, and the staff members who had built their careers in the field of adult education, focused on learning from experience.

The change process was characterized by a denial of the need for formal places and spaces for participants to debrief, mourn, and examine their experiences. This gave rise to a sense of betrayal by figures of authority and by an authoritative institution. This complex traumatic experience became part of the culture of the new organization. It is, therefore, likely to be perpetrated within the culture of organizations that replace it.

Conclusion

This chapter has summarized ideas on the perverse state of mind and its presence in work organizations. While I have elsewhere described perverse dynamics on a large scale in some failing corporations, I chose here to look at how perverse dynamics can occur amid what might be seen as more everyday and ongoing activities and decision making in organizations. In this case, while the senior authorities in the university chose to proceed without wider consultation in what they might have regarded as a relatively small change, they did this in a way that involved perverse dynamics. They acted as accomplices in a dynamic that was narcissistically and instrumentally driven, and involved denial when challenged. This was all done under the guise of a rational justification.

It is likely that the source of perversion at the systemic level of the organization was the widespread anxieties that followed the traumatic experience of failed dependency on the university as a system, with its increased pressure on academics to produce alongside increased difficulties in the administrative and compliance work surrounding teaching, in the context of economic and political changes in the wider society. The result was traumatic for staff and students. Earlier traumas might well have been repeated, and might well be repeated, because there continues to be little space in the modern university to reflect upon such trauma and to grieve losses in the academic "way of life".

Notes

1. It is hard to find the opposite to perverse. Should it be "normal", and, hence, invoke the psychiatric domain, or should it be "ethical" and invoke the domain of the law? That authorities have had trouble knowing where perversion fits in such schemes is indicative of problems with its recognition and treatment.

2. These ideas are drawn from general psychoanalytic theory with particular reference to Freud (1914c); Lacan (1977); Nobus and Downing (2006); Pajaczkowska (2000); Steiner (1993); Chasseguet-Smirgel (1984).

3. These indicators are taken from Susan Long (2008), in which they are described more fully.

4. It seems the lack of consultative process is rife amongst academic administrations. A recent failure to consult and inform financial stakeholders in the prestigious Melbourne Business School about a planned merger with Melbourne University's School of Economics prior to a recent Board meeting has led to many angry investors (Gluyas, 2009).

References

Bakan, J. (2005). *The Corporation: The Pathological Pursuit of Profit and Power*. London: Constable.

Benvenuto, S. (2006). Perversion and charity: an ethical approach. In: D. Nobus & L. Downing, (Eds.), *Perversion: Psychoanalytic Perspectives* (pp. 59–78). London: Karnac.

Chasseguet-Smirgel, J. (1984). *Creativity and Perversion*. London: Free Association Books.

Freud, S. (1914c). On narcissism: an introduction. *S.E., 14*: 73–102. London: Hogarth.

Gluyas, R. (2009). Establishment at war over school merger blunder. *The Australian*, 19 September.

Hopper, E. (1989a). Notes on psychotic anxieties and society: fission (fragmentation)/fusion and aggregation/massification. Paper presented to the Conference of the Royal College of Psychiatry, Cambridge.

Hopper, E. (1989b). Aggregation/massification and fission (fragmentation)/fusion: a fourth basic assumption? Paper presented to the VIII Conference of the International Association of Group Psychotherapy, Amsterdam, Holland.

Hopper, E. (2003a). *The Social Unconscious: Selected Papers* London: Jessica Kingsley.

Hopper, E. (2003b). *Traumatic Experience in the Unconscious Life of Groups*. London: Jessica Kingsley.

Lacan, J. (1977). *Ecrits*. London: Tavistock.

Lasch, C. (1979). *The Culture of Narcissism: American Life in an Age of Diminishing Expectations*. New York: Norton.

Long, S. D. (1999). The tyranny of the customer and the cost of consumerism. *Human Relations (Special Edition)*, 52(6): 723–743.

Long, S. D. (2002). The internal team: a discussion of the socio-emotional dynamics of team (work). In: R. Weisner & B. Millett (Eds.), *Human Resource Management: Contemporary Challenges and Future Direction*. An interactive digital book on CD Rom. Wiley, www.johnwiley.com.au.

Long, S. D. (2008). *The Perverse Organization and its Deadly Sins*. London: Karnac.

Miller, E. J. (1993). Power, authority, dependency and change. In: *From Dependency to Autonomy* (pp. 284–315). London: Free Association Books.

Miller, E. J., & Khaleelee, O. (1985). Beyond the small group: society as an intelligible field of study. In: M. Pines (Ed.), *Bion and Group Psychotherapy* (pp. 354–385). London: Routledge & Kegan Paul.

Newton, J., Long, S., & Sievers, B. (2006). *Coaching in Depth: The Organizational Role Analysis Approach*. London: Karnac.

Nobus, D., & Downing, L. (Eds.) (2006). *Perversion: Psychoanalytic Perspectives* London: Karnac.

Oxford English Dictionary (2011). Oxford: Oxford University Press.

Pajaczkowska, C. (2000). *Ideas in Psychoanalysis: Perversion*. Duxford, UK: Icon Books.

Steiner, J. (1993). *Psychic Retreats: Pathological Organizations in Psychotic, Neurotic and Borderline Patients*. London: Routledge.

Stoller, R. (1975). *Perversion: The Erotic Form of Hatred*. New York: Pantheon.

CHAPTER FOUR

Baked beans and mashed potato: the basic assumption of Incohesion: Aggregation/Massification in organizations treating adolescents with eating disorders

David Wood

Clinical vignette 1

It is teatime. A sixteen-year-old girl, face hidden by her long blonde hair, sits hunched at the table. She remains motionless. In front of her there is a plate on which there is a small piece of toast covered with a small amount of baked beans. She remains motionless. Her nurse, who is sitting beside her, gently encourages her to eat. She remains motionless. The girl is painfully thin. The processes of her spinal vertebrae are clearly visible through her clothing. The nurse reminds her that she has to eat. After a while, with painful slowness, she picks up the knife and fork. She moves one bean off the toast to the side of the plate. With exquisite care she slices the bean in half. There is a pause. The nurse encourages her again. She then slices each half of bean into a further half and then again until the bean is divided into eight. The nurse continues to encourage her. She moves one eighth of the bean on to the fork and very slowly moves it to her mouth. She repeats this eight times and then sits motionless. The nurse encourages her. She repeats the process with another bean. The meal has now taken forty minutes. The cycle is repeated until the hour allowed for tea is up.

Clinical vignette 2

It is lunchtime. A boy who looks about eight years old but who in reality is fifteen, sits in front of a plate on which is placed a small piece of fish, some peas, and some mashed potato. He begins to squash the fish with his fork. It looks as if he wants to grind it into the plate. He then starts to stir the fish into the mashed potatoes; he then mashes the peas and slowly stirs it into the mashed potatoes until the whole meal is one homogenized mash covering the whole surface of the plate. Inevitably, bits drop off the edge of the plate as he continues to mash until there is a ring on the table around his plate. This whole process takes about thirty minutes. Only when the constituents of the meal are completely unrecognizable does he begin to lift small pieces on to his fork and into his mouth.

Introduction

These scenes will be instantly recognizable to anyone working in a hospital that treats young people suffering from anorexia nervosa. They are more or less daily occurrences. Such behaviour is usually explained on the basis that it is a resistance to the act of eating, principally in order to avoid ingesting calories. However, while being true at a superficial level, this explanation does not help us understand why a baked bean might need to be cut into eight pieces or a meal homogenized into an indistinguishable mash. After all, it still has to be eaten. How can we try to understand these observations further? Might it be useful to consider the symbolism of cutting something up very small, or mashing food together until its components become unrecognizable? And what might be a possible link between the two; after all, both activities occur regularly, and that they occupy opposite poles of a continuum between cutting up (fission) and lumping together (fusion) is obvious.

The theory of (basic assumption) incohesion: massification/aggregation ((ba) I: A/M) as described by Hopper (Gantt & Hopper, 2008; Hopper, 1991, 1997, 2003) offers a rich and fertile context within which to understand these phenomena more deeply, and in ways which shed helpful light on many other phenomena that can be observed[1] in institutions treating young people with severe eating disorders.

Hopper states that his theory of incohesion is

formulated in terms of a fourth basic assumption [(ba) I:A/M], the component processes of which are personified by central persons whose identities can be described in terms of characterological protections against the fear of annihilation . . . which in turn is a product of traumatic experience within the context of traumatogenic processes . . . (Hopper, 2003)

It is, thus, necessary first to consider the role of trauma in the aetiology of eating disorders[2] before turning to explore further the application of Hopper's theory of Incohesion to observations made in an institution treating such patients.

Trauma and anorexia nervosa

It might not be immediately apparent that working in an organization whose purpose is the treatment of patients with anorexia nervosa inevitably involves working with people who have been traumatized. The literature on the aetiology of anorexia nervosa has not tended to emphasize the role of trauma, and, if mentioned at all, it tends to be defined in terms of catastrophic forms such as sexual abuse rather than the more subtle strain or cumulative types of traumatic experience.

A sophisticated "biopsychosocial" model of the aetiology of the restricting eating disorders is still under development (Nicholls, 2007). Connan, Campbell, Katzman, Lightman, and Treasure (2003) have proposed a complex neuro-developmental model in which early trauma (in particular, the role of suboptimal parenting in early life and its effects on the developing brain) takes a central (but not sufficient) role. In relation to trauma, Hopper (2003) makes the point that "logically a trauma must be defined in terms of both the wounding agent and the susceptibility of a person to the wound, [although] this is really more an axiom of psychoanalysis than an argument of substance". However, I would argue that this is particularly relevant to the study of trauma in anorexic patients, as there is evidence of a particular sensitivity and vulnerability to stressful events that would be far less disturbing to a more robust character. Young people who are more susceptible to wounds are *in fact* predisposed to developing anorexia nervosa.

Genetic vulnerability

Recent neurophysiological research provides clear evidence that genetic variations influencing the differential development of neurones might well underlie differences in individual experience of stressors. For instance, it has been shown that Rhesus monkeys who carry the "short" allele of the serotonin transporter gene are significantly more affected by maternal deprivation than those who carry the "long" form (Barr et al., 2003; Suomi, 2003).

In humans, a similar picture is found. The gene only reveals its influence when people experience adverse events, such as divorce, debt, unemployment, or other occasions of "threat, loss, humiliation, or defeat". Variation in only a single gene might be enough to explain why some people weather stressful events while others are plunged into depression, although the greater likelihood is that vulnerability is due to a number of complex gene–environment interactions.

Early trauma and the nervous system.

Further support for this hypothesis comes from data from animal models, which demonstrate that early life experience, akin to the attachment experience of human infants, might have a critical role in shaping the development of biological systems of the brain (Connan, Campbell, Katzman, Lightman, & Treasure, 2003). The hypothalamic–pituitary–adrenal (HPA) axis, the neuronal and hormonal system that plays a major part in mediating responses to stress, is modified by maternal behaviour (Francis & Meaney, 1999). Rat pups experiencing optimal levels of maternal care develop highly efficient central negative feedback mechanisms, which tightly regulate the HPA axis. In contrast, those experiencing maternal deprivation have a relative impairment in these systems and are left with hyperactivity of the HPA axis, the neurophysiological substrate for the psychological phenomenon of "oversensitivity".

Animal studies have shown that significant modulation of these systems can take place within the normal range of maternal care, *indicating that early life experience need not be within the realms of abuse to give rise to HPA axis modulation* (Connan, Campbell, Katzman, Lightman, & Treasure, 2003) and supporting the notion that trauma of the strain or cumulative type is just as important. It is also important to remember that these systems are developing during intrauterine life, and are susceptible to circulating maternal stress hormones that cross the placental barrier and influence the development of the HPA axis even before birth.

In anorexic patients, it is hypothesized that a complex interplay of these processes in turn leads to changes in the neurophysiological systems that control appetite regulation. It is important to maintain a sophisticated conceptualization of these processes, which are, in reality, highly complex, and which involve highly recursive feedback systems so that even early on it becomes impossible to distinguish what is "nature" and what is "nurture"; all experience of "nurture" is obtained through the filters of "nature" (or, more precisely, the genetically determined structures of the nervous system and its component neural networks that are responsible for the perception, processing, and regulation of sensory experience) and "nature" (or, more precisely, the expression of genes) is continually and constantly affected by the current context in which those genes exist, which particularly includes circulating hormones, many of which are under central nervous system control.

It is also important to maintain a broad conceptualization of "appetite". "Eating disorders" are commonly thought to be disorders that are entirely concerned with food, weight, and shape, but those more familiar with them are well aware that the issue is much broader and refers to the regulation of many different appetites, of which food and sex are, for obvious evolutionary reasons, the most important. Indeed "eating disorders" might be better termed "desire" disorders, as the central problem concerns the regulation of desire in all its manifestations.

Authors such as Minuchin (Minuchin, Rosman, & Baker, 1978) have hypothesized that there is a common theme in the structure of the families of eating disordered patients, characterized by patterns of *enmeshment, over-protectiveness, rigidity, and lack of conflict resolution.*

Later authors (e.g., Eisler, 1995) have argued that these patterns are as likely to be *consequent* to the experience of having a seriously ill child in the family as they are to be *causal*. It is not surprising that a family that is struggling with the anxiety of serious illness might "close ranks", adopt rigid patterns of interaction, and would become more than usually protective of their offspring.

There is further evidence that "enmeshment" might *predate* the onset of AN, but *follow* previous traumatic experiences, such as miscarriage, still birth, or illness in a sibling (e.g., Shoebridge & Gowers, 2000). In other words, prior experience within the family of traumatic loss understandably leads to heightened anxiety during a subsequent pregnancy and after, which leads, in turn, to more enmeshed patterns of relationship, "overprotection", and the avoidance of conflict.

Recent work in the fields of child development, neurobiology, and work with personality disorder has been brought together by Fonagy and colleagues (Fonagy, 2002; Fonagy & Target, 1996; Target & Fonagy, 1996) in their description of a model of the development of the self that is relevant to the current topic. In describing the processes that lead to the development of an autobiographical, agentive self, they discuss two modes in which young children might experience psychic reality before the development of the capacity to understand intentional states in self and others. They term these two modes "psychic equivalence" and "pretend". In psychic equivalence mode, the internal world is equated with the external.

> What exists in the mind must exist in the external world, and what exists out there must invariably also exist in the mind. *There cannot be differences in perspective about the external world* because it is isomorphic with the internal. (Bateman & Fonagy, 2004, p. 69, my italics)

Conversely, in "pretend mode", the child's mental state is "decoupled from external or physical reality, but the internal is thought to have no implications for the outside world" (ibid., p. 69). In optimal development, these two modes of experience become integrated into the more reflective mode of "mentalization", in which thoughts and feelings can be experienced as representations.

Development of mentalization is considered to occur most readily in the context of a securely attached and playful relationship with parents. When care is suboptimal, the capacity to mentalize either does not develop adequately or is fragile and vulnerable to collapse under stress, leaving the individual resorting to either psychic equivalence or pretend mode. "Failure to mentalize creates a kind of psychic version of an immune deficiency state that leaves these individuals extremely vulnerable to later sometimes quite brutal environments" (ibid., p. 82).

Of most interest in the present context is the observation that "the most characteristic feature of traumatization is *the oscillation* between these two modes of experiencing internal reality" (ibid., p. 93, my italics).

If functioning in psychic equivalence mode means that there can be no difference in perspective about the external world, then this mode of functioning would predispose towards fusion, confusion, and massification, whereas in pretend mode, the tendency to dissociation and decoupling from external reality would lead to fission, fragmentation, and aggregation.

From this clinical perspective, particular themes emerge, which are consequent upon the traumatogenic processes outlined above, but which also generate further traumatic experiences. These themes of exquisite sensitivity, terror of conflict, and greed and envy, are ubiquitous in the lives of these patients. Hopper has described how early experiences of profound helplessness, through defensive splitting of the primal emotion of "grenvy" (Coltart, 1989), give rise to states of intense greedy desire and malign envy. Both of these emotional states are experienced as terrifying and unbearable in their intensity, at least in part because of the sensitivity underpinned by the abnormal modulation of the HPA axis described above. Because of their intensity, they are also assumed to be "lethal" or catastrophic in their effects on others, and, thus, any form of conflict is terrifying because of its assumed consequences. Indeed, they can be considered to underlie the phenomenology of "eating disorders" in that the sensitivity gives rise to the experience of emotional states as overwhelming and "too big" to manage. Unregulated greed and envy are transformed into concretized belief systems that the body is fat and disgusting and out of control.

I will illustrate these themes briefly through some clinical vignettes:

Exquisite sensitivity

For these people, many events are experienced as overwhelming when most others would manage them: they are more like a delicate, fragile craft, such as a rowing skiff that is easily overwhelmed and submerged, as opposed to a robust fishing vessel that can weather most of the storms that life throws against it.

Alice, who had experienced severe emotional and physical deprivation as a young child, had begun to use her therapy sessions constructively after many months of silence and resistance. One day, her therapist was inadvertently detained on the telephone with a crisis and was just under two minutes late for her session. Alice felt crushed and rejected, and was unable to talk in her session again for a further six weeks.

The terror of conflict

Just as important and intertwined with the sensitivity is the sense of a family context that finds conflict problematic.

Betty's mother, Belinda, had experienced a childhood in which her own very rigid mother was unable to bear anything out of place, and would frequently lose her temper uncontrollably. Belinda grew up a very frightened and timid woman, for whom any conflict was terrifying. She had married a man who described a family life dominated by rows between his parents, culminating in his mother leaving the family when he was fourteen. Betty's parents could not remember ever having had a disagreement, let alone a row. All conflict was avoided in the most extreme way.

Greed, envy, and "grenvy"

At some point in treatment, most patients will make a shift from feeling themselves to be fat to talking about feeling greedy. They experience a profound sense of themselves as unbearably lazy, demanding, and selfish if they express any desire for anything pleasurable, even if it is only relaxation or basic needs.

Catherine, a sixteen-year-old girl with a long history of restricting anorexia nervosa, gradually moved from arguing endlessly and round in circles about how fat she was (despite being nearly half normal body weight), to tentatively discussing her intense feelings of greed, such that any appetite for anything was experienced as intensely shameful. She was unable to accept that it was possible to want anything without being greedy; to sit down was lazy, to go through a doorway first was selfish, and to eat anything was evidence of disgusting greed.

Anorexic patients are intensely envious, about which they feel profoundly ashamed and which is, thus, usually denied.

Catherine was also consumed with envy, about which she felt terrible. Although she could not easily make the connection, she took intense dislike to some other patients who shared the same therapist, or whose distress took the attention of staff away from her. She was unable to prevent herself making vicious envious attacks on others, and then would punish herself for being so bad.

Anorexia and "crustacean" and "amoeboid" characters

Tustin (1981) introduced the terms "crustacean" and "amoeboid" to illustrate two types of characterological defence against the fears of annihilation. The crustacean type develops a hard, impervious shell, which serves as a protection for an exquisitely fragile and vulnerable inner self, whereas the amoeboid type seeks merger and fusion in order to avoid the terror of dissolution or aloneness. Just as Hopper describes, patients with eating disorders oscillate between the two positions; at first the overwhelming helplessness is defended against by the development of the hard, bony shell, but the cutting off from the outside world and the isolation this induces gives way to a wish to merge or fuse with an external source of comfort. In turn, the fusion results in a fear of engulfment and a wish to cut oneself off again.

In the "crustacean" state, the patient seeks to cut herself off from the outside world for fear of being subsumed by it. She will enact this need to keep herself separate for the sake of survival by methodically cutting her baked bean into tiny pieces, or keeping the different foods on her plate separate, eating one at a time but never mixed. She will retreat into a remote uninhabited space, avoiding contact to the extent of looking at the floor rather than at a staff member, of not replying to questions, of sitting on the floor rather than on a soft chair. She will look admiringly at her hard, bony body, but hate any sign of softness, which is equated with vulnerability. She will deny that she is ill, as being ill means she needs something from outside of herself. She needs nothing from outside of herself, not even food or water. If you do not need anything, then you cannot be hurt, feel frustration, be rejected, or abandoned.

Catherine, who had considerable talent as an artist, brought her portfolio to her therapy session one day. In it were the most beautifully executed drawings of shells. She talked about her fascination with shells, their delicate curves, their hard edges and intricate shapes. She could not explain why she found them so fascinating, but just knew she did.

At the amoeboid pole, on the other hand, the patient seeks to merge with the other to defend against the terror of abandonment, isolation, and aloneness. She will mush everything together to annihilate any distinction between self and other, since, for her, *dis*tinction means *ex*tinction of any connectedness. She will deny having any thoughts of her own, but will compliantly agree with the views of others. She will find any sense of separation to be terrifying, becoming enraged if the staff member looking after her speaks to anyone else. She might even prefer to be fed by naso-gastric tube, as a concrete sign of a connection or fusion between inner and outer, and as an avoidance of the need to bite or cut (herself) off from the source of sustenance. She might express terror of being thought well, or that she is getting better, as to be well or to get better means that she will be forgotten and "dropped" by her carers.

Anorexic patients tend to more frequently demonstrate behaviour associated with the crustacean type, but in their material there lies evidence that this covers over amoeboid characteristics. Indeed, the intensity of their anorexic crustacean withdrawal will usually force the "outside world" to respond by becoming intrusive, invasive, or engulfing in order to save life.

Bulimic patients, on the other hand, tend to overtly demonstrate more behaviour associated with the amoeboid state. For them, the intense control that holds the anorexic patient together and prevents them from "dissolving" has given way to a more obviously oscillatory state. Anorexic patients often describe the fear of "letting the brakes off"; for the bulimic, the brakes have ceased to work properly and their "greedy" desire breaks free. The binge–vomit cycle replicates in the physical/somatic domain the internal situation in which they oscillate between a position experienced as one of intense, aching emptiness that cannot be filled up, however much they eat, and one of equally intense disgust at feeling invaded and filled with something horrible that has to be emptied out. They oscillate between unbearable emptiness and unbearable fullness. The emptiness is associated with acute loneliness (crustacean), whereas the fullness is associated with persecutory feelings of merger and loss of self (amoeboid).

Group processes in professional systems working with patients with eating disorders

I now turn my attention to a discussion of how processes associated with the fourth basic assumption (ba) I:A/M manifest themselves in an organization dedicated to treating patients with eating disorders. It is perhaps important to stress that the processes and phenomena described below have emerged despite enormous efforts on the part of the staff team to develop and maintain good "work group" functioning. It is testament to the power and inevitability of basic assumption processes.

Fourth basic assumption phenomena

I hope to have demonstrated that teenagers with anorexia nervosa (at least, those whose illness is severe enough to have required admission for inpatient treatment) are very often, if not always, profoundly traumatized, sometimes by devastating external events, but more usually by their exquisitely sensitive response to ordinary everyday stresses and strains. Their anorexia represents a desperate psychobiological way of attempting to cope with this, often manifesting primitive mechanisms that can be described in terms of defences against the fear of annihilation, oscillating between fission and fragmentation, and fusion and confusion. It is to be expected, therefore, that organizations providing treatment for such a group of patients will be very vulnerable to the processes that Hopper has outlined in his description of the fourth basic assumption: Incohesion: Aggregation/Massification. In presenting examples of these, the convention used by Hopper (2003) of discussing the features of aggregation and massification under the headings of communication, normation, and interaction will be followed.

Aggregation

Communication: inhibition, secrecy, sarcasm, bureaucracy, and euphemism

Hopper (2003) describes features of communication that are a sign of aggregation as inhibition, secrecy, sarcasm, bureaucracy, and euphemism. Those unfamiliar with work in a residential treatment setting for anorexia nervosa are often surprised, and sometimes quite shocked, at the profound silences in meetings, and the general painful difficulty in communicating. Staff arrive in the morning and politely say "Hi" to a young person that they pass in the corridor, only to be met with a blank stare that feels like a refusal to recognize their existence. To new staff, this experience can be profoundly disturbing and upsetting, and is often felt to be a personal attack.

More experienced staff who do not wish to accept this and actively request a response can be left feeling that they have attacked the young person if they insist on making contact, as if communicating is the same as stabbing with a knife.

Staff can often have a sense that something is going on behind their backs, the sense of a secret "contra" group that is plotting something.

A sub-group of patients, all of whom had been severely traumatized and for whom discharge was proving immensely difficult, formed a "secret" society, which they themselves chose to call "the Mafia". They would hold secret meetings and plot against the staff, usually planning destructive acts that would generate an immense amount of ill feeling that was hard to contain. It would feel as if any attempt to develop a therapeutic culture would be sabotaged, in much the same way that the Northern Ireland peace process was under attack from terrorism.

Newly appointed members of the staff team regularly express a sentiment such as, "I have never known anywhere that has such problems with communication". Under the sway of the aggregation pole of (ba)I:A/M, handovers between nursing shifts can seem to lack meaning, focusing on trivial banalities and ignoring significant information. Staff who do not work shifts and are present from day to day often find themselves wondering if yesterday really happened, as today's handover seems to be exactly the same as yesterday's, even though they know of important information that somehow seems to have got lost overnight. Communication between night staff and day staff is vulnerable to distortion and needs continual attention.

The use of sarcasm can be extreme and overtly humiliating and denigrating. Inexperienced staff, or those with little training, are particularly vulnerable to this and use hurtful and unprofessional language, such as telling a patient that they are "behaving like a looney", and then, if challenged, insisting that it is only light-hearted fun.

There is a tendency towards bureaucratization of procedures, whereby information is communicated with much more emphasis on its form rather than its content, such as that, at the end of a meeting, even though procedures have been followed, there might be difficulty in remembering whether anything significant was agreed. Perhaps of greatest significance is the "bureaucratization" of weight measurement as the apparently most significant bit of information about an individual. Clearly, a human being is infinitely more than just a number of kilograms, but sometimes one would be hard pressed to know this, as conversations become focused on the best and most accurate way of weighing someone and calculating their "thinness", thereby reducing the patient to a number (often to three decimal places!).

Patterns of normation: normlessness, ignorance, conflict, subcultures, normative taciturnity.

Building a therapeutic culture in which members of staff feel clear about what they are doing and why they are doing it seems profoundly difficult, and certainly more difficult than would otherwise be expected. It is difficult to agree policies in a meaningful way (that is, in a way that does not just feel bureaucratic). Staff members will often "do their own thing", seemingly heedless of whether it is consistent with what others do. It has been particularly difficult to achieve consensus over such basic issues as expectations of what needs to be eaten; although lip service might be applied to the principle, in practice, different staff apply different "rules" from day to day, sometimes directly countermanding decisions made by the previous shift without consultation. Subcultures arise, taking up different positions on a continuum of, say, that of firmness *vs.* leniency, but membership of each "culture" can shift from day to day so that someone forcefully arguing for greater firmness on Monday can be arguing for the opposite by Thursday.

Patterns of interaction: encapsulated sub-groups, ghettoization, and excessive role differentiation

It is a feature of any complex organization that, at any moment, there will be a number of sub-groups in existence. However, when the boundaries defining these sub-groups become overly rigid, their interaction with other sub-groups becomes impoverished and problematic. In inpatient units, a number of functional sub-groups are formed by different disciplines: nurses, teachers, therapists, etc. Further sub-grouping within disciplines arises, day and night staff, full-time and part-time staff, trainers and trainees, etc.

It has proved extremely difficult to get members of the nursing team to rotate between night and day shifts: the day staff and the night staff aggregate into encapsulated groups with little interaction. When a member of either group crosses over to the other, they frequently feel themselves to be out of sympathy with the other group, alienated and criticized or criticizing.

Relationships between the nursing staff and the teaching staff became strained during a phase of a team's development. There was much mutual recrimination and distrust, and retreating into rather rigid positions.

A common experience is that of a young person who will appear to be moderately cheerful and communicative with friends, but when she has to join a formal meeting, sits with her head down, her face covered by her hair, if possible on the floor, and refuses to say anything or to respond in any way. It is as if the group poses such a threat to identity that it cannot be faced.

Sub-grouping in the patient group is less obvious and less role defined, especially in units that only accept one diagnostic category, thereby eliminating sub-grouping by "diagnosis". However, sub-groups inevitably will still occur. Young people find it very hard to move between sub-groups, defined by positions taken up within the group, for example, the group of young people who always sit on the floor, the group who need feeding by naso-gastric tube, those who speak and those who do not, etc. Attempts to assist movement from one group to another provoke extreme anxiety and resistance.

Massification

States of aggregation give way to states of massification, as the anxiety related to the feelings of emptiness and loneliness in the aggregated state rises. A community meeting might start out in a state of aggregation, with much silence, failure to make eye contact, and individuals seemingly lost in their own worlds and unaware of the presence of the others in the room. At some point, it might become apparent that a shift is occurring; somebody speaks, using the "royal we", which is responded to by another, also communicating as if it is obvious that they are speaking for everyone and all in the room are of one mind.

Communication: magic and rites, cult speak, inauthentic mourning, affect contagion, pseudo morale

When a group is in the "massified" pole of (ba)I:A/M, patterns of communication could become ritualized.

In ward rounds in one clinic, when decisions were made which patients did not like, the patients were offered the opportunity to come to a further meeting to discuss the disagreement. This became known as the "court of appeal", despite deep misgivings about the unhelpful quasi-judicial language.

In a different clinic, despite the management team's clear view that decisions about care should be part of a collaborative process between patient and staff, the institution continued to refer to "*feedback*" that was handed over to patients following meetings, similar to an *ex cathedra* pronouncement from on high. In other words, anxiety about thinking together led to a ritualization of communication that generated further anxiety and pushed both patients and staff into ritualized roles.

At times, procedures that have been carefully thought about and designed to provide helpful structure, consistency, and predictability to a treatment programme can feel rather more empty and over-ritualized, with people "going through the motions". This needs to be seen as a sign that a massification process is operating rather than that the procedures themselves are unhelpful.

Patterns of normation: fundamentalism, total uniformity of beliefs

Patterns of normation in massified systems require total uniformity of beliefs, a fundamentalism that allows no curiosity or free thinking. This might be expressed by a propensity for those in senior roles to use the "royal we": "we always do this . . ." etc., and to speak as if there is no difference of opinion among the staff. At times, it can feel extraordinarily difficult to risk proposing an alternative point of view, as if one really is challenging orthodoxy. If one does, one can be made to feel extremely bad for having done so. It can feel very difficult to join a team, as if outsiders are automatically suspect of bringing contaminating views with them that are dangerous and threatening to stability.

In the patients' group the massification can be expressed through a profound intolerance of difference. Outrage is expressed at any perceived difference of treatment between one patient and another, and the notion that treatment plans might be based on individual needs of different patients is met with cries of "unfair". Of particular concern in this respect could be the difficulty a patient might have of moving out of a negative orthodoxy that views wanting to get better as akin to heresy. Wanting to get better is difficult enough for anorexic patients; when trying to make that shift involves challenging the normative beliefs of a massified group, it is almost impossible. This process can represent one of the very real "iatrogenic" adverse effects of inpatient treatment and it needs very active management from staff to help the group move out of it. It is important to remember that the opposite, apparently positive, norm of everyone expressing a quasi-religious fervour about getting better can result in an equally negative inauthentic "motivation" which is based on *getting better because the group demands it*", rather than a real shift in the patient's capacity to risk authentic change. Such motivation needs to be recognized as likely to be only "skin deep" and unlikely to last when the patient leaves hospital.

Patterns of interaction: imitation and simulation, minimal degree
of role differentiation, diffuse interaction, scapegoating

Scapegoating processes are rife and often severe. Without extremely hard work on the part of managers it is difficult for staff on the receiving end of these processes to survive, and the institution risks a succession of resignations.

For a period of about eighteen months, it felt as if there always had to be a scapegoat. The role moved around from one staff member to another, but it was observed that there was frequently a member of staff who felt "out on a limb", who dreaded coming to work in the morning, and who did not "want to work here any more". The scapegoat would feel devalued, attacked, at odds with the rest of the team, not listened to, and that other staff saw him or her as the source of all the problems. If only they would go away, then everything would be all right.

Unless these processes are managed very actively real damage can occur.

A nurse who had been appointed to the senior position in a clinic began to try to remedy some problems of communication and working practices that were interfering with the management of the patients. She found her authority continually undermined by another member of staff, who had been at the clinic for some time but who did not want the responsibility of the senior position. Despite support from the medical consultants, the senior nurse was eventually dismissed by management on grounds that were quite indefensible, but which were supported by a number of junior nurses and support staff.

It has been striking to observe how difficult it can be for the staff to accept role differentiation.

Although the principle of performance related pay was accepted eagerly on the basis that those working well would be better rewarded for their efforts, when it was introduced it met considerable resistance on the grounds that it would mean some being paid more than others. In particular, the notion that management could adequately differentiate staff on the basis of performance was difficult for some to accept, despite management being very closely involved day to day with a relatively small team that they knew well.

Staff find themselves stepping out of role; therapists take on nursing roles in actively comforting upset patients, nurses take on therapists roles by wanting to arrange lengthy private conversations with individual patients rather than be with the group, senior managers undertake straightforward administrative or maintenance tasks. Within disciplines, although there are inevitable individual differences in style (related to personality), allowing this to be acknowledged so that roles can be differentiated to fit individual's strengths has met with forceful resistance.

In a rather uncomfortable staff meeting, it was asked why A was allowed to take all her holiday in one go when B was not. The fact that A occupied a different role in the organization from B and that the effects of her taking four weeks' holiday together would have been, if anything, helpful to the organization, whereas it would have clearly been unhelpful for B to do the same, was not accepted as a valid reason.

It is important to remember that states of massification and aggregation oscillate from one to another, sometimes very rapidly.

Leadership and followership

Hopper (2003), drawing on Redl (1942), points out that "whereas 'work groups' have leaders, 'basic assumption groups' have 'central persons', and thus a so-called leader of a basic assumption group is really a kind of follower who is vulnerable to role suction . . .". A number of people come to occupy central roles in basic assumption processes, even though they are not leaders of the work group. They could be persons with a valency for roles such as "earth mother", "magician", "cheer leader", who take up roles as central persons in massified states, or persons with a valency for roles such as "purist", "control freak", "outsider", who take up roles as central persons in aggregated states.

Personification of leadership

In one setting, in which the team was led by two consultants over a period of two years, what started as minor characterological differences that could be understood as tendencies towards crustacean characteristics in one case and amoeboid in the other became exaggerated and increasingly problematic. A senior member of the team remarked with some frustration "one is a control freak, and the other disorganized". The two consultants felt themselves to be pushed more and more into polarized positions, one becoming a central person in a sub-group that tended more towards aggregation and the other in a sub-group that tended towards massification. These two groups became very polarized and considerable ill feeling was generated. Often attempts to think about this would be experienced as attacks and would attract retaliatory strikes.

The "crustacean" consultant was seen as "reliable but unapproachable", rigid, "snotty", anxious, controlling, and unsympathetic. The amoeboid was seen as "approachable but unreliable", chaotic, laid-back, funny (as in humorous), *laissez-faire*, and vulnerable.

Despite the polarity, both continued to get on well together, but shared a sense of overwhelming burden that left them feeling helpless, depressed, and exhausted.

Those gathered around the "amoeboid" central person found it very difficult to stay in role. Although their roles were in reality quite complex, they were senior experienced clinicians who should have been able to manage them appropriately. Instead, they often became caught up in taking up roles that belonged to others, thereby undermining them. They would hark back nostalgically to "how things were before", as if to a golden age which had been spoilt by the "crustacean" central person's insistence on what they saw as unnecessary rigidity and bureaucracy.

Followers of the "crustacean" central person found it easy to become drawn into taking up unnaturally rigid positions, or feeling isolated, rejected, and paranoid. They easily felt scapegoated, and worried that the organization would reject them for trying to stay in role, maintain boundaries, and insist on structure.

Character assassination of both staff and (particularly) parents has been a problem, with attempts to counteract this being met with sarcastic denigration and further victimization.

Clinical, managerial, and administrative implications

To work in an inpatient setting for the treatment of anorexia nervosa does not seem to be a popular career move. Recruitment and retention of staff is problematic in most, if not all, psychiatric institutions, but particularly so for those treating eating disorders. It is likely that much of what has been described above applies to other institutions dealing with traumatized patients, but attention to these processes is essential if a genuinely therapeutic institution is to be achieved.

First is the need for recognition that much of what happens day to day, which is so disturbing and discomforting, can be understood; that the frequent and often overwhelming experience of helplessness and hopelessness is the result of processes that have meaning can make the difference between wanting to stay in the job or leaving.

The institution needs to pay special attention to processes of communication, to the language that is used, to the maintenance of roles and boundaries, and to how all the disparate parts that go to make up the whole are relating. This is nothing new and certainly nothing that any well functioning institution would not already be doing, but understanding that all the things that happen that make it so hard to achieve might be manifestations of a fourth basic assumption allows the possibility of a more fruitful approach.

It is also essential to remember that no matter how hard the formal leadership of the organization strives to develop and maintain good work group practice, with staff acting in role and behaving in accordance with carefully thought out procedures designed to ensure adherence to the primary task of the organization, basic assumption processes will keep breaking through. This is inevitable, and needs to be understood to prevent demoralization in both the leadership and the wider community. It is also the case that good leadership in such organizations does not mean that the leaders are able to avoid feeling the consequences of this material and these processes, but that they are able to make creative use of what they are feeling in the service of the task (Hopper, personal communication, 2009). This is often very difficult, as the feelings associated with the fear of annihilation and its attendant defensive processes are intensely painful, and very difficult to bear. This requires considerable maturity and robustness, as well as sophisticated and skilled supervision and consultation when necessary.

Summary

Life in an organization dedicated to the treatment of young people with mental health problems is not easy. It can be an overwhelming, confusing, deskilling, exasperating, and thankless task. It can also be enormously interesting and rewarding. When the task of the organization is to treat young people with anorexia nervosa, staff seem to report considerably more of the former than of the latter. Managing these difficult feelings is problematic and requires particular qualities of robustness and maturity in staff.

I have outlined the theory of a fourth basic assumption as developed by Hopper, and applied this to the understanding of phenomena observed in institutions whose primary task is the treatment of individuals suffering from eating disorders.

Examples from empirical research have been given to support the notion that the individuals suffering from these disorders are more than usually susceptible to traumatic experience by virtue of their extreme sensitivity, and that patterns of defence arising from trauma are, thus, likely to be more than usually prominent.

The application of this theory has been illustrated with observations recorded during nearly two decades of work in such institutions, providing examples of the way processes of fission and fragmentation on the one hand, and fusion and confusion on the other, result in enactments of these processes in the behaviour of individuals, such as the dissection of a baked bean or the mashing of food, which otherwise appears deeply mystifying and irrational.

I have also provided illustrations of the way these processes become manifest in the unconscious life of the institution attempting to treat these disorders, and how this appears in the form of the fourth basic assumption. I have provided examples of the way processes of aggregation and massification determine various patterns of interaction, normation, and communication in the institution, and how these become personified in the various roles taken up by leaders and central persons in the institution.

The capacity to think about the unconscious life of the organization as a whole is essential, and being able to recognize what at first seem confusing and despair-inducing phenomena as manifestations of a fourth basic assumption of Incohesion: Aggregation/Massification has proved very helpful. The acknowledgement that these very painful experiences are understandable in terms of the trauma that has been, and is being, experienced by a very sensitive client group, and the consequent adoption of a fourth basic assumption as a defence against feelings of annihilation and overwhelming helplessness allows a distancing from the experience that promotes thinking, which in turn makes the containment of the powerful affects easier. The basic assumption group can move back to being a work group, at least for a while.

Notes

1. The ideas offered in this chapter are based on observations made over seventeen years of experience of working in two hospitals specializing in the treatment of adolescents with eating disorders, during which over 600 young people have been treated. It is difficult to know how many of these experiences are unique to these contexts and how many would be familiar to those working in similar institutions.

2. There are considerable problems with terminology in the field of the so-called eating disorders. As Nunn (2001) has pointed out, we do not

consider those suffering from obsessive–compulsive disorder to be suffering from a "cleaning" disorder, but we persist in labelling these conditions as "eating" disorders when they are far more complex and involve many facets of behaviour other than eating. However, we seem to be stuck with the terminology for now, and I have little choice but to continue the insult in order to be understood. For the sake of space, throughout this article it should be assumed that the words *anorexia* and *anorexic* refer to the psychiatric condition known as anorexia nervosa. It needs to be remembered that the word "anorexia" on its own, strictly speaking refers to a loss of appetite from any cause, whereas anorexia nervosa refers to a loss (or absence) of appetite due to "nervous" or psychological causes. As is well known, this is a severe misnomer, since people who suffer from anorexia nervosa do not actually "lose" their appetites; they are afraid of them, or the intensity of them, and, therefore, repress or deny them. I also do not like the term "an anorexic" when it refers to a person, as it objectifies them and reduces the complexity of their humanity to their symptoms. However, it is too cumbersome to continually refer to "a person who has been diagnosed as suffering from anorexia nervosa", so "anorexia" and "anorexic" will have to do.

References

Barr, C. S., Newman, T. K., Becker, M. L., Parker, C. C., Champoux, M., Lesch, K. P., Goldman, D., Suomi, S. J., & Higley, J. D. (2003). The utility of the non-human primate; model for studying gene by environment interactions in behavioral research. *Genes Brain Behaviour*, 2: 336–340.

Bateman, A., & Fonagy, P. (2004). *Psychotherapy for Borderline Personality Disorder: Mentalization-based Treatment*. Oxford: Oxford University Press.

Coltart, N. (1989). Personal communication. In: J. Berke (Ed.), *The Tyranny of Malice: Exploring the Dark Side of Character*. London: Simon & Shuster.

Connan, F., Campbell, I. C., Katzman, M., Lightman, S. L., & Treasure, J. (2003). A neurodevelopmental model for anorexia nervosa. *Physiological Behaviour*, 79, 13–24.

Eisler, I. (1995). Family models of eating disorders. In: G. Szmukler, C. Dare, & J. Treasure (Eds.), *Handbook of Eating Disorders* (pp. 155–176). Chichester: John Wiley.

Fonagy, P. (2002). *Affect Regulation, Mentalization, and the Development of the Self*. New York: Other Press.

Fonagy, P., & Target, M. (1996). Playing with reality: I. Theory of mind and the normal development of psychic reality. *International Journal of Psychoanalysis, 77*(2): 217–233.

Francis, D. D., & Meaney, M. J. (1999). Maternal care and the development of stress responses. *Current Opinions in Neurobiology, 9*: 128–134.

Gantt, S. P., & Hopper, E. (2008). Two perspectives on a trauma in a training group: the systems-centred approach and the theory of incohesion: Part II. *Group Analysis, 41*: 123–139.

Hopper, E. (1991). Encapsulation as a defence against the fear of annihilation. *International Journal of Psychoanalysis, 72*, 607–624.

Hopper, E. (1997). Traumatic experience in the unconscious life of groups: a fourth basic assumption. *Group Analysis, 30*, 439–470.

Hopper, E. (2003). *Traumatic Experience in the Unconscious Life of Groups: A Theoretical and Clinical Study Of Traumatic Experience and False Reparation.* Philadelphia, PA: Jessica Kingsley Publishers.

Minuchin, S., Rosman, B. L., & Baker, L. (1978). *Psychosomatic Families: Anorexia Nervosa in Context.* Cambridge, MA: Harvard University Press.

Nicholls, D. (2007). Aetiology. In: B. Lask & R. Bryant-Waugh (Eds.), *Eating Disorders in Childhood and Adolescence* (pp. 51–74). London: Routledge.

Nunn, K. (2001). In search of new wineskins: the phenomenology of anorexia nervosa not covered in DSM or ICD. *Clinical Child Psychololgy and Psychiatry, 6*: 489–503.

Redl, F. (1942). Group emotion and leadership. *Psychiatry, 5*: 573–596.

Shoebridge, P., & Gowers, S. G. (2000). Parental high concern and adolescent-onset anorexia nervosa. A case-control study to investigate direction of causality. *British Journal of Psychiatry, 176*, 132–137.

Suomi, S. J. (2003). Gene-environment interactions and the neurobiology of social conflict. *Annals of the New York Academy of Science, 1008*: 132–139.

Target, M., & Fonagy, P. (1996). Playing with reality: II. The development of psychic reality from a theoretical perspective. *International Journal of Psychoanalysis, 77*(3): 459–479.

Tustin, F. (1981). *Autistic States in Children.* London: Routledge & Kegan Paul.

CHAPTER FIVE

A study of trauma and scapegoating in the context of incohesion: an example from the oil industry

Ellen I. McCoy

Introduction

This paper describes a traumatogenic process in a large integrated oil company in an industry made turbulent by world events during the final third of the twentieth century. Turmoil in the politics of the Middle East and shifts in geopolitics relating to oil triggered economic disruption in the industrialized world. The resulting turmoil in the business landscape was imported into various companies and mirrored within their social systems. I illustrate this through the analysis of a particular American oil company with which I had long association in terms of Earl Hopper's theory of Incohesion: Aggregation/Massification (incohesion) as the fourth basic assumption in the unconscious "life" of social systems (Hopper, 2003b), and focus on scapegoating as an expression of aggression associated with massification.

Basic assumption incohesion describes a process of oscillation between the bi-polar states of aggregation and massification that results when a group and/or its members suffer trauma, which arises from failed dependency on people or situations. In this process, a group deteriorates into an aggregate (a collection of minimally connected people) whose members suffer anxieties based on isolation and lack of safety, which become so severe that the aggregate shifts to become a mass (a collection of people with maximal mutual attraction and little individuation) wherein its members now suffer merger-related anxieties such as fear of suffocation. The anxieties associated with massification precipitate a shift back to aggregation and a non-developmental oscillation between aggregation and massification ensues.

Aggressive feelings and aggression become especially problematic in masses and aggregates because the bases for interaction and standards of behaviour that regulate aggression are threatened along with the survival of the group. Scapegoating is a particular and ubiquitous form of aggression associated with massification, in which some members become targets for projections of the group's unwanted feelings and other "unacceptable" aspects. Scapegoating involves victims and perpetrators, and tends to become recursive, as perpetrators become victims and vice versa.

I was an active participant in the traumatized social system of the illustrative company in which scapegoating became a prominent feature, and it has taken years to develop sufficient detachment to become a credible reporter of the system's functioning and, specifically, to understand how a group of former colleagues could deteriorate into a lonely and defensive assortment of social isolates. The deterioration of the working environment occurred unevenly over time and across departments, so that a participant became aware of his or her lack of safety only when dependency on an assumption or a colleague failed. The experience of betrayal provoked self-protective behaviour that then led to failing others, producing a recursive pattern of trauma. The gifts of time and theory have helped me to understand this complex situation and my experience in it.

Background

Events culminating in the 1973 Arab oil embargo ushered in a new era of geopolitics in which forces in the Middle East became a powerful bloc that challenged the hegemony of the USA. America's excess capacity to produce oil had guaranteed energy security to the West during prior oil crises (including the Second World War) but, by 1973, this excess was exhausted, which assured the effectiveness of oil as a political weapon (Yergin, 1991). In 1978, a group of Iranian "students" entered the American embassy in Teheran and seized hostages, setting off a fifteen-month crisis that played out nightly on television and was punctuated by a failed hostage rescue attempt. Loss of the ability to dominate the world oil market and the humiliating hostage drama demonstrated America's vulnerability and eroded its world leadership role. The Iranian revolution and the bloody eight-year Iran–Iraq war that followed aggravated the instability of the Middle East and created chaos in oil production and logistics.

During this period, the balance of control over oil prices and supplies and associated political power shifted from large western integrated oil companies and their home governments toward producing nations, notably OPEC (Organization of the Petroleum Exporting Countries). Historically, oil had traded at publicly posted prices, and supply balanced demand sufficiently to support orderly trade. Following the tumultuous politics of the 1970s, OPEC raised prices precipitously and tried to support them by imposing production quotas to limit supplies. Fractious relations among OPEC members, however, led to cheating on quotas and secret price discounting, with associated price declines, until they would again resolve to limit production and maintain agreed prices, a process that resulted in extreme price volatility. Ultimately, lack of discipline among OPEC members meant that they lost control over pricing and oil joined other commodities in being priced by free-market mechanisms. After a decade during which oil prices increased nearly tenfold and producing countries gained enormous wealth, high prices encouraged increases in production and consumer conservation, which eventually led to a surplus of oil and a collapse in its price. Thereafter, although oil prices spiked periodically in relation to political and military conflict, essentially they remained at depressed levels throughout the 1990s.

Throughout this period of rapidly changing fortunes, producing countries used their wealth to penetrate downstream into the consuming world, traders entered the distribution chain through new spot markets, and producers and consumers contracted directly with one another without large company intermediation. In short, independent companies flourished in every sector from production, shipping, and refining through to distribution and retail sales, eroding the benefits of process integration that had allowed the large multi-national companies to maintain effective control of supplies. In retrospect, it is easy to see that the big oil companies had no option but to shrink. Initially, they responded by cutting costs and restructuring processes but, ultimately, some companies ceased to exist as their assets were spun off and others consolidated through mergers and acquisitions.

During a large part of this period, the illustrative company delivered good financial performance because it had strong management, solid financial and asset bases, well-established relationships with producing nations, and loyal and skilled employees. Interdivisional management processes, such as career development and strategic planning, had facilitated strong personal relationships and effective informal communication networks across the company; as a result, the company's social systems were "healthy" enough to weather the early years of price volatility and political shifts well. When end-to-end integration of the business process ceased to be a strong economic advantage, however, work groups became less interdependent and associated social systems began to fragment. The collapse in oil prices prompted intense profit pressure and severe cost cutting. By the 1990s, ongoing cost reduction measures within the company had compounded trauma from external sources and the human fabric of the company had become badly frayed.

A new President with an orientation toward the financial sector was named to lead the company. His immediate subordinates were Division Vice-Presidents (VPs), most of whom were near retirement. Divisions comprised major operating units, each led by a business leader of the generation expected to produce the next group of VPs. Within a few years of his appointment, the President concluded that external threats from new market realities were too great to survive alone and the company merged with another to ensure its long-term viability. This chapter focuses primarily on the executive group comprising the President, Division VPs, and business leaders during the period prior to the merger.

The theory of incohesion applied to this case

The theory of incohesion as a fourth basic assumption describes how groups and their members respond to traumatogenic processes.

Trauma is classified as either *strain*, similar to the Chinese water torture strain of daily life, *cumulative*, which is the "build up of small incidents into an overpowering wave of oppression", or *catastrophic* (Hopper, 2003b, p. 54), but trauma can be conceptualized as a mixture of these. People experience trauma when their dependency on other people, situations, or factors in the environment fail.

In individuals, trauma and failed dependency are likely to cause the fear of annihilation, which is also associated with profound shame and primitive forms of guilt. Fear of annihilation is experienced as intrapsychic fission and fragmentation (the feeling of falling apart) with associated anxieties that elicit the desire for merger (fusion and confusion with the lost object) as a defence; the state of fusion and confusion, however, is associated with psychotic anxieties such as fear of being smothered, trapped, or crushed, which then precipitate a retreat back to fission and fragmentation. As a result, fear of annihilation is characterized by a bi-polar oscillation between the states of fission–fragmentation and fusion–confusion as each extreme serves to defend against the anxieties of the other. Envy of the lost, abandoning, and damaging object is likely to arise as a protection against the fear of annihilation and primitive feelings of guilt and shame associated with it (Hopper, 2003b).

Groups of people can also be traumatized in a variety of ways that are often interrelated, such as management failures or other events that break the boundaries of containment and cause group members to feel profoundly unsafe (bank failures, civil wars, or earthquakes, for example), shared history of specific kinds of trauma, such as sexual abuse, regression of group members to an early phase of life, and/or importing and re-enacting traumatic experiences from other times and/or places through processes of equivalence.[1] Because group trauma involves social regression and the collapse of boundaries between people and their groupings, the concepts of personal trauma are closely related to social trauma (Hopper, 2009, p. 222). The group becomes fragmented into a state of aggregation, in which the organization seems to be (and often is) falling apart, relationships are in tatters, and overt aggression is rampant. As a defence against anxieties associated with aggregation, the group shifts toward massification, a state in which the organization appears to be coalescing but relationships are based on merger of the sort one might experience at a political rally or sports event, rather than authentic relatedness based on integrated interaction and communication that typifies an effective work group. Massification is dependent on various forms of aggression, which are often more covert than overt, especially scapegoating and other forms of marginalization. Massification generates its own anxieties, which then cause the group to shift back to aggregation. This repetitive process is not developmental, but results in a bi-polar oscillation of the group between aggregation, which is akin to fission and fragmentation in the individual, and massification, which is related to fusion and confusion. Hopper has conceptualized this group dynamic arising from traumatic experience as the fourth basic assumption Incohesion: Aggregation/Massification or (ba) I: A/M (Hopper, 2003b).

Trauma

The American public and the American oil industry suffered all three classes of trauma (strain, cumulative, and catastrophic) in the last third of the twentieth century when relations with Middle East oil exporting countries became vastly more difficult and oil became a weapon of politics. The general public and the oil companies experienced the initial trauma of the 1973 oil embargo as catastrophe from outside their borders; American consumers, however, soon shifted their focus to the oil industry, which they perceived as the enemy in their midst responsible for the loss of inexpensive and plentiful supplies of oil. Oil companies were required by key producers to enforce the embargo, which was particularly traumatic for American-based companies, since the USA was initially the primary target of the embargo. Trauma experienced by the oil companies from failed dependency on Middle East suppliers was compounded by hostility from the public and from the US government, which used Congressional hearings and punitive taxes to demonize oil companies as a displacement for alarm over America's loss of global influence.

When oil prices (and profits) collapsed, trauma in the subject company was exacerbated by internal initiatives taken to survive harsh new economic realities. The company shed assets and launched wave after wave of cost-cutting programmes. Trauma became more personal as some people lost jobs, most lost colleagues, and everybody lost confidence in their careers because they could no longer depend on the company and its management. The tacit cradle-to-grave employment agreement that offered security in exchange for loyalty had been breached. While trauma from internal events was catastrophic for some, cumulative trauma and that of daily strain had an impact on everyone.

Basic assumption life

Historically, the work group of this company was efficient, leading to its success for many years. The integration of business functions enhanced its economic strength and was supported by well-defined roles and processes that led to effective interdependence. Cross-divisional career development moves strengthened appreciation for success of the whole, and company-wide training programmes promoted common understanding of norms and bases for shared values. While elements of basic assumption phenomena sometimes occurred, they were generally channelled productively. For example, elements of fight/flight tended to be focused on competition, and elements of dependency and pairing supported leadership. Following the political and economic changes and company responses that have been conceptualized here as traumatic events, however, the organization began to evince incohesion.

Cohesion of social systems that are large and complex is based on the integration of their interaction system, so damage to the company's process integration ultimately compromised its social systems. Complex social systems are extremely vulnerable to trauma because integration means that if certain connections are broken, the system is likely to collapse (Hopper, 2005, p. 38). Organizational restructuring was undertaken individually by divisions and departments within them at different times, with little regard for co-ordinating results, protecting linkages, or recognizing shared agendas. This piecemeal approach to restructuring broke many connections, which damaged the integration of management processes and diminished interdependence in the social systems, thereby facilitating the move to aggregation.

Social damage was evident when company investment strategy meetings became individual competitions for capital and when secrecy became rife as business leaders kept operating problems hidden. Aggression among business leaders was apparent when, for example, one business leader provided flawed assumptions to another during the planning phase of a project and then sabotaged the presentation in public by pointing to erroneous conclusions based on the flawed assumptions. Informal networks across the company sustained damage and the former atmosphere of co-operation evaporated.

After years of cost cutting that generated increasing aggregation, the president shifted focus to raising profits through increased productivity of both the workforce and hard assets. Business units were challenged to raise profits through creative ways of doing business, and profit pressure generated ferocious competition among their leaders as each strove to outdo the other. Peer collaboration suffered as trust was replaced by envy and suspicion. Erosion of the integrity of management processes and the hierarchical structure showed further evidence of aggregation. For example, when one function was reorganized, a department manager who operated at the boundary between two divisions was documented to be fully accountable to both, a contradiction that superiors refused to resolve, so that the manager and his staff were unclear about their roles and responsibilities and unable to engage in decision making with any confidence when conflicting priorities were assigned. When hostility erupted openly between the respective division vice-presidents, the subordinate manager was held responsible and evaluated harshly on previously unseen criteria relating to yet a third set of priorities.

Further confusion ensued when the president bypassed his immediate subordinates and reached down into the organization to encourage hand-picked individuals to advance specific proposals; ostensibly, he intended to encourage entrepreneurship but, in fact, he blurred accountability. The president's involvement shifted attention away from screening procedures designed to insure robust investments, such as risk–return analyses and assumption testing by peer review, to seeking the president's favour. Business leaders were urged to take more risk while expert opinions that might curtail risky projects were viewed as obstructionist. In some cases, profit was pursued without proper risk management, with poor business results.

As confusion permeated the hierarchy and management processes, moral corruption crept into financial areas. People became more casual about expense accounts and financial irregularities became more frequent. Increased anxieties arising from unreliable standards of behaviour and interaction fuelled the contagion of corruption into personal areas as instances of excessive drinking and exploitative sexual relationships increased. Some executives used limousines at the company's expense so they could drink excessively at company functions, and several were disciplined for aggressive sexual behaviour. Private excessive alcohol consumption was obvious from morning-after signs, and sexual liaisons were evident at off-site meetings as people sought merger to ward off anxieties associated with aggregation.

A diversity initiative was launched in recognition of the forecast that new entrants to the workforce by the year 2000 would be dominated by women, ethnic minorities, and immigrants. The business leaders (all white American males) appeared to embrace the initiative with enthusiasm, apparently relieved to have an issue around which they could agree and simulate some of their former collegiality: that is, they could massify as a relief from the anxieties of aggregation.

The purpose of the diversity initiative was to engage the full productivity of all employees and to increase representation of women and minorities at more senior levels of the company. It aimed to eliminate systemic bias against particular groups and was advanced by a cross-divisional committee comprising the company's highest level diversity candidates and several high level white men who were committed to having a "healthy", diverse workforce.

The incoherence of diversity as a cause around which to massify was illustrated by the words of the initiative itself, which addressed the need to value differences while preaching "inclusion" of everyone in an undifferentiated sort of equality in nearly religious tones. In fact, focus on diversity at that time was probably aroused by underlying aggregation, because, even though ethnic and social categories are unrelated to productivity, they tend to take on fresh importance in traumatized social systems and become groups which form the basis of social identity for their members. In the eyes of the wider society, such groups ultimately become sub-groups and possible contra-groups: that is, sources of aggregation against which the only social defence is massification (Hopper, 2005, p. 38).

Aggression to maintain massification was soon apparent, as attempts to address the complex and nuanced issues inherent in authentic dialogue about diversity were cut off in the interest of political correctness. Visible executive perquisites were curtailed in an effort to emphasize equality and eliminate separateness, a move that required public embrace but caused private bitterness. The ill-defined concept of equality associated with "inclusion" raised unrealistic expectations for diversity candidates, who were disappointed when individualized, accelerated career development plans to redress perceived prior slights did not materialize. Ironically, one result of the diversity initiative was to further consolidate the massification of white American males and to encourage the rest of the employee population to take refuge in ethnic and social groupings, particularly evident in the company cafeteria.

In addition to using the diversity initiative to increase representation of women and people of colour at upper levels of the company, the President also used it to express dissatisfaction with current business leaders by implying the executive corps needed to be augmented due to the inadequacy of its current members. This exacerbated the fragmentation of the employee population by shaming the current business leaders and devaluing diversity candidates. Diversity groups became more acutely conscious of their marginal status and more envious of the group in power. White male business leaders were already shaken because they identified closely with business results that were declining, and implications that they had achieved their positions based on unfair advantage engendered hatred and envy toward diversity candidates, feelings that the bounds of political correctness did not allow them to express or even admit.

The early enthusiasm in support of the diversity programme gave way to intense negative feelings and threatened a shift back to aggregation, which required intensified aggression to maintain massification among the business leaders.

Scapegoating

A prominent form of aggression employed to maintain massification is scapegoating, in which groups purge themselves of unwanted thoughts and feelings and project them into certain of their members, whom they then marginalize; at the same time, they also project this unwanted "material" into other groups who are "different" and who are often regarded as inferior. Traditionally, scapegoating was regulated by sacred rites that functioned to cleanse a community of its unwanted elements. These elements were projected onto the scapegoat, who was then banished or killed in a ritualistic way. In the original Hebrew ritual, there were two goats; one was killed as an offering to cleanse the community of its sins and reconcile them to God, and the other was to bear projected guilt and evil and was taken into the wilderness, far from the community. While neither goat's fate was enviable, each performed a valued and sacred role for the community.

In secular life, scapegoats function similarly in that they carry the community's projections of "unacceptable and dangerous feelings, ideas, attributes and qualities. . . . These targeted people are then judged very stringently and perceived to be guilty. . . . Ultimately they may be shunned and even banished" (Hopper, 2003b, p. 79). Girard describes the function of the scapegoat in service to massification this way: "Where only shortly before a thousand individual conflicts had raged unchecked between a thousand enemy brothers, now there reappears a true community, united in its hatred for one alone of its number" (Girard, 1977, p. 84). What he calls "true community" is what Hopper calls massification. The scapegoat protects the society from descending into total violence by attracting violence to itself. Girard's discussion suggests the role has an element of sacredness because the "victim actually brings about communal cohesion" (ibid., p. 290), at least for a time.

As a result of the 1973 Arab oil embargo, American society was traumatized by the decline both in its global influence and in the supply of cheap gasoline to fuel big cars and the American way of life. Coming in the midst of the Watergate scandal, the catastrophic oil trauma threatened the fabric of society and the authority of government, resulting in unbearable aggregation. In an attempt at massification, the consuming public and the US Congress focused their anger and aggression over supply shortages and high prices on large oil companies, which served as effective scapegoats because they were perceived to have the ability to resolve supply problems but to have chosen not to do so. Further failed dependency on government agencies, such as the intelligence services, who failed to perceive the Iranian threat, and the military, who failed to rescue the hostages, continued to generate fear and helplessness and, thus, the need to maintain massification. Oil companies were well placed to play the role of scapegoat when their profits were high and seemed unable to escape this role long after profits fell.

Hostile projections from outside the company intensified the need for massification within the company because individuals were traumatized by persecution in their personal lives based on association with the oil industry, blurring the boundaries between personal and work life. When oil prices collapsed, profit pressure increased and the business leaders, each of whom aspired to be a future VP, were set up in a competition that fewer than half could win. At the same time, they were challenged to co-operate with one another for the greater good of the company, creating intolerable levels of anxiety and an intense need for scapegoats in order to protect their fragile massification.

Business leaders turned their attention to service functions and blamed them for eroding profitability. They were easy to blame because they were cost rather than profit centres and were not considered "core" to the business. Secret negotiations to outsource these functions as a whole were instigated without the rigorous analysis and evaluation of discrete segments that would be required to achieve a robust outsourcing arrangement. This premature effort was a rash attempt to rid the company of its profit problems: that is, as a way of sending projected hate, envy, and failure into the wilderness. The negotiations were foiled by internal opposition and the decision was taken to restructure the functions with audacious savings targets that would require enormous cost cutting and staff reduction.

A new process to select high-level executives had been developed in parallel with the study of the service functions and was used to select the leaders responsible for implementation of the restructured functions. It was a secretive, peer-based group process and replaced traditional hierarchical methods. The ostensible purpose of the new process was to encourage team spirit and co-operation but, in fact, secrecy diluted individual accountability and, in an environment rife with scapegoating, the selection group became a mass and sometimes a vehicle for lynching.

When staffing decisions were announced, the leader of the diversity initiative was not selected for a role commensurate with her level of seniority. Although such a position was available, it was left open while she was demoted into a lower-level job in an act of public shaming that was virtually unprecedented in the company. Because she was the company's highest-level woman, she had been perceived as having visibility and access to senior management beyond that which her position would normally warrant. She was like a privileged sibling and was, thus, a long-standing target of envy and well placed to be scapegoated as a displacement from the father/president with whom white male executives were enraged because of his perceived intent to promote diversity candidates at their expense. She was also scapegoated as a shaming mother/witch because she had "blown the whistle" on several men who had had sexual liaisons with subordinate women.[2] One such affair involved a senior executive who was hated because he had emasculated many male subordinates, reputedly to ensure he could not be replaced. The diversity leader might have expected collegial support for attacking this castrating object, but it was not forthcoming, and it is likely that she carried the projected unconscious Oedipal guilt of her male colleagues over their rage and desire to kill their superior. She was subsequently sent to a distant, nearly invisible project, like the scapegoat banished to the wilderness.

Simultaneous with the demotion of the company's highest-level woman, the other prominent diversity leader, a more junior woman, was selected to implement the major segment of the restructured functions, a significant promotion that meant she became the company's most senior woman. Her role required implementing unprecedented levels of cost cutting and redundancies, goals so extreme that either they could not be met, or, if they were, the associated pain and anguish to the organization would be greater than a career could survive. She was initially idealized as someone who could implement thousands of redundancies while keeping employee morale high, a virtual impossibility. While her promotion to this senior position might have been partly an attempt to atone for aggression toward the woman who was demoted, she was, in fact, set up in the role of assassin of the many people who would be made redundant, putting her in position to be assassinated in the future for either completing the assignment or failing to complete the assignment. She was also sent pornography from a senior executive in a clear warning that she, too, could be banished or demoted if she transgressed some unknown boundary.

As key leaders of the diversity programme and the most prominent women in the company, both were well positioned to carry projections of undesirable elements of the majority group: for example, the feminine, foreign, dark-skinned, homosexual parts. Including sexual orientation as part of the definition of diversity had been a particularly controversial element of the programme, and homophobia among the business leaders was no doubt heightened by attempts at massification.[3] Focus on race and ethnicity was a reminder of the dark-skinned Middle Eastern (and later African) suppliers who had once been dependent on these executives for development of their resource and income base, but who were now in a position to be courted because they had control over supplies. The impact of the shift in the balance of power was intensified within the company because it echoed the broader political reality. The new senior woman was an effective container for projections of distrust and betrayal associated with foreign, dark-skinned objects because she had previously served in commercial functions where she had dealt comfortably and successfully with many foreign suppliers. She was blonde and female with Aryan features: physically their opposite, which sometimes makes an ideal scapegoat.

In her new assignment to implement restructured support functions, she implemented large numbers of demotions and redundancies, and carried projections of murderous aggression and guilt associated with the culling effort that had initially been supported by the business leaders with enthusiasm. Within a couple of years, nearly everyone had a friend or colleague who had been affected, and the anguish of the organization was projected on to her; she was demonized and transferred to a distant location. Her transfer was accomplished quickly and smoothly, despite a complex chain of international transfers and office space reallocation, indicating a high level of planning. She and many of her staff and colleagues experienced it as assassination, "an illegitimate 'cutting down', associated with feelings of horror, terror, and rage" (Hopper, 2003b, p. 82). But what else can be done with an assassin after her work is done except to assassinate the assassin?

This figurative assassination is an example of the recursive nature of trauma in the context of incohesion. The organization was sufficiently traumatized by this event that external consultants were hired to interview perpetrators, peers, and subordinates, with the result that data were uniquely available in this situation. The data revealed that specific events occurring during the years prior to her appointment and involving a wide variety of people were projected on to her in a classic pattern of scapegoating. Further, this assassination, which itself was a response to the trauma of culling, triggered more trauma, as diversity candidates learnt that they were unsafe, executives learnt that support from the president was meaningless, and all employees learnt that prominence was dangerous.

Scapegoating and role suction

In this oil company, the drive to maintain massification generated a continual need for scapegoats. In his analysis of ritual sacrificial substitution, Girard points out that the victim must be sufficiently foreign to the community so that it is not attacking itself and propagating further violence, but must also be sufficiently connected to the community so that its expulsion can effectively carry away the community's sins: hence, the choice of marginal members as sacrificial victims (Girard, 1977, pp. 284–286). While they are generally ". . . drawn from the ranks of singletons and isolates (Roth, 1980), presumably because they are vulnerable and lack protective allies. . . . [S]capegoats are . . . central persons who carry the group's thoughts and feelings" (Hopper, 2003b, p. 80).

This process is, however, a bit more complex. Basic assumption processes arise as defences against anxieties that threaten the group's cohesion and they help the group hold itself together. The group then needs to create roles to support the basic assumption processes. In a dynamic that Redl (1963) calls "role suction", some group members are pressured to assume these roles through mixtures of projective and introjective identification (Horwitz, 1985, p. 29). Some people, notably those with a history of traumatic experience and a vulnerable sense of self, are more likely than others to assume specific roles and might even take part in creating and/or seeking them because they "offer a sense of containment and holding" and "bestow an identity within a field of turmoil and chaos" (Hopper, 2003b, p. 60). Perera notes that "in the scapegoat-identified individual there is a sense of being both chosen one and victim. . . . The individual feels affirmed . . . being the Christ-like, Chosen One, selected to the task" (Perera, 1986, pp. 50–51).

To the extent that the diversity programme itself became a source of aggregation, its advocates (as well as diversity candidates) were seen as personifiers[4] of aggregation, human impurities to be expelled in the service of massification. As such, they were ideally positioned for scapegoating, highly vulnerable to being sucked into a particular role in the service of maintaining the purity of massification. Within three years, despite careful adherence to antidiscrimination practices, all of the prominent advocates of diversity were targets of some form of marginalization: one resigned, two were made redundant, three were "sold" with assets, two were demoted, two were banished to far away posts, and one was side-lined.

The two prominent women in the company who led the diversity initiative were pressured to become scapegoats, but they also helped to create these roles and, in some sense, willingly assumed them. The fact that both women chose to build careers in an industry typically dominated by conservative men indicates they had an inherent desire to be special or to be the "only", a valued singleton, a role which provides a kind of automatic containment or protection against fusion. Their advocacy of diversity further highlighted their singular natures because they demonstrated their willingness to lead on a controversial issue and their ability (and probably their need) to maintain an independent identity even in (or especially in) a traumatized environment. It is ironic that "when massification prevails, the better the leadership . . . the greater is the desire for its elimination" (Hopper, 2003b, p. 102).

The role of leader of the diversity initiative was destined to be controversial by its nature, and the act of "whistle-blowing" isolated this particular leader further, although she appeared to feel invulnerable because she had been appointed by the president. Alford describes the motivation of the whistle-blower as "narcissism moralized", by which he means that the narcissist's sense of purity and perfection is wounded by association with moral corruption. The resulting narcissistic rage finds expression in exposing the corruption publicly, that is, whistle-blowing (Alford, 2001). Dialogue and education were generally the tools of the committee, but the Diversity leader was so indignant about several sexual liaisons that she took the unusual and aggressive step of reporting them directly to the president. Her outrage over misconduct at high levels, with apparent corporate tolerance, was no doubt fuelled by narcissistic wounding as described by Alford. She was envied and hated for her access to the president and for retaining her sense of self sufficiently to act on her indignation, attributes which also positioned her for the role of scapegoat.

When the other woman was appointed to her restructuring position, it was obvious that meeting her business targets would cause enormous organizational pain. While her appointment set her up to be scapegoated, she contributed to its likelihood by driving ruthlessly to achieve unrealistically ambitious goals even after she was warned of hostility swirling around her from the alarming numbers of redundancies. She was experienced enough to negotiate lesser targets and to court her enemies to protect her career, but she chose to pursue her assigned business objectives with apparent disregard for her peers' approval. She achieved a high profile outside the company and was featured in an industry publication, which attracted malign envy from the business leaders. Her unwillingness to seek dispensation from unattainable goals and compromise on more realistic targets might have been fuelled by narcissistic rage at finding herself in an untenable position, unable to deliver a perfect performance against an impossible target.

Both women seemed to believe that the president would protect them in their stubborn pursuit of the roles that he had given them. The president was a thick-skinned narcissist with a magnetic personality. Describing his impact, one subordinate said, "when standing in the president's glow, it feels so warm that it is easy to forget your backside is freezing." Many people, including these two women, fell under his spell. His abandonment might have so traumatized them and threatened their identities that they needed to find another skin of identity to protect their vulnerable selves against fragmentation, and, hence, sought the role of scapegoat.

The religious flavour in the writings of Girard and Perera referenced above seems apposite for these women. One is a strong practising Catholic, reputedly once a novitiate. The other, raised in a Protestant fundamentalist environment, struggles with the burden of sin. After leading the near-religious movement of diversity which failed to save the company, these Christian women both found roles where they sacrificed themselves (their careers, at least) for the good of the organization. Perhaps they were looking unconsciously for redemption, the love of the Father, or even hoping to replace the son on the cross.

Aspects of the "social unconscious"

The quality and intensity of scapegoating to maintain massification and the role suction of these women and their willingness to assume roles as scapegoats suggest that factors from the "social unconscious" of the broader society were imported into the company and fuelled the desire to "save" the company. The "social unconscious" refers to "the *constraints* of social objects that have been internalized, and to the *restraints* of those that have not" (Hopper, 2007, p. 286). The drive for financial success with little overt regard for the underlying social systems, the nearly religious fervour with which the diversity initiative was pursued, and the desire to "save" rather than adjust the organization, reflect particularly American values.

America's history and outlook is one of expansion of land, wealth, and power, supported by its social creed, which holds that there are no barriers to what one can achieve with enough hard work and raw desire.

While its value system encourages optimism and achievement, it also supports omnipotence and grandiosity. In its omnipotence, neither government policy nor public awareness comprehended the shift in the balance of power toward oil-exporting countries that began with the traumatic oil shortages in the 1970s, which is evident based on the ever-increasing size of vehicles and energy consumption since prices fell in the 1980s. The sense of grandiosity in the USA is evident from the persistent public conviction that the USSR collapsed as a result of pressure from President Reagan and his administration. More likely, the USSR, the world's largest oil producer, collapsed because it was bankrupted when oil prices fell by 75%. Grandiosity and omnipotence are obstacles to recognizing limitations and mourning losses and support the conviction that with a saviour (e.g., President Reagan) or the "right" course of action (e.g., the Iraq wars), supported by the "right" way of living (e.g., the Christian Conservative movement), America will retain its hegemony and the associated bountiful supply of cheap energy on which it depends.

The social penchant for optimism spills over into the financial markets, which demand positive forecasts and continual growth in order for management to be well regarded. In deference to this demand, the company announced their cost-cutting projects and culling programmes with enthusiasm regarding their financial advantages; acknowledgement of the human pain and suffering that would necessarily accompany them was perfunctory at best. This approach hindered the journey of mourning losses and limitations that would have been required to arrive at mature hope and capability. The executives had never come to terms with the inevitable need for the company and the associated power of its leaders to shrink. They appeared to subscribe to the promise offered by each cost-cutting initiative as if it would restore them to their former feeling of security and stayed in a regressed state, hoping to be saved by serendipity or magic, or by the scapegoats who stepped into this role. The difficulty, of course, was that no amount of scapegoating could return the company to its former state and that the search for a magical saviour was an obstacle to the authentic mourning that was necessary to develop realistic hope and mastery in the revised business conditions and to re-create effective work group functioning.

Summary and conclusions

The oil company described in this chapter was profitable and had effective social systems when the Western world and the oil industry within it was rocked by turbulent political and market forces in the early 1970s. In the ensuing years, company reactions to externally triggered crises compounded its internal turmoil. While the company survived well for some years, the traumatogenic process eventually led to severely damaged social systems in the context of incohesion, conceptualized by Hopper as the fourth basic assumption in the unconscious "life" of social systems.

The specific instances of scapegoating described were part of a larger pattern of aggression associated with incohesion, with scapegoating reaching epidemic proportions and leading to further debilitation of the company's social fabric. The frequency and intensity of aggressive attacks increased as the attempts to maintain massification became more desperate and less successful in the face of aggregation, demonstrating the recursive nature of trauma. The group assciated with the diversity initiative was targeted early and completely and, therefore, provided prime examples of scapegoating that became rampant in this company. Other scapegoats included people who could maintain an independent sense of identity, including prominent leaders and others who stood out in a variety of ways, such as in-depth knowledge and independent thinking. As a result, the cadre of competent leadership and technical expertise shrank at an alarming rate, compromising the ability of the company to redevelop organizational competence and recover effective work group functioning.

The top executives of the company believed that a significantly larger scale was needed to survive in the economic environment of the 1990s. Ultimately, the company merged with a larger oil company, which absorbed the ailing social fabric along with its hard assets. It is unclear whether senior management understood the extent of the damage to the social systems and associated management processes. In the end, the solution to the business problem essentially outsourced the social systems and management processes to the larger company.

The process of untangling the events described in this paper and creating a meaningful narrative took years of revisiting my own experience as a scapegoat. Locating the experience in a theoretical framework allowed me to explore the pain of others that turned colleagues into perpetrators and, ultimately, to reach the humbling recognition of my own participation as both victim and perpetrator. Analysis of the complex processes in this traumatized organization and my roles within it would have been impossible without the help of Hopper's theory to unravel the strands and find meaning in what often appeared as chaos.

Notes

1. The term equivalence refers to creating a situation that is "equivalent" to a previous one. People unconsciously tend to recreate situations that have occurred in another time and place. These situations are most likely to be those that have been traumatizing and have elicited primitive defences such as encapsulations. People "recreate traumatic situations in the service of expulsion and attack, and mastery and control . . . These processes are associated with the repetition compulsion and traumatophilia" (Hopper, 2003a, pp. 130–131). In this case study, global shifts in political power and the resulting social turmoil were enacted within the organization, which intensified the traumatogenic process.

2. Scapegoating

> may involve an unconscious attack on the Father (Money-Kyrle 1929), who is perceived to have failed the group and/or to have stopped access to the Mother. . . . Scapegoating also stems from

helplessness and envy of the Mother . . . on the basis of which 'she' is split into good and bad objects. The 'bad' target is attacked and ultimately banished. However, the 'good' target is killed and eaten, or at least incorporated symbolically, this initiating a process of atonement (Cohen and Schermer 2002; Maccoby 1982). (Hopper, 2003b, p. 79)

3. In massified social systems, one way "aggressive feelings are diluted and made more manageable" is "through their sexualisation or libidinalisation. . . . Competition is converted into banding, in which homosexuality becomes problematic" (Hopper, 2003b, p. 77).
4. Personification refers to the process whereby a person takes on a particular role that has been unconsciously created in association with a basic assumption and comprehends the concept of valence (sensitivity to role suction) along with the possibility for active interpretation of the role (Hopper, 2003b, p. 92).

References

Alford, C. F. (2001). *Whistleblowers: Broken Lives and Organizational Power.* Ithaca, NY: Cornell University Press.

Girard, R. (1977). *Violence and the Sacred.* New York: Continuum (originally published in French in 1972).

Hopper, E. (2003a). *The Social Unconscious: Selected Papers.* London: Jessica Kingsley.

Hopper, E. (2003b). *Traumatic Experience in the Unconscious Life of Groups.* London: Jessica Kingsley.

Hopper, E. (2005). Response to Vamik Volkan's Plenary Lecture 'Large group identity, large group regression and massive violence'. *Group-Analytic Contexts, 30*: 27–40.

Hopper, E. (2007). Theoretical and conceptual notes concerning transference and countertransference processes in groups and by groups, and the social unconscious: Part III. *Group Analysis, 40*(2): 285–300.

Hopper, E. (2009). The theory of the basic assumption of incohesion: aggregation/massification or (BA) I: A/M. *British Journal of Psychotherapy, 25*(2): 214–219.

Horwitz, L. (1985). Projective identification in dyads and groups. In: A. D. Colman & M. H. Geller (Eds.), *Group Relations Reader 2* (pp. 21–35). Washington, DC: A. K. Rice Institute.

Perera, S. B. (1986). *The Scapegoat Complex*. Toronto, Canada: Inner City Books.

Redl, F. (1963). Psychoanalysis and group therapy: a developmental point of view. *American Journal of Orthopsychiatry*, 33: 135–147.

Yergin, D. (1991). *The Prize: The Epic Quest for Oil, Money & Power*. New York: Free Press.

CHAPTER SIX

The survival and development of a traumatized clinic for psychotherapy for people with intellectual disabilities

Alan Corbett, Tamsin Cottis, and Elizabeth Lloyd

Introduction

In this chapter, we discuss various aspects of the structure and functions of an organization in which traumatic experience is ubiquitous. This organization exists in the highly specialized and minority field of intellectual disability. More precisely, this organization was established in order to provide psychotherapy for people with intellectual disabilities who had experienced or perpetrated abuse, often, but not always, of a sexual nature. Psychodynamically orientated interventions were also provided for those involved in the community-based care of patients, including paid staff and family members. We focus on the way in which traumatic aspects of intellectual disability impinged on the development of the organization and suggest some parallel processes between disability and how the organization functions. In addition, we will consider the significance of Hopper's (2003b) fourth basic assumption, "Incohesion: Aggregation/ Massification", or (ba) "I: A/M", in relation to the work of the organization, especially at a time of particular crisis. In (ba) I:A/M, Hopper argues that, as a result of traumatic experience, groups oscillate between a tendency either to split into separate, self-protecting, and isolated units, or to demonstrate extreme clinging, admitting no dissent or individual difference, diversity, or variety.

An organization whose clients are disabled is likely to be especially vulnerable to various failures of leadership. It might face several kinds of attack from its environment, such as funding restrictions and social and political disregard, as well as extreme challenges to its survival. Such an organization is under constant strain and exposed to cumulative challenges and disappointments, and occasional catastrophes in the ability of management and staff teams to deliver the services associated with the mission of the organization.

In common with other voluntary organizations, funding in the organization under consideration here was never secure, and the existence of the organization was always precarious. This organization, like others of its kind, needed strong leadership and secure containment and holding. Trustees, or board members, acting in a voluntary capacity, looked to a director to keep things in order and they relied on her to help them fulfil the obligations of their governance role. However, trustees as well as staff had strong needs for containment, holding, and protection with respect to the challenging demands of the work of the agency. Robust management procedures allied with high levels of trust and good communication between staff and trustees were required. These took a long time to develop and effort to maintain.

Especially important to the development of the organization was a set of highly damaging events (see below). In the aftermath of these events, the leadership sought to protect the organization from the basic assumption processes associated with traumatic experience, specifically the vicissitudes of (ba) I:A/M. However, eventually it was recognized that such an organization is likely to be especially vulnerable to such processes. In fact, there is likely to be a "maintaining cycle" which allows abuse—in its widest sense of the term—to occur repeatedly in such organizations, largely because the underlying causes of ubiquitous traumatic events have not been fully addressed, or serious losses fully mourned (Neill, 2008). Various measures were taken in an attempt to "earthquake-proof" the organization with regard to such experience in the future.

An organization in the field of learning disability is highly likely to be vulnerable to the vicissitudes of Hopper's fourth basic assumption processes, because the nature of its work involves what we would term a "trauma matrix", built from the following five features of its work:

- unresolved loss and mourning;
- societal marginalization and denigration;
- cognitive deficit;
- sexual trauma;
- sexual victimization/victimizing.

The impact on the organization of this "trauma matrix", inherent in intellectual disability and sexual abuse, will each be briefly considered in turn.

Unresolved loss and mourning

Working with intellectual disability involves fears of death and of dying and, both consciously and unconsciously, staff and management are asked to contain these fears. Hollins and Esterhuyzen (1997) and Blackman (2003) have described the obstacles, both societal and intrapsychic, that inhibit opportunities for people with disabilities to process the death of, or separation from, the figures to which they are attached. The experience of loss is commonplace. Parents can experience a profound sense of loss when they learn that their child has a disability. Their needs to mourn, grieve, despair, envy, and hate are often split off and encapsulated, both personally and in their family structures, as well as in the relationships of the family to the agencies of care in the surrounding communities. (It is unsurprising that organizations and, indeed, individuals who work with people with intellectual disabilities are likely to find themselves on the receiving end of projections and projective identifications that become subsumed into the culture of their organizations.) The problems that characterize the families of disabled children tend to be mirrored in the staff teams who support them. It can be very difficult for staff teams to maintain their morale and they might fall into states of despondency or into states of idealization, both of themselves and their work, and sometimes even of their intellectually disabled clients. Splitting within such teams is commonplace (Cottis & O'Driscoll, 2008; Menzies Lyth, 1988).

The nature of attachments between disabled children and their parents can be very fraught (Cottis, 2008). The cohesion of the families of disabled children is likely to be "inauthentic" in that the members of the family can become tightly bound together around the disabled child and caught in a feeling of being "on the outside" of society, associated with the social exclusion of the disabled. Alternatively, the family can hardly hold together and stay together as their relationships are likely to be based on denial and a failure to co-operate in order to manage the severe challenge to their ability to function. This applies to the relationship between the parents as husbands and wives, as well as fathers and mothers, and to sibling relationships.

Societal marginalization and denigration

The therapeutic process cannot be divorced from the political, social, historical, and cultural context in which it operates, and of which it is itself an expression. Thus, an ecological model of abuse and disability (Sobsey, 1994), in which vulnerability and trauma are experienced at a number of connecting levels is especially helpful in understanding traumatized organizations. This model is consistent with group analytical theories of open systems, foundation and dynamic matrices, and processes of equivalence, based not only on processes of projective and introjective identification, but also on processes of resonance, amplification, and mirroring (Hopper, 2003a).

The ego strength of a person with intellectual disabilities is also likely to be weak. The individual is vulnerable to abuse because attachments are weakened, and attachments are weakened in part because they exist in an environment that provides poor protection against abuse: research (Sobsey 1994) indicates that people with disabilities are 50% more likely to be abused than those without. People with intellectual disabilities are often devalued and the undesirability of a disability is communicated to the screened and tested foetus even before birth.

Cognitive deficit/annihilation fears

Sinason (1992) writes, "A child who is born with something wrong is often experienced as a disturbing challenge to our sense of biological autonomy and control". The attacks on the self and to society which may be carried through disability are likely to create very deep fears of annihilation. These will be brought about by

> ... (L)oss, abandonment and damage which spans generations and involves the relationships between victims and perpetrators and responses to the traumatised, failed dependency ... the Chinese water torture strains of daily life – the cumulative build up of small incidents into an overpowering wave of oppressions and/or the catastrophic violation of expectation. (Hopper, 2003b)

These fears of annihilation are carried unconsciously not only by the patients receiving psychotherapy from the organization, but also by the organization itself. The Trustees' ubiquitous mistrust of the directors and of the staff could be seen as an enactment of society's unconscious death-wish towards disabled people and those connected to them.

Although working with people with intellectual disabilities is not without rewards, these are often exaggerated and idealized. The cohesion of staff teams is likely to become highly inauthentic as a defence against facing the awful truth of the disability. After all, a cognitive deficit will not be "removed" by psychotherapy. Clinicians who work with such an inherent "lack" in the ability of their clients must face the reality that their work might not be valued by the wider professional community, or the community in general.

Sexual trauma

Fears of annihilation among people with intellectual disabilities are likely to be exacerbated by the experience of sexual abuse—especially incestuous sexual abuse in childhood. The long-term consequences of sexual abuse on mental health are well documented. Sexually abused patients might have enduring difficulties with authority and parental figures. Men are usually experienced as abusers or potential abusers and women as people who might have failed to protect them. In the clinical session, there are many expressions of these difficulties. The work of organizations that provide help for such patients has an interface between the trauma of disability and the trauma of sexual abuse.

Sexual victimization/victimizing

People with intellectual disabilities are not only at a greater risk than others of sexual victimization, they are also over-represented in the sex offender population. There is often an absence of an internal "benign" sexual couple, and sexuality is experienced as "malign" in both fantasy and reality.

These difficulties are likely to be "located" in the organizational structure. For example, gender issues are more than usually pronounced in staff relations and it might be difficult for a male member of staff to be experienced as a "good man". Staff might also project the suspicion of authority brought in by client material into their own governing body. This makes the relationships between staff and the Board of Trustees extremely difficult. In the same way that splitting is commonplace within families in which incest has occurred, and issues of blame and responsibility become part of the family culture, splitting is also a feature of organizations that work with trauma. In fact, there is a multiple splitting between staff and management, men and women, therapeutic and administrative staff. It can, therefore, be seen how extremely difficult it is for such organizations to develop authentic cohesion, both as a whole and in their parts.

All five elements in this matrix are illustrated in the following vignette, which also shows the severity of the various traumas experienced by the organization's psychotherapy patients.

"Susie", in individual psychotherapy for one year, was sexually abused by "John", the deputy manager of her day centre, over a period of two years. Aged thirty-five, and with moderate intellectual disabilities, Susie was the youngest of three daughters. Both her adult sisters were married with children of their own. As a child, Susie attended a special school and then progressed to a local day centre for adults with learning disabilities. She lived at home until the death of her mother, some three years before the abuse took place. At the time of the abuse, she lived in specialist supported accommodation with two other women with learning disabilities.

Susie talked in therapy of the way in which John groomed her for the abuse, taking her first on exciting day trips, then giving her special jobs to do in the centre, and spending time alone with her. The relationship only gradually became sexual, sex taking place in a computer room at the centre, and then, later, at Susie's flat. Susie described how

John persuaded her to keep their contact secret because he did not want his wife to find out about it. She talked of how he made her feel chosen, special, and attractive, and although he penetrated her with objects, and had anal sex with her, which she found shocking and shameful, she was thrilled by his attention. She believed that she was in a reciprocal relationship with him, and that the only obstacle to their being, as she said, "like a normal couple" was the fact that he was married.

However, following disclosure from another service user, it became known that John was sexually abusing at least four other female centre users. Susie was appalled to find she was not the "only one" in John's life and told her key worker what John and she had been doing together. In therapy, she became enraged, attacking a male disclosure doll, tearing at its hair and stamping on it. In addition to her sense of sexual degradation was a deep sense of betrayal.

Susie brought to therapy her feelings of being "on the outside" of normal family life, especially in relation to her two sisters. She was the victim of sexual trauma at the hands of John, and yet she felt the loss of the relationship with him acutely, made worse by the pain of his betrayal of her, as she saw it. These intense experiences of loss, shame, anxiety, disgust, and fear were generated and exacerbated by the five elements of trauma identified above.

As an example of parallel processes and equivalence, it was noted in supervision that Susie's staff team shared many of the Susie's feelings, including the fear that somehow they might have denied, or even colluded with, the abuse perpetrated in their midst. Notwithstanding the availability of regular clinical supervision, the discovery of abuse put the cohesion of the staff team at risk.

These parallel processes can also be seen in the organization itself. A senior member of the team (we shall call her X) who was in a leadership role defrauded the organization. We will not focus on the detail of the crime. We intend here to examine its ramifications for the organization. When confronted, X admitted her actions, describing them as symptoms of her wider "breakdown", and left the organization. When the fraud was committed, X had stopped being a work group "leader", and could be regarded as a "negative charismatic leader" rather than a "reparative charismatic leader" (Volkan & Itzkowitz, 1984). This shift in the form and style of leadership is typical of organizations in the hazardous world of the voluntary sector, in which leadership involves traumatic and potentially traumatizing material (Neill, 2008), and provides a special threat to new, or young, organizations. Additionally, and in another example of parallel processes at work, the changes in the behaviour and attitude of X went largely unchallenged by the Trustees and other staff. There was, in effect, a turning of a blind eye, a collusion.

We will now show how a tendency towards massification processes as a defence against the constant threat of aggregation processes associated with traumatic experience could be seen at various levels in the organization, including its clinical work. Our focus here is on two psychotherapy groups, one for men, which had been piloted and co-conducted by X, the other for women. Both groups embodied the trauma matrix, but the marginalization of the women was intensified through a devaluation enacted within the context of their abuse, which was internalized by the women themselves.

All the members of the group of women had suffered the most appalling failure of any containment, holding, and protection from abuse. Each member's experience of her own individual psychic skin, and of that of the group, was of a fabric torn and shredded beyond repair. They shared a sense of horror about their own bodies and a constant sense of boundaries being broken and their own bodily and psychic contents spilling out. Their traumata were re-enacted through harming their own bodies rather than those of others (Motz, 2001; Welldon, 1988).

With respect to aggregation, there were many references to the members' own experiences of being physically shut in, or trapped, in locked rooms, cupboards, wardrobes, and psychologically trapped in a learning disabled and sexually abused identity. Each member of the group seemed to be isolated from one another, even when they shared similar stories of their common histories. With respect to massification, they would insist that they were all completely the same, trapped and stuck in their group identities as learning disabled and sexually abused women. Very much later, at the most intensive and consistent phase in the group's life, the women discovered that their menstrual cycles had synchronized, their bodily leakage becoming harmonized as their emotional leakage became contained. However, in the swing away from the coalescence of massification, the group itself seemed to leak members; when the group finally ended, not one of the original members of it was present. It was impossible for the women to imagine an experience that was not one of laceration and leaking. In fact, it was often difficult to keep them all together for the hour and a half session, as though the skin of the group would not hold them together.

In the men's group, conflation of their cognitive deficits, sexual objectification by adults, and the encapsulated, isolated nature of their experiences resulted in a shared sexualizing of the world. In varying ways, they sought to relieve themselves of the unbearable pain of being a victim of sexual abuse by making others into victims who would carry their pain for them. It was decided that this group would be conducted by three people, rather than the more traditional one or two. The stated reasons for this were that to work with such a traumatized and traumatizing group of men should never be done by just one therapist, so the third therapist could help ensure that, even if one of the three was unavoidably absent through illness, then a couple would always be available. In retrospect, we would suggest that this apparently rational explanation of such a deviation from the traditional group analytic model disguised an unconscious desire or need to form a massified whole with which to counter the traumatizing nature of the men's pathologies. The notion that a single therapist or a healthy couple might conduct this group was unthinkable. In fact, the three therapists were unable to have independent thoughts about the clinical work of the group. Over time, their therapeutic attitude became one of punishment and control. Their authoritarian style allowed little space for the men's own experiences of victimhood and pain to be expressed and discussed.

Eventually, this group was conducted by only one therapist. In the session after it had been announced that X would not be returning, the therapist noted how unusually concerned the men seemed to be about each other: for example, one offered to bring another a glass of water. The therapist linked this with the fact of X's departure. This elicited a wave of manic laughter. The therapist interpreted that the men were terrified about another "parental loss". In response, the men became aggressive, insisting that the remaining therapist would be got rid of next. They articulated their rage at the therapist for evicting the "criminal" therapist from the group, but suppressed and repressed their terror that the remaining therapist might get rid of them next. The men's fantasies of being aborted were rarely far from the surface of communications in the group, but slowly they became more explicit as the men became more conscious of the fragility of the group's survival in parallel with the fragility of the organization's survival. The removal of the senior clinician had brought into consciousness their fears that the organization would not survive. It was impossible for this group to remain immune from these terrors, particularly since they echoed their own prevailing fantasies about nearly having been aborted themselves (Hopper, 2003b, p. 65; Sonne, 1994a,b).

At the "event horizon" of uncovering of the organizational trauma, this group found itself absorbing, feeling, and articulating the organization's internal collapse, in a complex interplay of parallel process and equivalence. While the employees of the organization were also undergoing their own processes of introspection, rage, collusion, guilt, and fear, the group also began to engage in a process of reparative work that mirrored and, in some instances, anticipated the reparative work of the outer organization. Themes of perverse heterosexuality and homosexuality, gender confusion, murder, abortions, damaged babies, and death continued to occupy the discourse of the group.

During the next three years of the life of the group, the participants were able to talk about their perverse fantasies and impulses rather than act them out—to an extent. In effect, a mourning process was instigated—in a way, kick-started—by the departure of X. Her departure had touched on all the men's core experiences of abandonment and, indeed, of being the victims of crime (abuse, neglect, and deprivation). On the basis of the conductor's interpretations of the group's response to this trauma, carefully relating it to the individuals' experiences as both victims and perpetrators of trauma, the group began slowly to voice a sense of hope.

It is important that the group conductor was seen to have stayed with the group and with the task. It is also significant that, notwithstanding the serious difficulties faced by the organization as a whole, in the wake of X's departure, the board of trustees decided to continue to run a group characterized by such complex forensic and analytical challenges. In retrospect, this decision can perhaps be seen to have been based on an unconscious knowledge that the seeds of organizational survival were, in fact, contained within the material of the group and its survival, the importance of which was acknowledged by members of staff. Such processes might be understood as fractal phenomena (Hopper 2003b; Procci, 2002). It should never be supposed that clinical work will not be coloured by the matrix of the organization under whose auspices and in whose context it is conducted. When trauma occurs in the frame of the organization, it is felt and enacted by both its patients and its staff.

Reparation

How, then, to recover? A process of reparation—a literal repairing of torn psychic skin—took place in the groups alongside, and, perhaps, as an essential part of, a process of reparation within the organization. Despite the varying pathologies exhibited by the men and the women in their separate but intertwined analytic spaces, a progression towards healing and recovery was made, alongside the healing of the organization. We now consider the reparative work that was undertaken in order to rescue the organization following the dismissal of the senior clinician, and describe the emerging sense of hope that allowed the organization to rediscover its creativity and continue to develop.

What the clinic team had lacked was a regular, designated opportunity to process the potentially toxic effects of working with severe trauma, on them as individuals, as members of a clinical team, and on the organization as a whole. As noted above, the clinic in question had been founded upon a "matrix of trauma" that was organizationally challenging on an individual basis, and potentially overwhelming when viewed cumulatively. A flaw in the birth of the organization was the lack of such an opportunity to consider, reflect upon, and process the individual and collective impact of the trauma. The clinic had recognized, in its work with the parents of their patients, the need for a space in which the parents could mourn the loss of the fantasized, non-disabled, perfect baby (just as they later needed a space in which to process the loss of their child's innocence in the crimes of sexual abuse perpetrated against, and sometimes by, them). In the same way, the clinic itself needed a space to examine the impact of the organization's close encounters with unimaginable loss, damage, and disappointment. Indeed, the failure to create such a space might have added to the likelihood of the senior clinician acting out her unconscious need to steal funds, perhaps, for example, to quieten her unconscious rage at her salary not being enough to compensate for the experiences of sexual abuse, abusing, and cognitive damage to which she was exposed on a daily basis.

It is important to consider her delinquent acting out, not only in psychoanalytic forensic terms, as a distillation of her own individual psychopathology, affected by her psychic history, but also as a group process; a fraudulent action on the part of others in the clinic whose internal sense of lack of compensation for the level of trauma to which they were exposed in their consulting rooms was as intense as hers. Her acts of financial misconduct were, perhaps, a voicing of a plea on behalf of the entire organization. In concrete terms, the plea was for money. In symbolic terms, it was for recognition and acknowledgement.

Organizational deviancy of the type perpetrated by this senior clinician could also be understood in terms of a failure to mourn. As described above, the rewards of psychoanalytic work with people with intellectual disabilities and forensic histories can be great, but slower and more difficult to absorb. This work brings with it a close intellectual and emotional contact with life experiences characterized by lack and deficit. To do such analytic work without mindfulness of one's own disappointment at the slowness of the brains we are encountering and one's rage both at the sexual abuses committed against our patients and, in some cases, perpetrated by them, threatens our capacity to regulate our sense of despair, despondency, and loss.

This was, perhaps, the most important lesson learnt in the aftermath of the acting out within the clinic. In order to address this significant absence from the matrix of the organization, a monthly "team dynamics" meeting was instigated. This became a close analytic observation of the group dynamic processes at work in the clinical team. In these sessions, the dynamics of a group of traumatized patients could be seen clearly to have a parallel in the dynamics of those working with them. It could do this because the framework for analytic reflection developed out of the existing clinical supervision of the group work programme. We were, thus, able to see instances where the dynamics of a group of traumatized patients had a parallel in the dynamics of those working with them. With this insight we were able, slowly, to weave the psychic skin of the organization into a new pattern, one that took account of the tearing and damage that had taken place, and work hard to mourn and integrate these experiences into a stronger fabric.

Questions about the organization

A set of questions emerged from this space, which had particular relevance for the clinic in question, and have wider relevance to other institutions working with patients whose core experiences involve disability, psychic damage, and abuse. These were:

1. Did X act out because she was dishonest or did the work cause a breakdown?
2. If she was dishonest, why did we invest her with power and, to some extent, collude in her dishonesty not being uncovered?
3. If the work caused a breakdown, are we all at risk of breaking down?

These were painful questions to answer, as they involved us in an examination of the deficits of the organizational structure, as well as our own shortcomings in not being more alert to the individual's valency to dishonesty or emotional vulnerability. The team dynamics sessions might be seen as the space in which thought could occur. Around them was a maelstrom of investigative and structurally reparative activity. And yet, even the establishing of such a healthy space did not obviate the risks of yet more splitting and fragmentation. It was important to ensure that the team dynamics space could include the voices of all the organization's personnel, not just the clinicians. (The absence of non-clinical staff, and trustees, from these meetings might be seen, retrospectively, as offering the potential for yet more splitting and fragmentation.) In response to this, the monthly team dynamic sessions were expanded to include first members of the administrative staff team at Respond and then, on an occasional basis, the trustees.

The group was facilitated by a highly experienced, deeply trusted, external facilitator. He was someone who could not only witness the painful place into which we had been plunged by the acting out of a colleague, but also equip us with a mutative space in which to construct new and more robust structures with which the clinic could not only survive, but prosper.

The second wave

There seemed to be a second wave of trauma—or aftershocks—that hit the organization a year after the director's dismissal, with fraught staff–trustee relations and splits in the trustee body itself, too. We were faced with the guilt of collusion. Just as with wider family members in the wake of incest disclosures, or as in Susie's staff team, the group had to undertake a processing of a possible collective and individual sense of responsibility for the fraudulent acts of the ex-colleague. The painful realization that it was not possible to project all the shame and guilt into the ex-colleague held a powerful grip on all involved in the group process, particularly those colleagues who viewed themselves and were viewed by others as having been close to the sacked team member. There existed a danger that this guilt would become a paranoid and paralysing one, robbing the organization of the ability to move on from the trauma and exercise authority in an untainted way.

There was a renewed sense of financial vulnerability and, for a few months, organizational collapse seemed likely but was, ultimately, staved off. Gradually, the financial situation improved with a series of grants for new projects. Robust financial procedures were put in place and trustee confidence and authority grew. A clinically led strategic report was adopted, with a range of projects outlined, and with regional development being seen as a long-term goal.

A series of changes also took place among the staff group. Previously, staff would either be sacked or would resign, in a blaze of fury and pain. These losses were rarely acknowledged, let alone mourned. Each of the subsequent departures was talked about and processed, in itself a remarkable indicator of the journey of a traumatized organization from despair to hope. The ability to process loss and mourning can be seen as perhaps the most vital part of recovery. It pervades all the others, and is linked closely to the phenomenon of working with intellectual disability.

A more authentic cohesion began to be felt, with a twin tracking of reforms: structural and financial safeguards were put in place, and there was the creation of a space which gradually allowed the team to feel able to claim a sense of healthy difference. A commonly stated view, in the early days of the organization and after the organizational trauma, was that the clinic staff all worked in very similar ways and this became seen as one of their key strengths. In fact, it can be seen as a form of unauthentic cohesion, a manic gluing together of ourselves in the face of fears of annihilation. Once the anxiety could be named and addressed, it became possible to acknowledge, share, and even celebrate difference.

In addition to fortifying the organization against the possibly cata-strophic impact of the "matrix of trauma", the capacity to work posi-tively and authentically with difference—that is, *in effect to challenge and resist the basic assumption processes of I:A/M*—could be seen as the touchstone of a society which seeks to be able to understand, support, value, and appreciate each individual person with learning disabilities who is a member of it.

References

Blackman, N. (2003). *Loss and Learning Disability*. London: Worth.

Cottis, T. (2008). Love hurts: the emotional impact of intellectual disabil-ity and sexual abuse on a family. In: T. Cottis (Ed.), *Intellectual Dis-ability, Trauma and Psychotherapy*. London: Routledge.

Cottis, T., & O'Driscoll, D. (2008). Outside in: the effects of trauma on organisations. In: T. Cottis (Ed.), *Intellectual Disability, Trauma and Psychotherapy*. London: Routledge.

Hollins, S., & Esterhuyzen, A. (1997). Bereavement and grief in adults with learning disabilities. *British Journal of Psychiatry, 170*: 497–501.

Hopper, E. (2003a). *The Social Unconscious: Selected Papers*. London: Jessica Kingsley.

Hopper, E. (2003b). *Traumatic Experience in the Unconscious Life of Groups: The Fourth Basic Assumption; Incohesion: Aggregation/Massification or (ba) I:A/M*. London: Jessica Kingsley.

Menzies Lyth, I. (1988). *Containing Anxiety in Institutions*. London. Free Association Books.

Motz, A. (2001). *The Psychology of Female Violence: Crimes Against the Body*. London: Brunner-Routledge.

Neill, C. (2008). Institutional abuse and pathological narcissism. Paper presented to Institute of Psychotherapy and Disability Conference: 'Beyond Institutional Abuse'. Chester, 7th November.

Procci, W. R. (2002). Chaos theory as a new paradigm in psychoanalysis a contribution to the discussion of models. *International Journal of Psycho-analysis, 83*(2): 487–490.

Sinason, V. (1992). *Mental Handicap and the Human Condition: New Approaches from the Tavistock*. London: Free Association Books.

Sobsey, D. (1994). *Violence and Abuse in the Lives of People with Disabilities: The End of Silent Acceptance?* Baltimore, MD. Paul H. Brookes.

Sonne, J. C. (1994a). The relevance of the dread of being aborted to models of therapy and models of the mind. Part I: Case examples. *International Journal of Prenatal and Perinatal Psychology and Medicine*, 6(1): 670–686.

Sonne, J. C. (1994b). The relevance of the dread of being aborted to models of therapy and models of the mind. Part II: Mentation and communication in the unborn. *International Journal of Prenatal and Perinatal Psychology and Medicine*, 6(2): 247–275.

Volkan, V., & Itzkowitz, N. (1984). *The Immortal Ataturk. A Psychobiography*. Chicago, IL. University of Chicago Press.

Welldon, E. V. (1988). *Mother, Madonna, Whore. The Idealization and Denigration of Motherhood*. London: Karnac.

PART II
LEADERS AND LEADERSHIP

Personal trauma and collective disorder: the example of organizational psychodynamics in psychiatry

Robert D. Hinshelwood

> "[The] helpful will unconsciously require others to be helpless while the helpless will require others to be helpful. Staff and patients are thus inevitably to some extent creatures of each other"
>
> (Main, 1975)

In this chapter, I give impressions of, and try to make a case for, the influence of unconscious psychodynamics on the task and performance of the organization itself. I make reference especially to the personal stress that results from working in mental health, and its effects on organizational function.

The personal impact of work, especially the professions caring for other human beings, can create an emotional strain, often not spoken of much, and greeted with an attitude of indifference. The strain is regarded as simply part of the work, an "emotional labour" (Hochshild, 1983). If the organization makes no special provision, the result might be unexpected "pathology" of the organization, which is inscrutable and intractable. The combination of a strain and the attitude of silence might amount to a stress that reaches the level of a trauma, and then clear maladaptive behaviour occurs, some aspects of which are known as "burnout" (Maslach & Jackson, 1982). In the interests of counteracting the traumatizing silence, this chapter discusses these experiences, their less apparent, unconscious roots, and the consequences for the organization and its work.

The recent history of psychiatry is of interest here. Major changes have taken place over the past fifty years, on the grounds that the old institutionalizing mental hospitals need to be replaced by a new kind of service which would prevent those deleterious effects. That new service is "community care". The reason why the old hospitals had disastrous institutionalizing effects was never properly investigated; it was assumed that large institutions simply had that effect. So, a simple policy change of getting rid of the institutions will get rid of institutionalization. As a brief survey of some results of community care confounds that expectation, it behoves us to engage in further reflection on what it is that caused institutionalization, and was missed in the planning of the new service in the community.

Institutionalization

Community care is, in effect, a far-reaching social experiment. The experimental question is: do the much smaller settings of community care protect patients from institutional effects? One of the early investigators (Denis Martin[1]) described institutionalization thus:

> ... the patient has ceased to rebel against, or to question the fitness of his position in a mental hospital; he has made a more or less total surrender to the institution's life ... he is co-operative. Here 'co-operative' usually implies that the patient does as he is told with a minimum of questioning or opposition. This response on the part of the patient is very different from that true co-operation essential to the success of any treatment, in which the patient strives to understand, and work with, the doctor in his efforts to cure ... [The] patient, resigned and co-operative ... too passive to present any problem of management, has in the process of necessity lost much of his individuality and initiative. (Martin, 1955, p. 1198–1199)

This describes the familiar personality distortion; vulnerable people are powerless within the institution. But they lost much more than just power; they lost significant aspects of themselves, of their identity—individuality, initiative, enquiry, and self-determination. They lost their *active* self. Martin conveyed almost a deliberate stripping of identity from these patients who are already vulnerable to losing their mind. Goffman (1961) described institutionalization similarly, in totalizing organizations; work, play and sleep, all the segments of the day, were regimented in the same place. How do these people fare in the new service, community care?

An assessment of community care

An assessment of the new service was conducted in 2005–2006 by the Health Commission (2007), in its "Improvement review of adult community mental health services".[2] Without being a swingeing rejection, the report highlighted eight areas where improvement is needed, including certain aspects of passivity in the users: (a) users are not fully involved in decisions about their own care, (b) people are not given enough choice about the type of medicines they take, (c) more focus is needed on physical health, and (d) people are not getting enough help with employment. These shortcomings suggest attitudes very similar to the depersonalizing surrender of patients in the old mental hospitals. As Angela Foster wrote just over a decade ago, ". . . institutionalisation which we are used to thinking of as a process that takes place within institutions . . . can also occur within the community" (Foster, 1998, p. 68).

After the closure of Friern Hospital in London, during the 1980s, Leff wrote,

> It is possible for patients to be living in the community but not to be socially integrated with ordinary people . . . To see whether this was the case, we defined a category of social contact, termed an acquaintance, who was involved in neither providing nor receiving psychiatric care. We found that there was an increase in the proportion of patients who knew at least one acquaintance, from 19 per cent in the hospital to 29 per cent in the community . . . It was reassuring to find that some patients had made social contact with ordinary members of the public, but they still represent only a small minority of those discharged. (Leff, 1997, p. 81)

According to this study, community care does offer a degree of de-institutionalization, but it is a very small effect. The large majority of discharged patients, over two-thirds, remained socially isolated and, in effect, similarly institutionalized, becoming non-persons within the community itself. The hypothesis that large institutions cause passivity, depersonalization, and institutionalization is not confirmed. If institutionalization is not an effect of organizational structure (large or small), we need a new hypothesis. The revised hypothesis is that the crucial factor appears to lie in the dynamics of the delivery of care in various structures, and, therefore, arises in the nature of the work with psychotic illness.

We will start from the observation that psychotic patients arouse a particular emotional stress in those who encounter them: relatives and friends, but also professional carers. That stress then reverberates within the dynamics of the organization itself, with unwanted effects on the staff, the organization, and, ultimately, we shall see, on the clients.

The mad hospitals

People went to work in the old hospitals with good intentions to care for the unfortunate. They ended up running dysfunctional organizations, foisting on vulnerable people a lifetime of inactive, institutionalized misery. How come so many staff became so caught up in something so alien from their intentions?

The dynamics of institutionalization

The unconscious dynamics have been investigated from the 1940s and 1950s (Goffman, 1961; Martin, 1955). Main (1946) was one of the protagonists for alternatives to the traditional hospital care for the mentally ill, declaiming, "health . . . is too often bought at the excessive price of desocialisation" (Main, 1946, p. 7). In later reflections, he described the process as a collusion of the patient with the institution (or, rather, with its staff):

> . . . only roles of health or illness are on offer; staff to be only healthy, knowledgeable, kind, powerful and active, and patients to be only ill, suffering, ignorant, passive, obedient and grateful. In most hospitals staff are there because they seek to care for others less able than themselves, while the patients hope to find others *more* able than themselves. The helpful and the helpless meet and put pressures on each

other to act not only in realistic, but also fantastic collusion . . . [The] helpful will unconsciously *require* others to be helpless while the helpless will *require* others to be helpful. Staff and patients are thus inevitably to some extent creatures of each other. (Main, 1975, p. 61)

There grew up a specific *dynamic of helplessness*. What patients lose of their healthy side accumulates in the staff. And what the staff lose in terms of their more negative attributes resurfaces within the patients. Like Martin, Main pinpointed how personality characteristics are redistributed in the social field, and between two groups: the group of patients vulnerable to losing their personalities, and the group of staff who want to build themselves up in successful medical and curative careers. This inadequacy and helplessness is juggled between groups in the dynamic of helplessness.

The trauma of personal stress

When society can no longer cope with an individual's madness, the psychiatric service exists to do what others have failed at: to contain a disturbance that is too much for the patient and for his immediate relatives, friends, and neighbours. This is no mean task. The impact of madness is striking—and numbing. When Samuel Beckett went to the Tavistock Clinic in 1934 for psychotherapy with the novice therapist, Wilfred Bion, he took an interest in mental illness and visited the Bethlem Hospital. Beckett later recalled his verdict on a schizophrenic patient he encountered: "[The patient] was like a hunk of meat. There was no-one there. He was absent" (quoted in Knowlson, 1996, p. 209).[3]

This is one aspect of the stress of caring for such persons. They have lost their active selves and, in a sense, have lost their moral agency to take responsibility for their decisions (Barrett, 1996). If the stresses arising from the impact of psychosis are not properly processed, they tend to undermine the sense of being benign and helpful which professional carers usually expect and need. The range of consequences can be extensive (Hinshelwood, 1998).

Experiences with psychotics

The crucial quality of psychotic anxiety leads patients to get rid of their experience by making the staff feel it instead: "Schizophrenia is an expertise in producing disquiet in others" (Berke, 1979, p. 23). Below is a brief list of some of those disquieting experiences.

1.   As Main, in the above quote indicated, being helpful is why most carers enter the work. They want to realize powerful intentions (and phantasies) of helping disturbed people to get better, but find that many patients do not. Mental health carers are too frequently left with those who remain permanently unhelped. Specifically, these experiences lead to feelings of inadequacy and unfulfilled responsibility, and, ultimately, the phenomenon known as "burnout".

2.   Feelings, especially the "disquiet", are not transmitted in words. A direct transmission of affect by some non-verbal route makes the interactions difficult to grasp, comprehend, and handle.

3.   Frequently, there is a connected feeling of fear. It is the fear of something going quickly out of control. This may be experienced as either madness or violence: a mind going out of control. Mental health workers live constantly with the risk that patients will become violent and injure us.

4.   There is another particular way in which we experience our patients. We have a sense that the patient's experience and anxiety have no meaning. Nature abhors a vacuum, and human nature abhors a vacuum of meaning. Similarly, Bion stated that "healthy mental growth seems to depend on truth as the living organism depends on food" (Bion, 1965, p. 38). The human mind needs truth and meaning to live, grow, and develop (Hinshelwood, 2004).

5.   Finally, the meaninglessness causes another reaction. We tend to pull away from the patient emotionally; that is the depersonalizing effect. We reach an emotional distance as if they are not properly human.

It is precisely because of the reasons that make us work with disturbed people that we can be so vulnerable. Invariably, we start with a special wish to help (Roberts, 1994), and a strong engagement and sensitivity, with very high hopes of restoring people from dreadful states back into whole and happy persons. Realistically, we can satisfy that ambition with only a small number of people. Reality is discrepant with the ambition, leading to a sense of failure (however unrealistic) and, hence, the need for Main's dynamic of helplessness. Very small changes for staff might be a great achievement for a patient, but might seem insignificant to staff seeking a higher level of change. Thus, a major and painful gap opens between the expected achievement and the realistically achievable. It often leads to acute personal difficulties, which go quite unrecognized, leaving an acutely lonely staff member in danger of "burnout". These demands can equally burden patients subjected to the insistence of a member of staff to "change", and "get cured", for the sake of that staff member.

Avoiding the trauma

Carers can put up with the numbing stress to a limit, but beyond that, they quickly institutionalize an emotional distance. If we reduce the "person" of the patient/client, we thereby reduce the emotional impact of "failing" them. This "depersonalization" is widely reported in examples of care organizations, starting with Menzies' study (1959) of a nursing service. An Australian psychiatrist, Rob Barratt (1996), made an anthropological study of the journey a patient makes through several stages in the course of admission and treatment in a mental hospital service. He concluded that there were four steps in that journey:

1. Initially, the patient is perceived (and dealt with) as an object, one who does not live in the world of ordinary meanings. He is no longer a person, because a disease entity has taken him over. His moral agency is discounted because his disease is held responsible for his behaviour and condition.
2. Then, he is dismantled into a set of symptoms and pathologies that can be recorded objectively.
3. This is followed by a reconstruction as a "worked-up" case, in which the patient's various "objective" signs and symptoms are recombined into a picture that is meaningful psychiatrically; he has a diagnosis, a set of treatment interventions, and a prognosis about his future.[4]
4. Only then can another piece of work start. As improvement begins, the patient needs to be reinvested with subjectivity and agency as a person again. This fourth step is interestingly

described by Barratt as involving the reactions of the professionals *as persons*. They begin again to see the patient as an agent with
volition. His volition requires moral evaluation from us; we like
or dislike, we agree or disagree, etc., with him, we start to hold
patients responsible again for how they are and what they do.
The patient is returned to being a person, and rescued from the
category of a "case".

For a major part of the admission, a patient is not a person, but a
disease. Although this is a helpful medical approach that determines
treatment, it has a collateral effect. It protects staff by supporting the
emotional distancing. They no longer have to think about the tortur-
ing *experiences* of their patients when they focus on the illness.

A similar blocking to the capacity to think about the person of the
client occurs in an example given by Davies (1996). Again, it is about
the level of the group dynamics of the team. I summarize as follows.

A disturbed man had a harsh mother as a child. She was violent
and humiliated him. When released from prison, where he had
finished a sentence for brutal sexual crimes, he asked to be kept inside.
The request was naturally refused. He subsequently engaged with the
helping network in a specific way.

He was dangerous, and a specific plan was set out at his hostel to
ensure that only male staff dealt with him. However, the arrangements quickly broke down for extraneous reasons—staff changed
jobs, or went on courses. He was taken into intensive counselling by
a female worker, and a female prison visitor who had visited him in
prison continued to see him, including taking him to her home, where
he assaulted her. Another female worker offered counselling, sometimes in evening sessions, and afterwards said she had forgotten he
was a rapist! The female staff had been drawn into taking up powerful professional roles with him, to be inviting, and then to withdraw
from him, giving him that intolerable feeling of powerlessness again.

The care network responded disastrously to his continuing disturbance, seeming not to realize that the arrangements had broken down.
What went wrong could be traced specifically to a repetition of the
experience of care the man received as a child. His mother was powerful, controlling, and continually made him feel powerless; he had
effectively no father with whom to identify. His sense of male power
was unpractised and uncontrolled. In the hostel, the male staff had

disappeared, like the ineffective father, and the female staff did their best to take over, as mother had.

The staff, unable any longer to think about the client realistically, or even to remember his case fully, succumbed to less than thoughtful re-enactment of care experiences involving violence and humiliation, and could not recognize either the risks or their origins in his early years.

Davies arouses our concern that, instead of understanding his plea for help, the carers became unthinkingly caught up in acting out his internal state; his plea for more restraint was neglected, and the frustration of powerful female carers was freely and insightlessly offered.

The deeply personal past, in which the man was trapped, came to be represented in actual terms by the present selection of people, not thoughtfully, in words and discussion, but impulsively, in actions. The man's needs were treated with a "care" response, but not a reflective one. No proper symbolization, conscious representation, or thought survived. Such dramatization by staff of the inner worlds of those in the institution is a very common (but unrecognized) phenomenon (Hinshelwood, 1987). Thus, the stressful experience of the work invaded the staff and, though dealt with by a kind of "not thinking about it", the impact, at an unconscious level, was sufficient to distort the work. Thus, the team and a whole service can be said to be affected by a process which, in a psychoanalysis, is called countertransference. These problems, which interfere with, and actually reduce, effective performance, affect all the team members.

I have traced dynamics from the level of individuals to interpersonal interactions between them, and I now want to move on to the organizational level. Individual disturbance, in the staff, distorts personal and group functions, but it also promotes sets of maladaptive cultural attitudes in the organization as a whole.

The "pathology" of the organization

Because of the stress in individuals, a number of things can go wrong in the working of the team:

1.   *Demoralization*: If many staff are subject to low job satisfaction and to feeling despair, then the team will become collectively

demoralized. People cannot give each other the ordinary support, encouragement, and praise that is needed if they themselves *feel* they are not doing a good job, *and* not getting the support they need themselves. There are many indices of demoralization: high rates of sick leave, absenteeism, and turnover of persons in the team. These effects of demoralization make the team feel unstable and unsupportive, and morale falls even lower.

2. *Stereotyped patients*: However, there are ways in which the team members can collectively help themselves. One is to deny the feelings of helplessness and despair. Then, it is very common for them to agree that those feelings are located in their patients—and *only* in the patients. A rigid perception of themselves and their patients grows up. Patients are unconsciously required to be (and remain) helpless and the "problem", as described in the quote above from Main.

3. *Scapegoating*: Sometimes, the sereotyping can be limited to just one patient, who is elected into a position to carry all the hopelessness. He is the "scapegoat", and usually gets worse clinically, thus confirming the way the staff have come to see him.

4. *Routine*: The meaninglessness of the patient's experiences and anxiety is very corrosive of the staff's ability to continue with sympathy and understanding. The emotional distance can then be institutionalized by a process of turning the work into a set of routines—one could say, meaningless routines.

5. *Paranoia*: Alternatively, the staff team can collectively change their direction of interest. Instead of feeling hopeless about their patients, a new attitude grows up: the patients could be helped, but the team is kept short of resources. The problem is believed to be the authorities or managers, who should provide more staff, or training, or money, and so on. Staff gain a new solidarity among themselves, but they feel as if under siege by their employers, who do not understand them, or who are stupid, or who might be deliberately malign.

6. *Splitting and fragmentation*: Another process is schism within the team. A sub-group of staff (for instance, one profession), absorbing the feeling of being helpless from the patients, exports it into another sub-group—the us-and-them strategy. A set of colleagues becomes the hopeless ones in contrast to using the patients in this way. The multiple professions working in psychiatry often

provide good opportunities for this kind of intergroup dynamic. The result is mutual denigration of each other, which is not openly expressed, so nobody can really get a proper picture of who is doing good work and who is not. Realistic perceptions and mutual support are lost. Commonly, this occurs between those who promote physical treatments (psychiatrists), and others (psychotherapists) who emphasize the human and relational aspects of the symptoms and the treatments.

7. *Fragmented agencies*: The intergroup dynamic just described leads to a splitting up, or fragmentation, of the service, and it might be especially prevalent in community care, where units and agencies are already geographically separate from each other. Different teams then get into the same mutual denigration of each other— the domiciliary team, the day hospital, the inpatient ward, etc.

    With these various phenomena occurring at the team level, the quality of the service must get worse. Changing staff, high levels of absence, and temporary staff, scapegoating of patients and staff, and splits within and between teams, all have a very bad effect on the work. This further effects morale, as staff realize that they do not give the best chances to their patients. Job satisfaction falls further, and all the negative opinions the staff members have about themselves, about each other, and about their employers are enhanced.

8. *Social defence system*: The intergroup processes are active defences against psychological distress, but at a collective level. Common perceptions of the work, or of each other, are driven by the need to avoid the anxiety and stress of the work. This is known as a social defence system (see Menzies' (1959) "case study" of a nursing service in a general hospital). These collective, or social, defences rely on the individual's primitive defence mechanisms—splitting, denial, projection. Such pressures towards the primitive have a rebound effect on the individuals, reducing them all together to less mature levels of functioning, leading to an experience of being deskilled. Above all, it is an unspoken, and unconscious, process.

9. *Anti-task*: One aspect of these defensive social attitudes and forms of practice is the way the overall task can be distorted with the aim to alleviate the direct impact of encountering psychotic people on a daily basis. In other words, an organization can

sometimes be diverted from its primary task to one which, instead, is less meaningless and stressful. Menzies (1979) described a residential school for emotionally and behaviourally disturbed children who had mostly suffered heart-rending neglect, and also often abuse, in early childhood. The pain of the neediness drove the staff, and, thus, the organization as a whole, to divert from its educational task to drift towards providing substitute parental love instead of education. An "anti-task" of this kind is sought to provide more job satisfaction than the actual task.

In a psychiatry setting, the strain of providing care for psychotic people can lead to a similar diversion of the task. Staff can silently prioritize self-care above treatment of patients. For instance, in the example quoted from Main, above, the self-care provided by an unconscious set of attitudes about the strength, knowledgeableness, and activity of the staff indelibly confirms the weakness and ignorance of the patients.

At the core of these cultural attitudes that give relief is the diminished emotional involvement, and this could be supported by the excessive "objectivity of a scientific approach to patients" of caring (as described in Hinshelwood, 1999).

Community care, for example

As with the old mental hospitals, we can consider the culture of community care and its relation to the "dynamic of helplessness". Some characteristics of the institutionalization in the old hospitals have carried over into community care. The work setting is radically changed. Patients have now been dispersed to be cared for in hostels, community centres, day care centres, and often to roam the streets, but institutionally trained staff, too, have been pushed out of the traditional tightly knit teams in the old hospital wards. Staff no longer have to tolerate specific patients on the basis of a whole seven-hour shift, and, therefore, have some relief from the previous stress. However, comparable work stress still occurs; staff now have to confront seriously disturbed patients, as well as their anxious families, on the doorsteps, in the alien environment of a domiciliary visit and an unfamiliar neighbourhood.

They are no longer on their home territory, and might lack immediate colleagueship, their regular procedures, and the hallowed traditions of the old institution. This is likely to cause increased levels of stress, with diminished support from a coherent team.

In addition, as Spillius (1976) pointed out in her anthropological study of a British mental hospital, psychiatry is at the focus of a three-way pincer movement. Relatives want relief through removal of the patient, patients want asylum from the stresses of life, and the professionals want the satisfaction of helping and curing. These demands are not necessarily consistent with each other, so staff do not please everyone all the time, and there is always an undermining element of displeasing someone.

Stress on staff in the community has several components: (a) the anxiety of uncertainty about the safety of their patients for long periods when they are out of sight, (b) a concern about a patient's unsocial, even disastrously dangerous, behaviour, (c) the pressures of the community itself on the psychiatric service. These anxieties tend to be much more public and to suffer the attention of the media and government. There is unlikely to be diminution of the impact of the work on professional carers, despite their greater distance geographically and, therefore, emotionally. The sense of helplessness or inadequacy is much more visible and publicly debated, often with a sharply critical, super-ego-ish edge.

If there is a "dynamic of helplessness" in community care as well, we can ask how it is coped with, and what organizational phenomena are manifest, comparable to the various manoeuvres and practices of institutional psychiatry. In fact, like institutional care, a number of features of community care can drift into maladaptive anti-tasks, and might, therefore, represent social defences.

1. *Professionalised care*: While intending that mentally ill people should be inserted back into networks of ordinary (or genuine) human relationships in their communities, in practice, ex-patients are inserted back into a community of professionals: professionals who continue to "need: their dynamic of helplessness. The human needs industry seems increasingly to occupy the place of ordinary human relationships.[5] While specific training has important benefits, it can also institutionalize once again the familiar "dynamic of helplessness".

2. *Skills-based training*: While training is a major contributor to staff support, in increasing confidence, it is mostly restricted to the individual's skills. Like scientific psychiatry, skills-based training can, by its mechanistic approach, avoid attention to the care relationship. Once again, the side-effect of this well-intentioned input is to support the collusive depersonalization and institutionalization, and diminish job satisfaction.[6]

3. *Risk management*: In community care, there is increased risk when patients are out of sight for much of the time. Particularly since the well-publicized Ben Silcock and Christopher Clunis cases, risk assessment and its management in psychiatry has been strongly promoted by the Department of Health, via the 1995 Act (*Mental Health (Patients in the Community) Act*). Ten years after the Act, Higgins and colleagues (2005) found that 60% of Trusts in England and Wales had instituted formal risk assessment procedures. However, it has also been considered from a critical perspective (Petch 2001), and Smukler (2001) contended that risk assessment is notoriously inaccurate when the risk incidence is very small: "Rare events are inherently difficult to predict. Even a test with an impossible 0.9 accuracy for both true positives and true negatives will be wrong more than nine times out of ten at a base rate of 1%" (Szmukler 2001, p. 75).

    These technical assessments of risk are important. However, we can also study and learn why the drive for risk management is so imperative (Power, 2007). Risk reaches deep into unconscious aspects of people's reactions, both professionals and the public. It touches on deep-seated imperatives to outrage, fear, and guilt. In the face of public concern, levels of administration, up to government level, can indulge in the assumption that all risks can—and, therefore, should—be eliminated. In fact, they cannot. The toll in life and injury of this belief can only be partially ameliorated by risk management. The debate should be about what level of risk is acceptable for the continuance of community care, an almost completely silent debate. Discussion on how to eliminate risk altogether is back in the stratosphere of unrealistic ambitions. In addition, attention needs to be paid to the degree to which the coping mechanisms, such as emotional distancing and depersonalization, actually enhance risk.

4. *Care and "narcissism"*: If professional carers have to take care of
    themselves, they will focus on their own personal survival and
    development. They withdraw inevitably from a concern for the
    "other", from patients in need of care. The implicit task of the ser-
    vice can then vacillate over who is to be cared for. Staff care for
    patients better if cared for themselves. Individual carers, therefore,
    have a difficult, double kind of job: they do need to ensure care for
    themselves, but, at the same time, must prioritize care for their dis-
    turbed patients/clients. But the risk is always that this will get out
    of balance, and there is no debate about what is the right balance.

5. *Survival anxiety*: There is currently an increasing trend for organi-
    zations to present their future as an uncertain one; an organiza-
    tion must make strenuous efforts to survive. Survival anxiety is
    increasingly prevalent in all enterprises, public and commercial,
    because it is seen as a motivating force. However, uncertain
    survival could threaten to overwhelm and hinder performance,
    as well. Although the assumption is that people will work harder
    if anxious about their jobs or income, that is motivating only up
    to a limit, and beyond this it can become counter-productive.
    Hence, in already stressed professionals and workers in care
    organizations, the effect of increased anxiety needs careful evalu-
    ation. Psychiatric care organizations might be especially vulnera-
    ble to excessive anxiety; after all, they are organizations whose
    specific work is to contain anxiety itself. The concern is that the
    development of community care, coinciding with the develop-
    ment of survival anxiety in working organizations, has pushed
    many services to this counter-productive level. The overgrowth
    of anxiety needs constant appraisal, but such evaluation is rarely
    done, rarely even recognized as needed.[7]

6. *Multi-disciplinary teams*: Multi-disciplinary team working has been
    promoted for a long time. Rightly, the coherence of disparate pro-
    fessionals needs careful attention, and is important especially for
    the care of fragmented personalities. Surprisingly, however, good
    interdisciplinary working is hard to achieve. Communication is
    often inhibited and sometimes infected with dismissive or deni-
    gratory attitudes. Stokes (1994) has suggested there are natural
    fault-lines between the disciplines: nurses, for instance, inter-
    preting their role as dealing with dependent patients, social work-
    ers often seeing themselves as fighting the "system" on behalf

of their clients, and therapists might engage in rather cosy exclusiveness on a one-to-one basis—these drift in the task, matching Bion's basic assumptions. Such palpable variation between disciplines is, unfortunately, not always regarded as a source of rich collaboration; quite the reverse, since distinctive features can give easy opportunity for the projective "dynamic of helplessness" among staff. While Stokes has shown this interesting differentiation between disciplines, Hopper's fourth basic assumption, incohesion, would seem to apply to the whole team—a kind of coherent fragmentation, where it would seem the groups stick together in order *not* to respect each other and work together.

I propose to discuss this last feature in more detail, as it seems to give evidence of a continuing existence of the dynamic of helplessness beyond institutional psychiatry, into community care. In other words, the way of dealing with inadequacy by seeing it in others remains, while the "others" in whom it is seen, might be different—other staff rather than patients/clients.

Multi-disciplinary working

Multi-disciplinary working aims at mutual support by enriching with multiple perspectives. The opposite could easily happen, and, particularly in the community, the deeply unsupportive "dynamic of helplessness" might pollute the work. Then, "inadequacy" is attributed to other staff and not owned by anyone. Such a process can lead to a debilitating mutuality of disrespect. In fact, community care is at greater risk of intergroup systems because its groups and units are geographically dispersed.

Despite the teamwork requirement, there is little evidence of specific training to work in a multi-disciplinary way (Whyte & Brooker, 2001). It seems to be generally assumed that collaborative working will routinely emerge, but little research has been done to corroborate that assumption. Where formal research has been done, it appears that the intuitive assumption is not the case (Atwal & Caldwell, 2002; Burns & Lloyd, 2004). For instance, a systematic study of music therapists showed a high rate of burnout, for which the MDT did not offer protection (Hills, Norman, & Forster, 2000). This might be a feature of the less powerful professions within the team. Verbal contribution to team discussion tends to vary according to discipline and the discipline's standing within the team. Sanson-Fisher, Poole, and Harker (1979) showed that occupational therapists spoke less than nurses or doctors. A pecking order and interdisciplinary threat between occupational therapists and nurses was confirmed by Jones (2006). Jones found quite disturbing results in a study using participant observation and semi-structured interviews in a psychiatric team (in East London): "To protect their role, clinicians attempted to protect role boundaries and function. This has also been described by Davies (2000) who found both medical and nursing staff intransigent in working towards collaborative ways of working" (Jones, 2006, p. 25).

"Intransigent" is a strong word, considering the self-evident benefits of working together. This is alarming because lack of support and interdisciplinary criticism and rivalry contribute to low morale (Janssen, Jonge, & Bakker, 1999; Maslach & Jackson, 1982). Peck and Norman (1999) describe the different acculturation processes in the different disciplines, which they take to be the source of the problem of working together.

Such a state of affairs, when we are all up against the same problem, is difficult to explain in rational terms, and must be one of the powerful imperatives for looking at the unfortunate "irrational" dynamics. This chapter has attempted to provide the explanation of non-collaborative working, finding it in the unconscious and collective reactions to the stress of working with psychosis.

Conclusions

The intention here has been to argue that insufficient attention has been paid to one whole area of organizational function. The gist is that the stress of encountering and working with psychotic people is not attended to, and that it then emerges as organizational "pathology", in the old mental hospitals, as the phenomenon of institution-alization, but in the newer community care as a persisting social isolation and passivity in patients. I have identified a transport from the closed institutions to community care of an unconscious dynamic of helplessness. Depersonalization, redistribution of personality characteristics, narcissistic intergroup relations, and organizational schism become apparent and even common, together with ensuing problems of social pathology, such as absenteeism and high turnover rates, together with a restless series of policy changes, such as risk management, legal provisions for compulsory detention, etc.

While it is entirely understandable that such stress should be denied, it would seem better to confront the problem. The distress might feel as insurmountable as it is unbearable, but this might be an experience necessarily transmitted by psychotic people; it might not, therefore, be the case in reality. Many problems that comprise psychosis are today significantly manageable with medication, psychological treatments, and social care. However, it is important that the reality of care is robustly acknowledged. The felt experience, based often on unrealistic ambition, might not accord with the real achievement. Ideally, the apparent conspiracy of silence, so common in dealing with stress and trauma, would be counteracted by a new culture in psychiatry that can both recognize the despair and demoralization while not accepting it as realistic. The tragedy is that silence results in extra harm to the functioning of the service. This is unfortunate, since breaking the silence and engaging in shared recognition of the numbing encounter at the heart of the work, the limited achievements, and the real benefits of meagre improvements, could release many teams from demoralization and fragmentation.

The changes in psychiatry in the UK from the large mental hospitals of the 1950s to the community care of the 1990s are a natural experiment that can show us the stressful impact of the care of psychosis, and its impact on individuals, teams, and the service as a whole.

It is worth considering that such kinds of self-defeating organizational effects could exist in any high-stress occupational organization, including education and the emergency fire–ambulance–police services. The endless search for solutions to mysteriously recurring, mutating, and intractable organizational problems, wherever they occur, suggests that, with their unconscious motivation, they are consigned to silence.

Notes

1.   See also Barton (1959).
2.   The report is most easily available on line: www.healthcarecommission. org.uk/_db/_documents/Community_mental_health_-_full_report.pdf;

and similarly the Commission's summary: www.healthcarecommission.
org.uk/_db/_documents/Community_mental_health_-_summary_
report.pdf

3.   Consider another revealing comment about psychotic people:

> I did not like those patients . . . They make me angry and I find
> myself irritated to experience them so distant from myself and
> from all that is human. This is an astonishing intolerance which
> brands me a poor psychiatrist. (Freud, 1928, quoted in Dupont,
> 1988, p. 251)

The quote comes from Freud's private letter to Istvan Hollos, who had
sent Freud a copy of a book he had authored.

4.   This dismembering process, conducted in a conscious scientific way,
parallels the unconscious schizoid processes of the individual. The depersonalization is a kind of "aggregation" of symptoms and features. The
elements are not related, but collectivized into an aggregate. Hopper (2009) described aggregation as one of the poles of incohesion, the
opposite pole being massification, and described these two socio-cultural
states in oscillation between them as a fourth basic assumption (added
to the three that Bion (1961) introduced). Similarly, my "Attacks on
the reflective space" (Hinshelwood, 1994) describes a group unrelatedness.

5.   Craib (1994) has argued that professionalizing the response to human
experience has been advancing rapidly in contemporary society.

6.   The point about job satisfaction here is that professional carers going into
the business to help other people lose emotional contact with the person,
while dealing with an "object of study", and, thus, lose the possibility of
achieving their own need to help other persons, a point made strongly by
Menzies (1959).

7.   Elsewhere (Hinshelwood, 2004), I have spelled out how survival anxiety
is that of the paranoid–schizoid position of Melanie Klein. It is the fear of
annihilation of the self, central to traumatic experience, whereas the anxiety of care is probably more aligned with depressive position, and the
fear *for* the other.

References

Atwal, A., & Caldwell, K. (2002). Do multidisciplinary integrated care
pathways improve interprofessional collaboration? *Scandinavian
Journal of Caring Sciences, 16*: 360–367.

Barratt, R. (1996). *The Psychiatric Team and the Social Definition of Schizophrenia*. Cambridge: Cambridge University Press.

Barton, R. (1959). *Institutional Neurosis*. Bristol: Wright.

Berke, J. (1979). *I Haven't Had To Go Mad Here*. London: Penguin.

Bion, W. R. (1961). *Experiences in Groups*. London: Tavistock.

Bion, W. R. (1965). *Transformations*. London: Tavistock.

Burns, T., & Lloyd, H. (2004). Is a team approach based on staff meetings cost-effective in the delivery of mental health care? *Current Opinion in Psychiatry*, 17: 311–314.

Craib, I. (1994). *The Importance of Disappointment*. London: Routledge.

Davies, C. (2000). Getting health professionals to work together. *British Medical Journal*, 320(7241): 1021–1022.

Davies, R. (1996). The interdisciplinary network and the internal world of the offender. In: C. Cordess & M. Cox (Eds.), *Forensic Psychotherapy, Volume 2* (pp. 133–144). London: Jessica Kingsley.

Department of Health (1995). *Mental Health (Patients in the Community) Act*. London: Department of Health.

Dupont, J. (1988). Ferenczi's 'madness'. *Contemporary Psychoanalysis*, 24: 250–261.

Foster, A. (1998). Psychotic processes and community care: the difficulty in finding the third position. In: A. Foster & V. Roberts (Eds.), *Managing Mental Health in the Community: Chaos and Containment in Community Care* (pp. 61–70). London: Routledge.

Goffman, E. (1961). *Asylums*. New York: Doubleday.

Health Commission (2007). *No Voice, No Choice: A Joint Review of Adult Community Mental Health Services in England*. London: Department of Health.

Higgins, N., Watts, D., Bindman, J., Slade, M., & Thornicroft, G. (2005). Assessing violence risk in general adult psychiatry. *Psychiatric Bulletin*, 29: 131–133.

Hills, B., Norman, I., & Forster, L. (2000). A study of burnout and multidisciplinary team-working amongst professional music therapists. *British Journal of Music Therapy*, 14: 32–40.

Hinshelwood, R. D. (1987). *What Happens in Groups*. London: Free Associations.

Hinshelwood, R. D. (1994). Attacks on the reflective space. In: V. Shermer & M. Pines (Eds.), *Ring of Fire: Containing Primitive Emotional States* (pp. 86–106). London: Routledge.

Hinshelwood, R. D. (1998). Creatures of each other: some historical considerations of responsibility and care and some present undercurrents. In: A. Foster & V. Roberts (Eds.), *Managing Mental Health in the Community: Chaos and Containment in Community Care* (pp. 15–26). London: Routledge.

Hinshelwood, R. D. (1999). The difficult patient: the role of 'scientific' psychiatry in understanding patients with chronic schizophrenia or severe personality disorder. *British Journal of Psychiatry, 174*: 187–190.

Hinshelwood, R. D. (2004). *Suffering Insanity*. London: Routledge.

Hochschild, A. (1983). *The Managed Heart: Commercialization of Human Feeling*. Berkeley, CA: University of California Press.

Hopper, E. (2009). The theory of the basic assumption of Incohesion: Aggregation/Massification or (ba) I:AM. *British Journal of Psychotherapy, 25*: 214–229.

Janssen, P. M. P., Jonge, J. D., & Bakker, A. B. (1999). Specific determinants of intrinsic work motivation, burnout and turnover intentions: a study among nurses. *Journal of Advanced Nursing, 29*: 1360–1369.

Jones, A. (2006). Multidisciplinary team working: collaboration and conflict. *International Journal of Mental Health Nursing, 15*: 19–28.

Knowlson, J. (1996). *Damned to Fame*. London: Bloomsbury.

Leff, J. (1997). *Care in the Community: Illusion or Reality?* Chichester: Wiley.

Main, T. H. (1946). The hospital as a therapeutic institution. *Bulletin of the Menninger Clinic, 10*: 7–16. Republished in Main (1989), *The Ailment and Other Psychoanalytic Essays*. London: Free Association Books.

Main, T. H., (1975). Some psychodynamics of large groups. In: L. Kreeger (Ed.), *The Large Group* (pp. 57–86). London: Constable. Reprinted in Main (1989), *The Ailment*. London: Free Association Books.

Martin, D. (1955). Institutionalisation. *Lancet* 1955/2: 1188–1190.

Maslach, C., & Jackson, S. E. (1982). Burnout in health professions: a social psychological analysis. In: G. S. Sanders & J. Suls (Eds.), *Social Psychology of Health and Illness* (pp. 227–251). Hillsdale, NJ: Lawrence Erlbaum.

Menzies, I. (1959). A case study in the functioning of social systems as a defence against anxiety. *Human Relations, 13*: 95–121. Republished 1960, *The Functioning of Social Systems as a Defence against Anxiety*, Tavistock Pamphlet No. 3. Republished in Menzies (1988), *Containing Anxiety in Institutions*. London: Free Association Books.

Menzies, I. (1979). Staff support systems: task and antitask in adolescent institutions. In: R. D. Hinshelwood & N. Manning (Eds.), *Therapeutic Communities: Reflections and Progress* (pp. 197–207). London: Routledge and Kegan Paul. Republished in Menzies (1988), *Containing Anxiety in Institutions*. London: Free Association Books.

Peck, E., & Norman, I. J. (1999). Working together in adult community mental health services: exploring inter-professional role relations. *Journal of Mental Health, 8*: 231–243.

Petch, E. (2001). Risk management in UK mental health service: an over-valued idea. *Psychiatric Bulletin, 25*: 203–205.

Power, M. (2007). *Organised Uncertainty: Designing a World of Risk Management*. Oxford: Oxford University Press.

Roberts, V. (1994). The self-assigned impossible task. In: A. Obholzer & V. Roberts (Eds.), *The Unconscious at Work* (pp. 110–119). London: Routledge.

Sanson-Fisher, R. W., Poole, A. D., & Harker, J. (1979). Behavioural analysis of ward rounds within a general hospital psychiatric unit. *Behavioural Research Therapy, 17*, 333–347.

Spillius, E. B. (1976). Hospital and society. *British Journal of Medical Psychology, 49*: 97–140.

Szmukler, G. (2001). Violence risk prediction in practice. *British Journal of Psychiatry, 178*: 84–85.

Stokes, J. (1994). The unconscious at work in groups and teams. In: A. Obholzer & V. Roberts (Eds.), *The Unconscious at Work* (pp. 19–27). London: Routledge.

Whyte, L., & Brooker, C. (2001). Working with a multidisciplinary team in secure psychiatric environments. *Journal of Psychosocial Nursing & Mental Health Services, 39*: 26–34.

CHAPTER EIGHT

Disorganized responses to refusal and spoiling in traumatized organizations

Christopher Scanlon and John Adlam

"All the King's horses and all the King's men
Couldn't put Humpty together again"

(Traditional nursery rhyme)

A substantial literature attests that practitioners who are charged with the delivery of health and social care to the homeless, the dangerous, the disordered and others who find themselves at the margins of society, frequently become themselves traumatized and interpersonally *dis-ordered*, while the teams, agencies and organizations in which they work become *dis-organized* (Cooper & Lousada, 2005; Foster & Roberts, 1998; Hopper, 2003 *inter alia*). This systemic "dis-order" and "dis-organization" frequently mirrors, or reciprocates, the difficulties and distress of the client population, and sometimes generates or exacerbates their clients' difficulties. A root cause of this dis-order and dis-organization, we contend, is that many "evidence-based" policies, interventions, and treatments aimed at people with severe mental health and social problems depend upon, and, indeed, at times problematically assume, levels of motivation, pro-social aspiration, and reality oriented engagement from those towards whom the help is targeted. However, it is the fate of many socially organized responses to founder upon the rock of the *refusal* (Adlam & Scanlon, 2009; Billow, 2007; Scanlon & Adlam, 2008a) of this chronically excluded population. Not only do they refuse to "come in from the cold", but, in their refusal, they are also experienced as *making a mess* of society's best (and, perhaps, sometimes worst) intentions and interventions.

In this chapter, we take as a paradigm for these psycho-social dynamics, severe disturbances of eating that become manifest in the feeding pair and the spoiling and refusal of food in severe anorexia nervosa. We explore what happens when traumatized dis-organizations, who identify themselves as would-be helpers, become bound up with identifications in which they experience themselves as inhabiting the providing role. We examine what happens to them when their *food* and provisions are refused, messed around with, and thrown back at them by clients who, none the less, remain famished, emaciated, and in desperate need of nourishment. To express this in different language, we explore the nature and impact of problematic processes of projective and introjective identification between the "would-be helpers" and the "refuse-to-be helped" clients when the relationship between them comes to be characterized by interpersonal dis-order and collective dis-organization. We also examine the ways in which the mutual hatred and reciprocal violence which inevitably emerges is projected into the would-be-helping *organization,* both from inside (the reasonable and unreasonable expectations of the staff), and from outside (the reasonable and unreasonable expectations of the general public, the clients, the funders, and other stakeholders). Collective identifications with these projections result in the traumatized dis-organization.

Borderline and antisocial relations: the psycho-social context

> "And in that Heaven of all their wish,
> There shall be no more land, say fish."
> (Rupert Brooke, 1915, *Heaven*)

Our use of the paradigm of the disturbed feeding dyad by no means assumes a benevolent, effective or organized provider, nor, for that matter, a malevolent and dis-ordered refusing client. Just as the starving anorexic might have good cause to regard the proffered food as poison rather than *medicine*, so, too, might the homeless, the dangerous, and the disordered have good reason to refuse and to spoil a societal provision which is at best inadequate and entrapping and at worst perverse or malign (Bauman, 2004; DeClerck, 2006; Gilligan, 1996; Žižek, 2008). Our paradigm, then, also represents the problematic psycho-social and socio-political relationship between "us" and "them": between an in-group and an out-group—what in Main's (1957) terms might be described as a societal *ailment*. In Foucault's historical account of this relationship, he proposed that "we are at war with one another" across a front line or caesura running through society "continuously and permanently" (Foucault, 1976, p. 51). The system of care and the dis-organizations that comprise it are deployed paradoxically by the in-group both as an *invitation to an out-group to join* and as a *means of exclusion*. Of course, this out-group is already chronically excluded and, as such, has come to represent a problematic and feared "other"-ness.

Our disordered eating paradigm is also manifest in a use we want to make of Lévi-Strauss's (1955) categorization of responses to "otherness" into two fundamental types (see also, among others, Bauman, 2000; Young, 1999): one type, the "anthropoemic" response, involves the "vomiting out" of difference, in which the included wash their hands of the excluded. We might think of this as rooted in a fight/flight basic assumption state in the in-group (Bion, 1961) in which *meaningful* differences must be got rid of or got away from. The other type, a kind of converse position, is the "anthropophagic" response, in which difference is abolished through ingesting, devouring, and coercively assimilating. We might think of this forced incorporation of the irritant as rooted more in a dependency driven basic assumption. As the American critic Art Buchwald said, "If you attack the establishment long enough and hard enough, they will make you a member of it", and so, by extension, dependent upon it.

Similarly, organizations that exist in order to deliver societal goods and services to the out-group tend towards a view of their allocated task that is either more "caring" and, therefore, dependency oriented and anthropophagic, or more "custodial", more fight/flight oriented, and more dismissive and anthropoemic. In thinking about the relationship of violence to our societal metaphor of refusal in disturbed eating, our attention was also drawn to contrasting societal responses to two different and notoriously violent men, both of whom went on hunger strikes in response to what they experienced as the violence of this societal response to them. The first, Bobby Sands, a member of the provisional wing of the Irish Republican Army (IRA) was in a British prison, convicted of crimes against the state. When this Irishman took up his hunger strike, the "anthropoemic" response of the criminal justice system was to look away, to let him fade away and to die as if it were a just desert for his crimes. The other example, Ian Brady, a notoriously sadistic serial child killer, was in a British maximum secure mental hospital. When this "sadist" took up his hunger strike, the more "anthropophagic" response of the mental health system was to force-feed him out of his hunger strike, to keep him alive, to incorporate him into "the system" so that he might continue to go on suffering at the hands of a widespread social vilification.

Using our paradigm, we hope to show that it is the out-group's spoiling and refusal of the proffered nourishment or punishment *combined with* the unconscious projections into these organizations of an offended citizenry or "general public", that generates these disorganized responses. The anthropophagic response yields to the impulse to force or coerce the more feared members of the dismembered out-group to leave their places of refuge and enter *proper accommodation*. This often includes over-using statutory powers, such as mental health legislation, "preventative detention", and criminal justice disposal. The anthropoemic response, although sometimes straightforwardly violent, as in the example of Bobby Sands, can, at other times, also wear the cloak of seeming indifference, involving the impulse to wash one's hands of the won't-be-helped and to leave them out in the cold. This experience is often associated with the under-use of statutory powers, so that men and women who are of little or no immediate threat to "us", except in their "other"-ness, are left uncared for, while the real and present danger that they present to *themselves* goes seemingly unnoticed.

Borrowing from Bion (1961), we have elsewhere (Adlam & Scanlon, 2005, 2009; Scanlon & Adlam, 2008a,b, 2009) offered the concept of "disturbances of groupishness" to explore the difficulty that can be encountered in all of our attempts at taking up our membership of any and all available societal groupings, ranging from the nuclear family to national and global citizenship. Some of us, however, experience more severe and distressing disturbances of groupishness, which, although infinitely variable in their manifestations, give rise to distinctive states of mind. For example, some of us, in what we would describe as a more *antisocial state of mind*, take up our membership of *the social group* in opposition to it, by violent occupation of it or by standing outside "in the cold" and refusing to join in. Others of us take up our membership of society in the liminal spaces at the edge of these social groupings, in what we might describe as a more borderline state of mind that involves a "tightrope" walk of fear, ambivalence, and self-loathing. The *refusal* and *spoiling* emerging from antisocial or borderline *relations* can then be understood more in terms of an interpersonal *location of the disturbance* rather than an intrapsychic one.

The German word *Schwellenangst*—that intense anxiety which is on or at the *threshold*—expresses succinctly this *set of relations*, the state of mind associated with it, and the ways in which the individual is so trapped as to be unable to move significantly one way or the other. To move further out and away from the group is to feel abandoned and aggrieved; to move further in and towards the group is to feel intrusive or intruded upon and equally aggrieved. In their personal and interpersonal painfulness and in their psycho-social disturbance, these entrapping modes of relating become a painful double bind. They are the realization of the intrapsychic processes which Rey (1994) described as the claustrophobic–agoraphobic dilemma and which Glasser (1996) described in terms of the "core complex". As Foucault (1961) suggests, "[the madman] cannot and must not have another prison than the threshold itself" (p. 9).

At the heart of this psycho-social positioning is a powerful *refusal* to be and *to feel* included that goes beyond more straightforward notions of psychological resistance. Billow (2007) points out that such refusal is much more like "a willful nonparticipation in offering or responding to material that can be symbolized". This refusal remains a problem both for the excluded, imprisoned in their antisocial or borderline relations, and for society as a whole. Even though there are significant numbers of excluded and severely distressed people who do manage eventually to "come in from the cold", we contend that this residual problem of refusal is intractable. Policy initiatives that *optimistically, or cynically, envisage a future when all of us will be socially included*—that would seek, for example, to eliminate rough sleeping in

Central London altogether (and conveniently in time for the 2012 Olympic Games) (Department for Communities and Local Government, 2009)—are themselves innately cynical. These ideas, as a reflection of the refusal that they purport to address, *involve an equally stubborn and institutionalized* refusal *to face up to the complex reality of these problems.*

"Let them eat cake . . ."

Individual practitioners and the agencies who attempt to accommodate the needs of the homeless, the dangerous, and the disordered are faced daily with people whose relationship to the "including" or "outreaching" in-group is, or is construed to be, both a refusal to join in and an implicit or explicit rubbishing or spoiling of their invitation. It is experienced as aggressive, sometimes violent, and, in turn, invites a frustrated, aggressive, and sometimes violent response. The individual worker, team, or organization becomes caught up in a reciprocal relationship analogous to that which obtains between a food refusing child and the rejected and frustrated parents. The latter are caught between the neglect that would be a consequence of their collusion with the refusal or spoiling, and the coercion that would be inherent in their insistence that "the food" must be appropriately consumed.

This is, in essence, the "forensic dilemma" in which the would-be provider, as representative of the societal in-group, is caught between the rock of force-feeding and the hard place of allowing and permitting starvation. While it is possible and might be thought to be sometimes necessary to force a severe anorexic to take in a certain amount of nourishment against their will, using a naso-gastric tube, for instance, it is quite impossible to force somebody to consume food orally if they do not want to. You can take a horse to water but you cannot make it drink. Similarly, the treatment-refusing patient, if found or caught, can be forced into treatment but cannot be forced to change. This is the case whether we are speaking of people with severe eating disorders who refuse to eat (or to stop eating), homeless people with complex needs who refuse to be settled, people with drug and alcohol problems who refuse to stop damaging themselves through dangerous addictions, recidivist offenders who refuse to be corrected, disaffected young people who refuse to be educated, or dangerous or perverse people whose persistent violence or intrusive-ness presents a risk to others. There will always be people who will continue to refuse, and if there never was any bread to begin with, why, indeed, would we repeat Marie Antoinette's apocryphal error and expect those of us who are hungry to devour her reparative but inherently suspect cake?

It is also interesting, perhaps, to consider how some aspects of the societal response to refusal and spoiling, expressed through the typi-cal anorexic phenomenon of over-exercise, come to mirror the over-active and exhausted exertions of the more cynical policy initiatives. In this context, these initiatives can be understood as a physical or "muscular" evacuation of the problem, rather than a more reality oriented, "depressive" incorporation of its intractability. Eating disor-dered patients on inpatient units are particularly prone to over-exer-cising but, in our experience, staff, too, are relentlessly busy, missing out on their own lunch breaks and constantly "innovating" as they breathlessly present one new therapy after another to famished but understandably suspicious and hesitant lips. Viewed from this perspective, we might imagine the patients' "pathological" over-exer-cise to be a parody of the in-group's preoccupation with "busy-ness". Likewise, their hoarding of food (or of the waste products of food), or the hoarding of the homeless "bag lady", can be understood as a parody of the preoccupations of those of us who live in an acquisitive world obsessed by goods and chattels. "Diogenes' syndrome" is an informal term for this kind of "problematic" hoarding, and we have elsewhere made extensive reference to the story of Diogenes of Sinope and his philosophical questioning of the values of the society whose accommodation he had refused, preferring instead to live in his (literal and metaphorical) barrel (Adlam & Scanlon, 2005; Scanlon & Adlam, 2008a; see also Navia, 2005).

Although our proposed paradigm of refusal and spoiling can also be understood in terms of early life experiences in the feeding pair, our focus is on the presentation of antisocial and borderline relations at the organizational and societal level. We are interested here in the impact of the social equivalent of food refusal and spoiling on indi-vidual workers', teams', and organizations' capacity to provide appro-priate services. What happens when all the king's horses and all the king's men are still not enough, because our *un-balanced* Humpties *seem* to prefer their fragmented, dis-membered state to being put together again? We focus on the frustration, hatred, and despair that is engendered, and the extent to which the societal response becomes dis-organized in ways which echo and mirror the antisocial and borderline relations whence the refusal and spoiling emanate. There is a complex reciprocal relationship between those of us who experience ourselves as "included" and those of us who experience ourselves as "excluded", between society's members and those whom society *dis-members, between* the *housed* and the *unhoused*. The violence of this relationship has particular implications for individual workers, staff teams, and organizations that are tasked with attempting *to house, re-member*, or otherwise *to accommodate* such people, both in their minds and within the systems of care in which they live and work.

Shame and the traumatizing response

> For leaning out last midnight on my sill,
> I heard the sighs of men, that have no skill
> To speak of their distress, no, nor the will!
>   (Wilfred Owen, 1990, "The Calls" (unfinished))

The excluded people whose plight we are concerned to highlight are those whose *shame* is that they have become psycho-socially *dis-membered* and *unhoused* as a result of the complex reciprocal relationship played out between "us" and "them" within "our" families, communities, and societies, yet who are *unable* to live with any meaningful personal awareness of the extent of their humiliation. Gilligan (1996) writes that he "has yet to see a serious act of violence that was not provoked by the experience of feeling shamed and humiliated", and he argues that the violence always represents an "attempt to prevent or undo this 'loss of face' no matter how severe the punishment" (1996, p. 110). In our terms, their refusal or incapacity to think about and communicate their experience of the unbearable states of mind which arise from this psycho-social positioning gives rise to their becoming psychically unhoused and dis-membered, which in turn results in their becoming actually homeless, really dangerous, and truly disorderly.

In this chapter, although we are attempting to eschew the language of "us and them" and so to invite "us all" to approach these questions collectively, we find it nearly impossible to hold on to the "we" as we founder upon the *jointly imagined*, problematic relationship between "us" and "them", and the mutual hatred, reciprocal violence, and hostile dependency which drives it. In this probably inevitable breaking down of "we" into "us" and "them", battle lines are drawn—a *caesura* across which hostile projections are directed. The sufferers in the out-group whose predicament we are evoking are less like the historical Diogenes, with his integrated, witty, and eloquent philosophical critique of his world, and more akin to the distressed soldiers in Wilfred Owen's poem, who cannot—or will not—metabolize their experience, and so cannot—or will not—express their protest more articulately.

A question evoked from this analysis of traumatic experience is: what then becomes of those of us who, as practitioners, or, for that matter, as citizens, experience our *authority* as being thwarted or disrespected by others' refusal? It is not only the "won't-be-helped" out-group who might struggle to articulate its feelings or who might feel shamed by the inability to do so. The "sighs" of those who seek to provide *the food* on society's behalf are often no less loud than those who feel they must spoil the food, no matter how hungry they are. Faced with this "forensic dilemma", do we force-feed the "won't-be-helped" patient up to a body mass index that she finds absolutely intolerable, or do we cut her adrift to die of starvation, since she will not dine with us on our terms? Of course, depending on the nature of the presenting danger and its impact upon us in our differing social and professional role, it might be possible for some of us to be able to do some of these things, while others of us must do another, opening up the inevitability of a split response within the system (Gabbard, 1989). Too often, our individual and organizational minds break down under the strain of this dilemma.

Our attention, thus, is drawn not simply to the *unhoused*, the dangerous, or the disordered mind, but to the relationship between these dis-membered individuals and other *normal* members of a society who seem to consider the differentials between the rich and the poor, the haves and the have nots, the housed and the unhoused, to be normative and acceptable. The social world so constructed is one of institutionalized and reciprocal humiliation and disrespect *between* the haves and the have-nots. Each fears the other and, in their different ways, inflicts violence upon the other, through either violent action or impoverishing omission. It can feel unthinkable for either party to give up the terrible and painful grievance that is an expression of their own version of this refusal, because to do so would be to face up to the *unbearable* grief that underlies the projections of the greed and envy that has brought us to this.

Steiner (1993) coined the term "psychic retreat" to refer to ways in which we can all, at times of extremes of painful contact with the external world, withdraw into states of mind that are "often experienced spatially as if they were places in which the patient could hide" (1993, p. xi). Armstrong (2005) developed this using an organizational analogy to explore the ways in which aggrieved persons, at times of difficulty, withdraw and refuse to take up their proper role and appropriate authority in organizations and in the world more generally. In our previous use of the image of Diogenes' retreat into his barrel, we suggest that there are many and varied psycho-social equivalences that are exactly such places for people whose experience of feeling unhoused is one of actual humiliation and real psycho-social dismemberment. These *places* and *appointments* are made because some of us do not yet have the capacity to communicate *our* dis-appointment, and because others of us do not yet have the capacity to understand others' offensiveness and refusal to be both a cryptic and a straightforward publication of their dis-appointment. Social-psychic retreats as sanctuaries and as rubbish dumps have been discussed by Mojović (2011).

Rather than being seen as traumatized through shaming experiences of poverty, deprivation, neglect, and abuse, our refusers and spoilers are construed by those of us who imagine ourselves to be included as delinquent, deviant, and/or offensive. In the face of this presentation, the impulsive societal and institutional response, which operates both defensively and offensively, oscillates between opposing and irreconcilable impulses to "chew 'em up" or "vomit 'em out". Given the power and pervasiveness of these psycho-social dynamics, societal institutions and systems of care tend mindlessly to mirror wider social prejudices. Ever more elaborate ways of excluding or forcibly including such people from our services and from our minds form a kind of malignant mirroring of the wider social attitudes, rather than, as might be hoped for, being able to provide a more realistic mirroring that could reflect these hypocrisies and prejudices back to wider society. Societal institutions struggle to understand the needs of "outsiders" *and* their own need for there to be such outsiders, because concepts like "cultural integration", "successful resettlement", "safe and secure disposal", "treatment and rehabilitation", "proper accommodation", and other ideas about what constitutes a "positive outcome", such as "punishment and retribution", are predicated upon the *workers'* experiences of what "housed" and "secure" states of mind and "safe communities" might be. Meaningful enquiry into what the won't-be client might actually understand by *feeling safe and included* is eschewed. The problem for the worker is that such unhousedness, insecurity, and nihilism cannot be split off or got rid of because, no matter how muscular or explosive the projective evacuation, there are parts of *all* our minds and all our communities that remain insecure, unhoused, and intensely frightening to one part(y) or another (Foster & Roberts, 1998).

Incohesive responses to refusal and spoiling

> Things fall apart; the centre cannot hold;
> Mere anarchy is loosed upon the world . . .
> The best lack all conviction, while the worst
> Are full of passionate intensity . . .
>   (W. B. Yeats, 2000, "The Second Coming")

Individual workers, teams, and organizations working with traumatized persons, like the wider society from whom they take their authority, invariably and inevitably find themselves caught up in the "forensic dilemma" manifested by oscillating tensions: for example, between espoused notions of "client-centredness" and "helping", and social realities of being agents of social control. This leads to day-to-day dilemmas and conflicts about how to make sense of, and so how to exercise, a proper "duty of care". They come to feel a sense of helplessness that is both a real and an imagined threat to their effectiveness. In this dangerous and endangered state of mind, the workers' capacity to manage themselves effectively in role is threatened. Their demand that these feelings of helplessness will be accommodated by their teams and organizations becomes ever more urgent. As this pervasive and collective sense of helplessness tightens its grip, it comes eventually to overwhelm organizations' capacities to think about and to manage these tensions and contradictions. Staff members find themselves feeling increasingly unhoused and dis-membered from their team and within their organization. These teams and organizations then become prey to the type of incohesive basic assumption functioning highlighted in this volume and previously described by Hopper (2003). In these circumstances, we have observed how the emergent groupings then begin to evince characteristic disturbances in their capacity to be "a team" and to be "organized" as they oscillate between more *aggregated* or more *massified* patterns of relating (Hopper, 2003). These two modalities again find an echo in our paradigm of the spoiling behaviours displayed by eating disordered patients, who often respond to the shaming prescription of food either by cutting it up into tiny pieces so that it is unrecognizable as an integrated and cohesive meal, or by mashing all the foodstuffs together into an undifferentiated (and sometimes disgusting) blob, so that it is unrecognizable as to its constituent parts, as described so incisively by Wood (Chapter Four).

The more aggregated patterns of relating typically lead to individual team members experiencing themselves as more atomized, monadic, and nomadic, increasingly distanced and alienated within themselves and from their colleagues and from their clients. In Hopper's terms, this increased sense of nihilism becomes a socially organized defence against helplessness rooted in their experience of the organization's failure to contain their dependency needs. An example of how this aggregation is expressed is the way in which practitioners retreat into what they experience as the *relative* safety of their own "case-loads", over which they imagine that they have some control. From this position, we have observed how they begin to extol the virtues of individual advocacy for their "own(ed)" patients, whom only they "really understand". As "key workers", they often begin to behave *as if* this notion had come more literally and concretely to mean "key-holder" or "gate-keeper" of their own privatized fiefdom, a role that they attempt to fulfil by, for example, autonomously deciding who is to be held on to, who is to be admitted, and who is to be discharged; who is to be chewed over, who is to be incorporated, and who is to be vomited out.

Either way, this every-person-for-himself attitude sucks workers increasingly into identification with the projections of their "chosen" clients and so involves them in taking up an essentially "antisocial" position in relation to the primary task of the organization, which cannot accommodate their anxieties. This antisocial attitude typically becomes manifest either by practitioners apparently "taking the patients' side" against an unthinking and uncaring system, or by excluding, controlling, and mistreating the patients that they are charged with helping. As one would expect in such fragmented teams and systems, there are inevitably strong undercurrents of disagreement and unexplored differences and hostilities (Gabbard, 1989). On one side of the polarization, we have often observed how those "filled with the passionate intensity" born of a powerful identification with the anger of the "alienated outsider" take up particular roles. Even in their dress and demeanour their self-presentation becomes a powerful emblem of their identifications, which itself communicates a confusion of vulnerability and aggression that mimics rather than reflects the world of the clients (Adlam & Scanlon, 2005). It is as if the communication is rooted in an "identified" wish to work what is, for the most part, a pseudo-altruistic, macho deception that says to "the wider" system "I, unlike you, *really* know what it is like to be one of 'them'". On the other side of the split, other staff, perhaps more strongly identified with the more schizoid and nihilistic part of the patient experience, come to "lack conviction". In this state of mind, they exercise a prerogative to avoid all emotional or participative connection with their patients, with their colleagues, and so with the life of the organization. They are cynical and dogged in their determination to avoid "work", their case-load is *secretly* dormant, low in number or neglected, and they give an impression of vacancy, laziness, or quasi-moral superiority. On each side of the splits that characterize these aggregated patterns of relating, the attitude is one of "each to their own", every man for himself: a "lone ranger", frontier mentality where the dynamics of growling protectionism and self-interest prevail.

At other times and in other teams, we have observed the emergence of different, more "massified" patterns of relating, arising from constant exposure to the clients' refusal and the resultant hostile dependency that is played out between them. A quasi-morale is presented that is rooted in an apparently groupish basic assumption that the survival of the individual member relies upon "sticking together" and directing their shared hostility against an external enemy. Again, there is something essentially *antisocial* and gang-like about the relational patterns which emerge. For example, we have observed situations in which teams, like perverse Robin Hoods and merry men, *stick together* in order to try to cheat the system, to take from the rich to give to the poor, or, like predatory gangsters, they *stick together* to rob from the poor to feed their own sense of impoverishment. Either way, there is a pervasive and unspeakable hostility towards a jointly imagined "persecutory" *system* within which *the team* is inadequately "housed" and from which it becomes increasingly isolated. These patterns of relating are again driven by a problematic identification with the oppressive–oppressed client group, and often involve a flight from professional accountability into a spuriously gratifying war on authority. These massed gangs then come to experience themselves as part of *a special project for special people*, and the rhetoric and language in which they state this position is critical and dismissive of the efforts of others. In their antisocial positioning, they are oppositional and see themselves as the "team" who likes to say "yes" when the wider organization or the wider system has said "no", or vice versa.

As Hopper (2003) suggests, group members in massified social systems make various attempts to reinforce the delusion that all share the same view of what is being said or assumed. As we have illustrated elsewhere (Scanlon & Adlam, 2008a), the implicit demand of the individual member is to become a colluding member of a corrupt association and collectively to look away from the abuses and misdemeanours that are perpetrated within it. Sanctions for "thinking one's own thoughts" are severe (Gabbard & Wilkinson, 1994, pp. 71–91). In our observation, these massified social systems often unconsciously select a particular *cause célèbre* that is taken up as a "politically correct" symbol and representation of their shared assumptions about the cause of their own and/or their clients' oppression, while simultaneously defending against a more *authentic* awareness and appreciation of their shared helplessness and the very real violence that erupts from it. The *cause célèbre* becomes a "politically correct" and defensive "non-problem", which, none the less, must then be taken very seriously (Garland, 1982), a psycho-social dynamic similar to what, in the wider socio-political sphere, has been described by Volkan (2002, 2004) as a "chosen trauma".

In our use of Hopper's formulation, we have observed that each of these incohesive patterns of relating—aggregation and massification— involve a mirroring of different aspects both of the divided experience of the refusing and spoiling clients' fractured and fragmented experience of themselves *and* coincidentally reflecting the inherently split and contradictory demands of the various societal stakeholders. The more the "difficult" would-be–won't-be client refuses the anthropoemic invitation to vomit them out, or the more anthropophagic invitation to take them in, the greater the pressure of these "external" demands on the individual isolated worker, the sub-group, or team. A sort of dance is set up, in which the lead is constantly moving back and forth across a boundary characterized by the oscillating needs and desires of the worker(s) and client(s), respectively. The possibility of a more empathic understanding of the helplessness is replaced by the workers' constant *unconscious* attempts to defend themselves and/or each other against the anxiety that emerges in the face of their clients' incapacities and refusals. As the irresistible force meets the immovable object, the *organization* that was established to house and re-member traumatized and dis-membered people with unhoused minds becomes itself a traumatized dis-organization employing the *services* of dis-membered staff in correspondingly unhoused states of mind. This traumatized dis-organization has itself become a mirror image of its relationship to the dangerous and endangered social world, within which it becomes increasingly poorly accommodated and from which it becomes increasingly dis-membered. In effect, the organization-as-a-whole and its individual members are paralysed, caught between the *behavioural* violence of their clients and the *structural* violence (Gilligan, 1996) of a wider establishment. With nowhere to hide, they find themselves retreating into basic assumption functioning in a futile attempt to free themselves from this terrible and potentially terrifying bi-polarity.

One operational example of this dynamic that we have frequently encountered in dis-organizational life lies in the confusion between what are seen as "rights and responsibilities" of the workers and the clients, respectively. On the one hand, there is an insistence, from both the clients and the wider system, that all clients have a right to be seen regardless of how they behave, thus violating the rights of staff through threats and intimidation. On the other hand, there are co-existing confused and confusing "politically correct" *zero tolerance* policies that expect the homeless, the dangerous, and the disordered to respect the rights of the staff by behaving in *sane and responsible* ways in order to access the help. Often, these operational confusions are played out between different agencies, some operating so-called "open-access" while others are more selective; however, our experience has shown us that both these positions co-exist within the same organizations, setting staff against each other, with the result that the split off and forgotten trauma of the clients is re-created and painfully replayed between different factions within the staff team(s). Some workers or teams, identified with our *passionate intensity*, come to see themselves as "lean and mean" and become cast in the role of the hero, doing a dirty job under difficult circumstances in order to clean up somebody else's mess, while detached and demoralized others end up *lacking conviction*. In our view, neither position is better or worse than the other; rather, both are manifestations of the deeply divisive and profoundly painful splitting processes that lie at the heart of our troubled societies and institutions. (This is similar to good/bad or malignant administrative groups in a large complex hospital described elsewhere in this volume by Rosenbaum and Winther).

". . . including the consultants"

In this dangerous and endangered state, the kinds of group activities—staff meetings, supervision, training, etc.—that would usually provide staff members with a sense of cohesion and personal identity become a source of tension, and those activities such as management, supervision, or consultancy, whose functions are associated with these tasks, are attacked or avoided. In this state, any sharing of workers' *experiential* understanding of the pain of "the would-be–won't-be client" is denied, so that both clients and staff teams can then *only* take up conversations within which it is assumed that all *knowledge* of all *distress* and *dis-ease* is *dis-membered* from the body of their shared experience. The uncoupled hostility is then either channelled by staff into a spuriously gratifying fight with "the establishment", or, more worryingly still, is inflicted upon the vulnerable people that they are charged with "helping". Either way, instead of re-membering the trauma and pain inherent in *refusal* and their own disturbed relationship to it, the organization-as-a-whole finds itself only able to accommodate a problematic *identification* with, or *detachment* from, the plight of the socially excluded.

In attempting to manage, supervise, or consult to these problematic dynamics, we, too, invariably find ourselves facing corresponding and parallel dilemmas. Caught between our own rock and hard place, as would-be-helpers, we have found ourselves coming under pressure to give up our questioning attitude and instead to accommodate or collude with more energetic and muscular activities rooted in an idea that "the enemy", represented as either the client(s) or *the establishment*, or both, is "at the gates", or "without". Whereas, if we can remain in our proper place, being neither anthropophagically pulled in nor anthropoemically pushed out, and *think our own thoughts* (Gabbard & Wilkinson, 1994), only then can we take up the challenge of fielding, metabolizing, and reflecting back the hatred and anger that comes with that position, and allow for the possibility of a more creative conversation about the inevitable helplessness that we encounter in our contacts with our own and our clients' refusal and with the profound psycho-social traumatization that underpins it.

However, in the absence of meaningful cohesion, our experience is that these conversations, which are difficult at the best of times, are simply refused or spoiled, a *grievance* is passed through the organization without being digested, and "the shit hits the fan". Sometimes, this shit is shovelled onwards and upwards into "the system", sometimes downwards into retaliatory action against the aggrieved staff or the would-be–won't-be clients. Frequently, it just goes everywhere. If it is shovelled upwards, the aggrieved service which complains to, or about, the system of care is then seen by the wider system as *troublesome, damned by association* with a population that it purports to serve, and, in a parallel process, becomes itself subject to the anthropophagic–anthropoemic oscillations described above. Attempts are made to incorporate it or "take it over", or vomit it out and "close it down". And so, at every level, the perverse dance continues: professional "goods and services" are apparently exchanged, but the net result is a *zero sum game* in which there is no movement, no change. Our social systems, and its members, at every level, become more impoverished, more ashamed, and, consequently, more aggrieved. At these points, no matter who has ended up in which position, for whatever reason all have finally achieved the basic assumption objective of *forgetting* the painfulness associated with the traumas of the most vulnerable among us. Of course, it is also at these points that serious (re-)enactments occur that cause very real offence, affront, or injury within or to the organization, manager, worker, client, or citizen, depending on whom, in the wider scheme of things, has found themselves to be in the wrong place at the wrong time: so, a vicious circle is perpetuated.

Some concluding remarks

Franz Kafka's short story "Ein Hungerkünstler" ("A fasting artist") (1996) offers an imaginative portrayal of the borderline and antisocial relations between the food-refusing individual and the excluding society that we have attempted to outline. The protagonist has turned his fasting into an art form in which the performance of the fast depends upon the participation of the audience, even though only he himself could be "a wholly satisfied spectator of his own fast" (because only he has the experience of it twenty-four hours a day). As part of the acknowledged ritual between the fasting artist and his audience, guards watch in shifts to ensure that he does not "cheat", even though he would never have taken in food "even under coercion", for "the dignity of his art forbade it". For Kafka's protagonist, it is not just the groupish demands of his audience that spur him on to renewed feats of starvation endurance: Kafka suggests that "he may have become so thin purely out of dissatisfaction with himself". When his audience neglects him, moving on in search of other gratification, it becomes clear that it is not the fasting artist who is cheating (he continues to starve himself), but, rather, it is the world that cheated him. At the last, he explains that he could not after all have stopped fasting, even had he wished to, because he had never been able to find food that he could want to eat: "[i]f I had found it . . . I'd not have made this fuss but would have eaten my fill the same as you and everyone else . . .".

In this chapter, we have explored some of the dynamic processes emerging from working with difficult clients in difficult circumstances, using the paradigm of a feeding pair in which the process of giving and receiving food within a reality oriented and reciprocally rewarding relationship is replaced by an escalating cycle of reciprocal violence characterized by spoiling and food refusal in one party and by rapid oscillations between chronic neglect and force-feeding in the other. Our observations have been that these dynamics are themselves a reflection of a wider dynamic played out between a societal in-group and a won't-be-helped out-group, between the food refuser and his audience. We have suggested that ideas of psychic "unhoused-ness" and psycho-social "dis-memberment" might be useful ways of conceptualizing the presenting difficulties of the "food" refusing clients as well as also describing the complementary experiences of staff members working in these very difficult settings. We have also explored how we might understand the interaction and transaction of reciprocal helplessness of both parties' experiences, and how the projection of others' shame and humiliation reconstitutes a constant cross-fire along a troubled frontier/caesura, so that the potential for empathy and understanding of the societal audience for the refusing, spoiling outsider gets lost in the shell-shock that lurks under the smoke and chaos of the battle.

Bion (1992) draws our attention to the bi-polarity in the mind of the individual (patient) between narcissism and "social-ism" and the conflicting impulses towards either pole that account for splitting in the psychoanalyst (in our terms, in the system of care). He particularly emphasizes the importance of the analyst (the food or care provider) being able to sustain a mindful connection to his social grouping. Under such pressure, the capacity of any *organization* to offer what Hopper (2003) calls an optimally *cohesive* approach to care is conse-quent upon the capacity of individual workers to be helped to develop a necessary and sufficient *social-ism*, or "groupishness", within which individual authority and competencies are valued. In other words these workers need to be helped to become *members* of the teams, organizations and wider communities in such a way that they can feel *housed* (or, at least, think about the ways in which they remain unhoused) and within which they can establish formal ways of metab-olizing their experience.

References

Adlam, J., & Scanlon, C. (2005). Personality disorder and homelessness: membership and 'unhoused minds' in forensic settings. *Group Analy-sis, 38*(3): 452–466.

Adlam, J., & Scanlon, C. (2009). Disturbances of 'groupishness'? Struc-tural violence, refusal and the therapeutic community response to severe personality disorder. *International Forum of Psychoanalysis, 18*(1): 23–29.

Armstrong, D. (2005). *Organization in the Mind: Psychoanalysis, Group Relations, and Organizational Consultancy*. London: Karnac.

Bauman, Z. (2000). *Liquid Modernity*. Malden: Polity.

Bauman, Z. (2004). *Wasted Lives: Modernity and its Outcasts*. Cambridge: Polity Press.

Billow, R. M. (2007). On refusal. *International Journal of Group Psychotherapy*, 57(4): 419–449.

Bion, W. R. (1961). *Experiences in Groups*. London: Routledge.

Bion, W. R. (1992). *Cogitations*. London: Karnac.

Brooke, R. (1915). *1914 and Other Poems*. London: Sidgwick and Jackson.

Cooper, A., & Lousada, J. (2005). *Borderline Welfare: Feeling and Fear of Feeling in Modern Welfare*. London: Karnac.

DeClerck, P. (2006). On the necessary suffering of the homeless. In: R. Scholar (Ed.), *Divided Cities: The Oxford Amnesty Lectures 2003* (pp. 161–175). Oxford: Oxford University Press.

Department for Communities and Local Government (2009). *Ending Rough Sleeping by 2012: A Self Assessment Health Check*. Available at: www.communities.gov.uk/publications/housing/selfassessmenttoolkit

Foster, A., & Roberts, V. (1998). Not in my back yard: the psychosocial reality of community care. In: A. Foster & V. Roberts (Eds.), *Managing Mental Health in the Community: Chaos and Containment* (pp. 27–37). London: Routledge.

Foucault, M. (1961). *Madness and Civilisation*. London: Routledge.

Foucault, M. (1976). *Society Must Be Defended*. London: Penguin.

Gabbard, G. O. (1989). Splitting in hospital treatment. *American Journal of Psychiatry*, 146: 444–451.

Gabbard, G. O., & Wilkinson, S. (1994). *Management of Counter-transference with Borderline Patients*. New York: Jason Aronson.

Garland, C. (1982). Taking the non-problem seriously. *Group Analysis*, 15(1): 4–14.

Gilligan, J. (1996). *Violence: Reflections on our Deadliest Epidemic*. London: Jessica Kingsley.

Glasser, M. (1996). Aggression and violence in the perversions. In: I. Rosen (Ed.), *Sexual Deviation* (pp. 278–305). Oxford: Oxford University Press.

Hopper, E. (2003). *Traumatic Experience in the Unconscious Life of Groups: The Fourth Basic Assumption: Incohesion: Aggregation/Massification*. London: Jessica Kingsley.

Kafka, F. (1996). *A Hunger Artist*. Prague: Twisted Spoon Press.

Lévi-Strauss, C. (1955). *Tristes Tropique*. Harmondsworth: Penguin.

Main, T. (1957). The ailment. *Journal of Medical Psychology*, 30: 129–145.

Mojović, M. (2011). Manifestations of psychic retreats in social systems. In: E. Hopper & H. Weinberg (Eds.), *The Social Unconscious in Persons, Groups and Societies, Volume 1: Mainly Theory* (pp. 209–232). London: Karnac.

Navia, L. (2005). *Diogenes the Cynic.* New York: Humanity Books

Owen, W. (1990). *The Poems of Wilfred Owen.* London: Chatto and Windus.

Rey, H. (1994). *Schizoid Modes of Being.* London: Free Association Books.

Scanlon, C., & Adlam, J. (2008a). Refusal, social exclusion and the cycle of rejection: a Cynical analysis? *Critical Social Policy, 28*(4): 529–549.

Scanlon, C., & Adlam, J. (2008b). Nursing dangerousness, dangerous nursing and the spaces in between: learning to live with uncertainties. In: A. Aiyegbusi & J. Clarke (Eds.), *Relationships with Offenders: An Introduction to the Psychodynamics of Forensic Mental Health Nursing* (pp. 127–142). London: Jessica Kingsley.

Scanlon, C., & Adlam, J. (2009). 'Why do you treat me this way?' Reciprocal violence and the mythology of 'deliberate self harm'. In: A. Motz (Ed.), *Managing Self Harm: Psychological Perspectives* (pp. 55–81). London: Routledge.

Steiner, J. (1993). *Psychic Retreats: Pathological Organisations in Psychotic, Neurotic and Borderline Patients.* London: Routledge.

Volkan, V. (2002). September 11 and societal regression. *Group Analysis, 35*(4): 456–482.

Volkan, V. (2004). *Blind Trust: Large Groups and Their Leaders in Time of Crisis and Terror.* New York: Pitchstone.

Yeats, W. B. (2000). *Selected Poems.* London: Penguin.

Young, J. (1999). *The Exclusive Society.* London: Sage.

Žižek, S. (2008). *Violence.* London: Profile Books.

CHAPTER NINE

Trauma and leadership succession: congregational leadership transition in the context of socio-cultural change

Louis B. Reed

"We have this treasure in earthen vessels . . ."

(St Paul, II Corinthians, 4:7, *The Holy Bible*)

"How can this be happening to us?" Tears well in the eyes of an elderly parishioner as he grips my hand at the church door. "We used to be such a happy family."

Introduction

Less than a year into his tenure, the minister to Queens Road Church has collapsed emotionally under relentless attack upon his character and leadership by an *ad hoc* group of congregants. His abrupt and outraged resignation is accompanied by most of those who have supported his initiatives. Devastated by the sudden loss of their new pastoral leader and one third of the members of this once thriving and prestigious "church family", the remainder are shocked at the intensity of the rupture among long-time friends and neighbours. They fear that their church family will not survive. The only matter on which all parties can agree is that the other side is to blame. "We have nothing to ask forgiveness for," they argue. "We've done nothing wrong."

Although a primary psychosocial function of a religious organization is to foster cohesion among its constituents through shared belief, ritual, and moral norms, eruptions of self-destructive aggression are not at all uncommon among religious congregations following successions of pastoral leadership. Notorious in ecclesiastical circles are serial "clergy killers" (Rediger, 1997), unruly and dysfunctional flocks who trample a succession of shepherds charged with their care and guidance. More surprising is the sudden outbreak of a violent stampede within an apparently harmonious and functional congregation during an ordinary and normal transition in leadership. Survivors, surveying the damage inflicted upon itself and its new leadership, are left to wonder how this can be happening to them. The following study describes and explores the onset, outbreak, and consequences of catastrophic internal conflict in one such congregation, as manifested during my tenure as its interim minister, in light of sweeping transformations occurring within its socio-cultural environment. Earl Hopper provided consultation regarding unexpected difficulties encountered by the congregation and myself during that time.

Destructive effects of internal conflict increasingly concern ecclesiastical leaders, most notably among mainline Protestant denominations whose congregational cultures celebrate harmony and frown upon dissonance. Analyses of church conflict focus largely upon congregations whose lives have become snarled as a consequence of imagining themselves as idealized extended families, in the absence of sufficient understanding of certain realities of organizational life in modern society. Extreme and uncontained bursts of internal conflict break the hearts of devoted constituents, overwhelm and discourage clergy caught in the middle, and frustrate denominational authorities unable to contain them. Bindings of shared belief and ritual unravel as pressure from virulent survival anxiety overwhelms communicants and pits them against one another.

The vessels in which these tempests rage, like teacups, are relatively small, often fragile, and frequently antiquated, often with more sentimental than practical value within their social environments. Still, religious congregations constitute an essential thread woven into the social and cultural fabric of their respective times and places. Beyond the immediacy of their theological and parochial interests and concerns, they play a larger role as *mediating structures* that filter the relationship between dominant institutions of a society and its members through layers of transcendent imagery (Berger & Neuhaus, 1977). St Paul metaphorically characterizes churches as vessels holding and disseminating a treasure (*The Holy Bible*, II Corinthians 4:7). When an ecclesiastical vessel is cracked or shattered, the treasure is sure to spill and likely to spoil. Hopper's personal anecdote of his memory of a shattered vase as a kind of individual and collective self-object conveys the poignancy that accompanies damage to or loss of a treasured transitional or evocative object (Hopper, 2003, p. 15). Ecclesiastical leaders who attempt to pick up and reassemble the jagged pieces are susceptible to nasty cuts.

Anxiety within congregational systems

Family systems theory currently provides a preferred model in ecclesiastical circles for diagnosis and treatment of church conflict by bringing the character of a congregation as an *emotional system* into bold relief. While a church congregation is commonly equipped by denominational polities with organizational structures designed and differentiated to enable it to manage itself and attend to its mission, events that threaten the stability of its emotional system can pull its constituents into the quicksand of emotional enmeshment endemic within pathogenic family groups. Since responsibility for maintaining systemic boundaries lies in the hands of pastoral leadership, it is essential that those hands be steady. The *non-anxious presence* of self-differentiated leadership, it is widely held, is effective in *inoculating* a congregation against the virulent spread of anxiety within its emotional system. When emotions spin out of control and things get scary, it is essential that leaders remain "calm and courageous no matter what" (Steinke, 2006).

Accumulated experience of ecclesiastical officials supports and confirms the efficacy of calm, disciplined self-management by leadership in restoring and maintaining congregational equilibrium under conditions of mild to moderate internal conflict. Quite a different picture emerges, though, in cases where internal divisiveness has become deep, pervasive, intractable, destructive, and out of control. Participants at a clergy resource centre where I serve as consultant,

most with track records of effectiveness in church leadership, com-
plain repeatedly of incomprehension and despair at the ferocity
directed toward them as they attempt to engage maliciously combat-
ive congregations in addressing their problems and negotiating their
differences. Unable to avoid triangulation and to maintain composure
and focus under fire, overwhelmed by the intensity of anxiety
and aggression swirling around them that they can neither contain
nor escape, some succumb to exhaustion and depression, some to
somatic disorders or sexual misconduct, others to deterioration or
destruction of family life or career. For their part, bereft congregations wither, splinter, or drift while awaiting the arrival of messianic
leadership.

At the very least, cases in which exceptional levels of anxiety
pervade the emotional system of a congregation present a formidable
challenge to the abilities even of skilled and seasoned pastoral leaders
to maintain a sufficiently calm and courageous presence to halt the
spread of infection. Mainline Protestant churches typically function
both as fellowships and as work groups, combining democratic attributes of a voluntary membership society with legal and financial
structures of a non-profit corporation. Clergy, likewise, occupy dual
roles that add dynamic complexity to their work, but are susceptible
to tangling and snarling as well. On the one hand, a congregational
minister is responsible for the care of souls, and on the other, with
their spiritual and functional leadership. While pastoral care and
leadership roles might be complementary and mutually reinforcing
under ordinary conditions, none the less they require different and
frequently contrasting skill sets and orientations. Balancing these responsibilities requires that the left hand know what the right hand is
doing, and, in the midst of emotional chaos, who can be sure? As
structural boundaries dissolve in the acid of anxiety, dynamic tensions
inherent within the dualities of congregational culture and of pastoral
role are exacerbated into dilemmas that defy resolution.

Effects of traumatic events upon the social
unconscious of a congregation

Insufficient consideration has yet been given to the church congregation as a *mental*, as well as *emotional* and *social* system, and to the

effects upon those systems of events that overwhelm a congregation's ability to think about and learn from them. The effects of such traumatogenic events and processes are psychically and somatically encapsulated within the social unconscious of groups as well as within the personal unconscious of individuals, rendering them inaccessible to symbolization, hence, communicable only through concrete enactment.

Studies of unconscious effects of catastrophic failure of dependency within group and organizational life provide a psychoanalytic and group analytic perspective, congruent with systems theory, that facilitates attention to details of congregational dysfunction wherein both God and the Devil lurk. Hopper demonstrates that catastrophic failure of a *basic assumption of dependency* within the social unconscious of a group or organization traumatizes its participants, evoking and exacerbating psychotic anxieties of annihilation that shatter internal cohesion and devolve complex emotional and social systems into primitive forms focused singularly upon survival. Extending Bion's view of unconscious basic assumptions that underlie and shape group function (Bion, 1961, pp. 14–16), he proposes that an organization infected with annihilation anxieties tends to reconstellate around a fourth basic assumption of *incohesion*, two forms of which are *aggregation* and *massification*. As the fourth basic assumption of Incohesion: Aggregation/Massification prevails, differentiation and development are sacrificed for the sake of escaping primitive, unconscious fears, and capacity for work group function is accordingly impaired, if not destroyed. A group whose internal bonds of basic trust have broken, saturated with unbearable fears of destruction, achieves the appearance of a steady state through oscillation between paranoid fantasies and enactments of aversive shattering and indiscriminate clinging (Hopper, 2003, Chapter Three). It remains helpless, though, to manage its affairs, and unable to address the problems and threats that face it. Ensuing conflicts are concerned not with *dependence, fight/flight, or pairing,* but with *survival.*

The basic assumption reflected in phenomena of *dependency,* Bion explains, "is that the group is met in order to be sustained by a leader on whom it depends for nourishment, material and spiritual, and protection" (Bion, 1961, p. 147) Bion observes that churches are particularly susceptible to the influence of basic assumption: dependency (Bion, 1961, p. 167), echoing the controversial argument of early nineteenth-century Protestant theologian Friedrich Schleiermacher that the essence of religion resides neither in beliefs nor morals, but in *feelings of unity or absolute dependence* (Schleiermacher, 1999, p. 12). Schleiermacher's conviction that religious sentiments are grounded in such primal sentiments helps account for the urgency and ferocity— even intractability—manifest in intense religious and ecclesiastical conflicts. Hopper emphasizes that, when dependency fails, "the emergence of the basic assumption of Incohesion indicates that the survival of the group is in doubt" (Hopper, 2003, p. 85). The stakes are very high, or at least seem so.

The following study is constructed from elements of my experience as interim minister to Queens Road Church and from reports by participants in the events that unfolded there. It traces the devolution of the mental, emotional, and social systems of a homogeneous, functioning congregation faced with emerging socio-cultural threats to its survival over which it had no control, through regression into a corporate fantasy of dependency upon benevolent leadership ultimately unable to deliver its promise of safety, and thence into the shredder of annihilation anxiety for recycling into an object more bizarrely decorative than useful. Devoid of both the capacity to manage itself and of the protection of an idealized care-giver, the congregation explodes in rage at its helplessness, is stunned into incomprehension at the force of its self-destructiveness, splits apart in despair and distrust, relentlessly attacks itself and its leadership upon whom it relies for rescue, and lives in alternating dread of abandonment and destruction. While failure of absolute dependence defies absolution, it can be described as a state of *incohesion,* manifested in the oscillating forms and processes of *aggression* and *massification.*

Identities are disguised to preserve confidentiality. The term *congregation*, as employed here, refers to the *group-as-a-whole.*

Queens Road Church

"QR Church", as colloquially known by its constituents, is a suburban British Free Church located in the Midlands of England. As participation in religious organizations expanded rapidly following the Second World War, QR thrived in influence and prestige within its community and denomination, growing to a peak of 500 members, many of whom were actively involved in community leadership and support of social services. A stately new church building was constructed in the heart of the business and professional class neighbourhood from which its constituents were drawn in order to facilitate and accommodate membership growth. Expansion took place largely through inclusion of extended multi-generational family groups who, over time, became entwined through socializing and intermarriage within a church to which almost everyone could walk from home. Grandparents watched their children and grandchildren grow up and remain within its fold. Such is the lore of "happy family" held within collective congregational memory.

QR Church governs itself through a set of bureaucratic structures prescribed by denominational polity consisting of democratically elected officers and committees with limited terms and a governing council with final authority over congregational policies and operations. Pastoral ministers are selected collaboratively by congregational and denominational authorities, with defined responsibilities for both pastoral care and leadership. Unofficial responsibilities of clergy spouses are established by local custom. This plan provides for structured differentiation of a hierarchy of roles intended to optimize and regulate congregational ability to manage its affairs and to carry out its mission. It is understandable that, as unconscious fantasies of family life entertained by congregants and pastoral leaders leak into such familiar and time-worn structures, they will colour and animate them, but will blur their boundaries and oversimplify their purposes as well. As the balance of congregational attention shifts from mission toward internal maintenance, its structural muscle atrophies, leaving it insufficiently equipped to address problems and threats that inevitably follow.

This study begins in midstream, with the surrender of the QR congregation's capacity for self-regulation into the hands of an idealized pastoral minister, accompanied by regression into profound emotional and functional dependency upon him. These developments unfolded concurrently with the onset of a seismic shift in the congregation's socio-cultural environment that profoundly altered thirty years of largely homeostatic existence and led rapidly to traumatic failure of that dependency and consequent loss of internal cohesion.

Toward a culture of dependency

Social historian Callum Brown traces declining participation in British churches in recent decades to a sudden consequence of a cultural paradigm shift initiated by the 1960s generation, in which awareness of the relevance to ordinary life of the language and practices of religious institutions diminished rapidly (Brown, 2001). By the late 1970s, as young families drifted away and few took their places, the membership of QR had shrunk by 30%. Its remaining core of largely middle-aged to elderly congregants, bewildered by the disappearance of their offspring and worried about consequences of the greying of the congregation, anticipated the pending retirement of their popular and beloved pastor with dread. Concurrently, the character of the neighbourhood surrounding QR Church began to change from professional to working class. Loyal constituents maintained family-like ties by continuing to commute to QR by car from their new suburban homes, taking little interest in welcoming new arrivals to the neighbourhood into their closed system.

As events beyond the comprehension and control of the QR congregation threatened the survival and perpetuation of the familial culture upon which its members relied for nurture and safety, Reverend Gregory assumed pastoral leadership of a congregation only beginning to grieve the loss of its beloved and newly retired minister. Congregants described Reverend Gregory as endowed with a charismatic and dominating personality who was resolved to win the affection of a flock who, it must be said, did not quickly warm to him. "What's the matter? Don't you love me?" he pressed inactive congregants. During his decade at the helm of QR Church, Reverend Gregory compensated for the affection denied him by steadily extending the range of his dominance and control over its affairs, displacing its internal lay leadership and assuming chairmanship or control of congregational committees and societies by offering assurance that its future was safe in his hands. Pews vacated by resigning church members were filled by transfer of membership of loyal followers from his previous congregation.

Prior to his retirement, he installed a member of one such family, overwhelmed by the terminal illness of its patriarch, into a position that placed control over administrative and financial records in her hands. Through her, he was able to extend his dominance behind the scenes with the tacit consent of the congregation. Endowing Mrs

Harris with scarcely warranted authority as an expert on ecclesiastical polity, the congregation continued to re-elect her to that position well beyond statutory time limits, intimidated as well by fear that she would fall into suicidal depression if relieved of office. Within that role, she embodied the continued influence of Reverend Gregory over congregational life well beyond his retirement, enabling the congregation to sustain its culture of dependence upon him throughout the terms of his successors, as well as its depressed and helpless state. "QR is a great church," Reverend Gregory pointed out to me over lunch. "It's *my* church, and it will *always* be my church." At the time, I failed to recognize the narcissistic force with which he was marking his territory. That did not become fully apparent to me until the morning following my final day on the job.

By the time of Reverend Gregory's retirement, QR Church was left seriously depleted of its capacity to manage its affairs and address its mounting problems related to loss of membership. "He made every decision in this church," related an amused congregant. Why might a congregation with a history of successful self-management and a sizeable remnant of members experienced in and competent at work group functioning willingly forfeit its authority and responsibility to a pastoral leader acting far beyond the boundaries of his defined role? Evidence suggests that abandonment anxiety evoked by the retirement of his esteemed predecessor during a time of threatening cultural change was assuaged through enchantment by Reverend Gregory's assurances of preservation of its fantasy as a happy and secure church family through submission to his beneficent protection and control. Its work group function atrophied, role distinctions blurred, operational rules overlooked, and internal communications ritualistic, the QR congregation contracted with centripetal force around the minister occupying the centre of its life as a personification of *familias*. The culture of dependency that had given shape and energy to its work became an end in itself, salving shared narcissistic wounds of congregation and minister.

Holding the church together

In defiance of denominational regulations, Reverend Gregory, following retirement, continued to participate actively in QR Church. Through exploiting his ongoing personal relationships with friends and allies nurtured across a decade, and with the aid of his agent, Mrs Harris, in control of agendas and records, he covertly undermined efforts of his successor to restore authority and responsibility for self-management to the congregation. Reverend Mansfield—a skilled, experienced and savvy church administrator with a conciliatory personality—recognized that he was faced with a formidable adversary to his leadership and set about avoiding confrontations with Reverend Gregory that he knew he would lose. Yielding to his predecessor's behind-the-scenes control of congregational life, Reverend Mansfield turned his energies to pastoral care and socializing with congregants, allowing him to succeed in steering clear of conflict with Reverend Gregory. A handful of new families affiliated with QR Church, attracted by his easygoing and affable bearing, joined other members in beginning to vie with Reverend Gregory's allies for influence over congregational affairs. "Reverend Mansfield played a lot of golf," a parishioner told me. "His wife did the work."

Indeed, a talented and extroverted Mrs Mansfield exhausted herself to the point of illness in attempting to fill gaps in church life opened by Reverend Gregory's retirement but avoided by her husband. Her service as a personification of parental devotion to the care of her church family provides a measure of rising tides of engulfment and abandonment anxiety within the congregation. With Reverend Gregory no longer openly micromanaging church life, attempts on the part of some congregants to stretch their wings exposed the fragility of the homeostasis that Reverend Gregory's allies sought to preserve. Internal tensions grew as a sub-group began to coalesce around Reverend Gregory's agent, Mrs Harris, asserting its authority over church life and attempting to quell emerging attempts at differentiation.

Recognizing that dark clouds were gathering, Reverend Mansfield sought assignment to another congregation before the completion of his term. "We don't understand what we did wrong," the Mansfields later reflected to me. "We tried our best to hold the church together." It shattered upon the arrival of its next minister.

Failure of leadership transition

An ecclesiastical supervisor told me that, in being recruited to lead QR Church, Reverend Naismith felt he had been duped. Having been charged to promote recruitment of younger families into its depleted membership, he recognized with one look at the tapestry of grey and white hair in the congregation that he would be sailing in rough seas. It is no secret that elderly congregations do not readily welcome the involvement of younger people, whom they claim to want and need to pick up the reins which they can no longer hold. Friends and sympathizers of Reverend Naismith observed that he seemed to try too hard to overcome obstacles to his goals and challenges to his authority and leadership mounted by Reverend Gregory's allies.

Reverend Naismith was a second-career minister, experienced in authoritative corporate management, mindful of both his mandate as an agent of change and of the difficulties posed by the transparent influence of Reverend Gregory. Realizing that denominational authorities were unwilling to enforce rules limiting participation of retired clergy, Reverend Naismith took it upon himself to insist that Reverend Gregory leave. Although essential to the restoration of internal boundaries, his unilateral action provoked denunciations by Mrs Harris and her circle and anxious silence from his supporters, probably sealing his fate. Increasingly isolated and defiant in the face of attacks by Mrs Harris's allies, Reverend Naismith threw petrol on the fire by ousting several Sunday School teachers who outspokenly opposed his initiatives to reform a stagnant educational programme. Angry teachers and parents, joined by Reverend Gregory's loyalists, instead forced closure of the Sunday School and resigned *en masse* from church membership in protest at the imposition of pastoral authority with which he challenged their domain. Chastened, Reverend Naismith subsequently set about attempting to salvage his revitalization programme by pressing ahead with a proposal for architectural renovations intended to attract prospective young families, anticipating that the congregation would unite behind it. They did not.

The breaking point came with disclosure that the renovation plan involved the relocation of a choir pew that a prominent and esteemed member of the congregation had occupied until his recent sudden death. An eruption of outrage from members of the choir was joined and amplified by Reverend Gregory's circle of devotees. The majority of congregants who supported his proposal largely kept quiet in the face of a torrent of furious denunciations and attacks upon his character. "You're destroying our church," a council member shouted as Reverend Naismith pushed his proposal. "Hitler!" charged another.

Mrs Harris openly accused him of misappropriating funds. Her allies began planting anonymous hate letters in church pews for worshippers to find, conspicuously turning their backs on Reverend Naismith during services and refusing to speak to him, while his frightened supporters looked away in silence. His spouse was excoriated by members of the women's society for taking a job and for looking after her small children rather than leading their meetings as expected. Reverend Gregory subsequently volunteered to me that Reverend Naismith was "evil and has no business in the ministry".

Mrs Naismith initiated the end game by defiantly resigning from church membership and joining another congregation. Nine months into his tenure as minister, her husband broke emotionally under the force of relentless and withering attacks to which he was subjected. His letter of resignation, accusing his adversaries of "unchristian behaviour", was received without discussion by the governing council. Denominational authorities quickly mobilized an emergency response team to restore order in the congregation, but were denounced by congregants for interfering in their affairs, and threatened with a lawsuit by Reverend Naismith for failing to exonerate him.

Following the resignation of most of Reverend Naismith's supporters in protest at his treatment, a small group of former lay officials volunteered to serve as an interim management team in an attempt "to save the church", now dwindled to 175 stunned members, "from closing". Their efforts drew guarded support from marginal members whose interest lay mainly in keeping the doors open, and ominous silence from allies of Reverend Gregory. Mrs Harris continued to hold her position at the centre of the congregation following its rupture, maintaining close emotional ties with her sponsor as he maintained friendship and pastoral support to her traumatized family.

One of his critics told me that Reverend Naismith did not appear to understand the differences between a business and a church, that his assertions of authority were abrupt and heavy-handed where a delicate touch was required. His suggestion testifies to the fragile state of the congregation's mental, emotional, and social systems, in which the emerging necessity of work-group leadership disturbed its collective fantasy of itself as the object of pastoral nurture. Clearly, Reverend Naismith sensed danger to his leadership from the outset, and his efforts to assert it set in motion an escalating spiral of anxiety that neither the congregation nor he could endure. Indeed, the virtually simultaneous emotional and functional collapses of congregation and minister seem to mirror one another, and presage a calamitous split occurring at the close of my tenure, during which the delicate touch did not work any better.

It is noteworthy that, even as Reverend Naismith's capacity for emotional self-management was overwhelmed, he continued to act within his role as pastoral leader until the break occurred, neither abandoning it to soothe the sentiments of his adversaries, nor retaliating to their attacks. Although his rising anxiety clearly exacerbated the congregation's, tensions over growing differentiation had already reached critical mass before his tenure began, and dawning recognition within the congregation that it was in need of a transfusion of new blood had led to his selection and mandate as minister. Like his predecessor, Reverend Naismith quickly recognized that QR Church belonged to Reverend Gregory, but failed to realize that he was as helpless to dissolve Reverend Gregory's ownership as was the congregation itself. Having established its influence at the centre of congregational life, an enclave of loyalists anxiously and furiously defended the perpetuation of a culture of dependency upon the care and protection of Reverend Gregory, while advocates for differentiation moved quietly to the margins. Now isolated, Reverend Naismith was rendered helpless to engage the congregation as a large group in acting in its own interest, to protect it from threats to its survival, and to control outbreaks of aggression such as shunning, character assassination, and scapegoating. Reverend Naismith's reaction to these attacks likewise reflects fantasies of being crushed by the mass attacking him, and abandoned by the aggregate of bystanders.[1]

My entry into this emotional and social system of QR Church commenced a year following the resignation of Reverend Naismith, during which its remnants operated under the authority and supervision of denominational officials. I am a semi-retired American pastoral psychotherapist and administrator with an interest in dynamics of congregational life. Having determined that the congregation was in no position to entertain placement of another minister through regular channels, denominational and congregational officials invited me to serve as interim minister for a period of two years to provide holding and support for its efforts toward recovery and reparation. In contrast with Reverend Naismith, I was not charged with responsibility to facilitate changes in the congregation's social system, neither was I dependent upon success in this assignment for my livelihood and career development. Nevertheless, denominational polity places formal responsibility and authority for liturgical and administrative leadership in the hands of its designated minister. Liturgical responsibilities include the conduct of worship services, administration of sacraments, and other ritual observances. As chief administrative official, the minister is required to preside at congregational and governing council meetings.

Manifestations of incohesion

Within an hour of our arrival at Queens Road Church, my spouse and I are drawn directly into the heart of the predicament of this leaderless and dysfunctional congregation. Each member of the lay management team gathered to welcome us announces their immediate departure for a fortnight's holiday. As the door closes behind them, my spouse and I look at one another in confusion and alarm as realization dawns that we have been left alone within a country, culture, and congregation unfamiliar to us, abandoned in the dark about our respective responsibilities in keeping with customary liturgical and administrative practices. Hasty enquiries directed to other congregants are met with alarmingly polite dismissal: "Just do whatever you want to." During the coming year, it becomes apparent that whatever we choose to do is wrong.

The contours of this introductory encounter contain a fractal of the congregation's unstable emotional and social systems. Whereas congregational social gatherings within which the presence and leadership of the minister is not central seem relaxed and convivial, appearances of solidarity and *bonhomie* as congregants gather for worship or business meetings dissolve quickly into passive or active acrimony as the opening hymn sounds or the gavel falls. Profound dependency upon leadership for nurture and protection from threatening exigencies of self-management is trumped by fear of betrayal. Interactions between congregation and interim minister occurring along the arc of the pendulum between fusion and fission reveal both the tenacity of congregational longings for nurture and protection and their fragility, disseminating apprehension throughout the system with each rotation. A warm and inviting welcome ceremony is followed by repeated brush-offs when I enquire about local customs. I am not informed of meetings I am expected to attend, then told that I should have known. I am unexpectedly placed in charge of each meeting I attend, then shamed for failing to know in advance what I am expected to do by congregants who themselves are unable to think of what to do except to place their leader upon a pedestal and wait for him to fail.

No written records of traditional liturgical practices exist. Vague hints, when pieced together, portray a service in which congregational attention is centred passively upon performance by the presiding minister. Prior to my first worship service, the church's senior official is speechless when I ask him to tell me where the minister customarily stands and sits; instead, he awkwardly pushes me physically from place to place as the service unfolds. Two-thirds of the congregation sit scattered loosely through the fifteen rows of pews on the pulpit side of the central aisle, arms folded across chests, with the remainder huddled tightly together against the back wall in four rear pews on the lectern side. I become mildly disorientated. I ask an usher why the foremost pews on the lectern side are vacant. "That's where the Sunday School sits," I am told. "Where's the Sunday School?" I ask. "It closed a year ago," he replies.

Week after week, lively conversation buzzes among worshippers as they await the beginning of the service, but a grey pall seems to settle over the congregation as I enter the room and the organ sounds the opening hymn, through which I can hardly make out the features of the people. Congregational singing is muted and reluctant, dragging and funereal. While a few worshippers smile weakly at my attempts to reach them, I feel isolated and threatened by pervasive unresponsiveness on the part of the people in front of whom I stand like a second-rate nightclub comedian sweating in the spotlight and thinking, "Somebody help me. I'm dying up here." My sense of continuity fails, and I struggle to remember what comes next in the service. It seems not to matter what comes next, only that I am the one who does it and as long as it is wrong. The congregation and I are united in a sense of helpless distress as we stumble through communal enactment of familiar rituals. I am vaguely aware that I am vulnerable to being "killed off".

Currents of apprehension likewise permeate governing council meetings, issuing in rapid shattering of initial appearances of conviviality and orderliness. A lively and pleasant conversational buzz fills the room until the meeting is convened, at which point a thick, tense silence descends upon the group. Movement into the agenda quickly sets off sparks on the part of a small circle of allies of Mrs Harris, who heatedly challenge any proposal on the table and divert attention to extraneous issues, while the remainder of council members retreat into nervous silence, eyes cast downward, avoiding contact. My efforts to focus attention upon the agenda instead provoke verbal attacks upon my competence, launching the meeting into chaos that I am able neither to contain nor interrupt. Mrs Harris herself attempts to take over one meeting by declaring the Chair out of order! An ally shouts in my face that I am driving people away from their church. My observation that the council is too upset to be able to proceed with business is shunted aside. "We don't want to embarrass anyone," a previously silent member explains, closing the subject. I am swamped by confusion and fear for my safety, yet unable to abandon my responsibilities to them in their distress. Buzzing continues on the doorstep as I leave, dazed and depleted. My short walk home is filled with doubts about my competence and helplessness that continue through the night as I pace the floor of my study. On one occasion, I become dissociated and lose my way home. The phone rings later that evening. "The trouble is starting again," the caller whispers. My spouse reports that, likewise, her initiatives to volunteer her services are met either with silence or with bemused contempt and humiliation. She informs me that she has "disappeared", and senses that she is on the verge of illness unless she, like Mrs Naismith, leaves.

Recognizing the futility of our position, I offer my resignation to the management team, who refuse it on the grounds that "the church will surely fall apart if you leave us." Fearful now of re-enacting our predecessors' abandonment of the congregation, I argue with my spouse that we are morally obligated to stay the course. We have incorporated the polarities of aggregate and mass in which we are immersed, and are likewise able neither to arrive at a synthesis nor an exit. The fabric of interaction between leaders and congregants at QR Church assumes the colouration and texture of personalities involved, as they are woven conjointly upon an unconscious warp of apprehension and helplessness. It embodies a bizarre illusion of cohesion, too fragile to put to work, yet too evocative of primal dependency to deconstruct or discard.

The response of the QR congregation to my attempts to fulfil the rudiments of the role of pastoral leader highlights the significance of a letter from a congregant prior to our arrival: "We're so glad you're coming to take care of us." Filtered through subsequent experience, her greeting signifies longing for the restoration of pastoral nurture and protection lost with the retirement of Reverend Gregory. The force of emotional and social pressure exerted by the congregation upon me to identify exclusively with the role of pastoral care-giver persistently overcomes my capacity for self-differentiation, essential to asserting work-group leadership. I begin feeling uneasily that "it's all about me", and that "it" is not good enough. I seem both immensely important and helplessly inept, an incompetent plenipotentiary who becomes stupid, hapless, lost, and humiliated in the presence of a shattered congregation that paradoxically manages to appear enchantingly solid, composed, confident, and self-contained. The urgency I feel to protect the congregation from narcissistic shame blinds me to its helplessness and magnifies my own. I soon feel isolated, trapped, and desperate. I am unable to sleep or think clearly, dreading the approach of each worship service and administrative meeting, and increasingly withdrawing into long walks and day trips to collect myself. The urgency of my predicament leaves me oblivious to theirs.

Despite differences in personality, temperament, and job description between Reverend Naismith and myself, patterns of interaction, normation, and communication reflective of loss of cohesion that emerged during his administration have continued seamlessly into mine. The congregation has become polarized between an encapsulated sub-group devoted to the overthrow of pastoral leadership and restoration of a failed culture of dependency and a loose alliance of advocates for differentiation, with others scattered at the margins waiting to see who prevails. Norms of conduct disappear into all-out conflict while appearances of unity and solidarity remain undisturbed. Affective dissonance is disseminated through symbolic equation and projective identification. Dissent is inhibited and secretive. Pastoral leaders are subjected to intense pressure to repair and reinforce damaged fantasies of nurture and comfort, while being isolated and vilified as they exercise leadership functions for which they are responsible. Immersed in an emotional and social system permeated by the unbearable helplessness and isolation of its constituents, both Reverend Naismith and I are subjected to denigration in order to preserve idealization of Reverend Gregory—not an uncommon problem in processes of leadership succession in traumatized organizations.[2]

Role differentiation

Faced with persistent failure to develop a working alliance with a tattered congregation, I shift my focus to restoration and management of boundaries of role and responsibility between minister and congregation as defined in denominational polity. Acknowledging our inability to work together effectively, I explain that the balance of my tenure shall be devoted to fulfilling my basic statutory responsibilities toward the congregation while endeavouring to understand and appreciate their predicament. The congregation, accordingly, shall be responsible for managing its affairs as prescribed by polity as it is able. Worship services will be structured to invite active congregational participation, and governing council meetings will be conducted strictly according to parliamentary procedure. Working committees shall meet only as chaired by an elected member, and responsibility for congregational care will be restored to its appropriate lay committee.

Understandably, my imposition of pastoral authority to restore role boundaries provokes an initial reaction of consternation and resistance, followed soon by unexpectedly marked improvement in functioning. As each committee hesitantly complies by installing its own leader, it quickly begins to attend to its business. After procedural boundaries are thoroughly tested, the governing council starts to employ parliamentary procedure to move through its agenda and arrive at decisions. The congregational care committee reluctantly resumes its responsibility for visiting the sick and disabled, referring to the minister for intervention as warranted. Liveliness and vitality start to appear in worship services as congregants gradually intensify their vocal participation, undisturbed, as Mrs Harris continues to give me the evil eye while surrounded by her protectors. A handful of worshippers drift into the Sunday School's empty pews. Attendance and financial contributions pick up noticeably. Requests for copies of sermons appear. A successful plot is hatched to remove Mrs Harris from office. Plans for architectural revisions are revived and approved. Denominational officials take notice of improved morale and functioning in the congregation, and decide to risk assignment of a pastoral successor. I begin to relax, enjoy my work, sleep at night, feel competent and effective, and reconnect with my spouse. My assumption that improved functioning signifies repair of internal cohesiveness, though, proves illusory.

"It's starting to feel like it used to," says the tearful elderly parishioner at the church door, and a shadow of doubt falls after all across my confidence in the congregation's resilience. While I am enjoying the appearance of recovery of work-group function in the congregation, he announces recovery of a fantasy of primordial unity evoked as he and his church family sing, pray, and read *en masse*. The congregation's ability to co-operate with authoritative pastoral management, while supported by the external skeleton of denominational polity, is fleshed out by reawakened fantasy of euphoric experience of submission to enchantment and protection at the hands of an omnipotent former minister who is both envied and feared. Improvements in capacity for collaborative work in response to strict management prove to emanate not from repair of internal bonds of trust, as I had hoped and imagined, but from recovery of such a fantasy. I am subsequently taken by surprise by an abrupt and overwhelming surge of abandonment anxiety in both the management committee and myself when I propose that we begin planning together for my termination.

Near the conclusion of my term, I suggest that the management team conduct an exit interview to begin preparations for transition to new pastoral leadership. Following a lengthy silence and averted eyes, a team member hesitantly explains, "Well, some things might be said that would better be left unsaid." I put on my therapist hat: "Perhaps you're concerned that I'll feel hurt by something you say." "No," comes a sharp reply. "You'll just attack us." The fragile fantasy of massification that the congregation and I have enjoyed shatters as we face the end of my tenure. I am too stunned by the force of unexpected fear and hostility to hear their confession of abandonment anxiety and the guilt and shame that accompany it. I am unable to take in and comprehend what has happened. I tell my denominational supervisor that I have done all I can and am too depleted of strength and will to carry on until the end of my term. He is unsurprised, and arranges for my termination one month early.

Despite my determination to avoid re-enacting my predecessor's angry abandonment of the congregation, I have done so. While Mrs Harris's allies celebrate, the remainder of the congregation reacts with surprise, hurt, and bewilderment. I attempt to recover by organizing the final service of worship around a litany of termination in which minister and congregation ritually express gratitude, declare release from further expectations of one another, and say goodbye.

The next morning, my spouse and I attend the funeral of a parishioner whom we had befriended. We sit toward the rear, and few people speak to us. Reverend Gregory is officiating. As he postures in the pulpit, extolling the congregation's greatness, worshippers are spellbound.

*   *   *

Following the conclusion of my term as interim minister, a dozen additional members of QR Church transfer their membership to other congregations, replaced by an equivalent number from two other nearby congregations that had closed. An active member reports that the congregation has resolved "to put the trouble behind us and move forward". Acrimony appears to have subsided, enabling the congregation to proceed with construction of the architectural modifications that precipitated its rupture, and the succeeding minister to complete his tenure without incident.

Trauma and leadership

Our study traces the development and consequences of catastrophic conflict within the Queens Road congregation through a series of leadership successions during two decades of social and cultural instability. Arousal of primitive fears of abandonment and annihilation shatter a congregational culture unified in shared unconscious fantasies of dependency, degrading its ability to function and threatening its survival. Declaration of resolve "to put the trouble behind us and move forward" marks a heroic attempt to mask dissociation by simulating recovery of cohesion through collective willpower. Unable to reflect upon its experience, the congregation survives by splitting, projective identification, and clinging together in innocence: "We have nothing to ask forgiveness for. We've done nothing wrong."

As this traumatized congregation devolves into an undifferentiated mass, the reparative potential of forgiveness, with its antecedent, confession, is foreclosed. Opportunities for engagement with leadership to address emerging threats and opportunities dissolve into enactments of survival anxieties, drawing leadership via projective and introjective pressures into identification with its fears and helplessness. Such conditions are hardly favourable to the reparation of damaged basic trust and serve as serious, if not terminal, limits to the capacity of a traumatized congregation and its leadership to collaborate in recovering vitality of mission, maintenance, and life together.

Recovery from traumatic experience, whether personal or corporate, is long, arduous, uncertain at best, and replete with hazards to the emotional, professional, and family lives of those entrusted with its care and leadership. Unable to follow the lead of leadership, a traumatized QR congregation instead warily submits to imposition by pastoral authority of firm role boundaries, management of gatherings, and restoration of orderly behaviour that evoke fantasies of "feeling like it used to": harmonious, secure, and powerful in the enduring care and protection of its shepherd, while dreading its inevitable failure.

Notes

1. Bollas (1992) characterizes the moral void dominated by a drive for certainty that requires purging the mind of contradiction to an idealized, militant principle or leader as *the fascist state of mind*. Oppositional mental contents are projectively identified into a victim who must be viciously annihilated. The resulting loss of self fuels delusional narcissism and, ironically, exacerbates intolerable uncertainty.
2. Industrial sociologist Alvin Gouldner (1954, pp. 79–83) characterizes these phenomena as bureaucratic enactments of "The Rebecca Myth", as derived from Daphne Du Maurier's novel.

References

Berger, P. L., & Neuhaus, R. J. (1977). *The Role of Mediating Structures in Public Policy*. Washington, DC: AEI Press.

Bion, W. R. (1961). *Experiences in Groups*. London: Tavistock.

Bollas, C. (1992). The fascist state of mind. In: *Being a Character* (pp. 193–217). New York: Hill & Wang.

Brown, C. G. (2001). *The Death of Christian Britain*. London: Routledge.

Gouldner, A. W. (1954). *Patterns of Industrial Bureaucracy*. New York: Free Press.

Hopper, E. (2003). *Traumatic Experiences in the Unconscious Life of Groups*. London: Jessica Kingsley.

Rediger, G. L. (1997). *Clergy Killers*. Louisville, KY: John Knox Press.

Schleiermacher, F. (1999). *The Christian Faith*, H. R. Mackintosh & J. S. Stewart (Trans.). Edinburgh: T & T Clark.

Steinke, P. L. (2006). *Congregational Leadership in Anxious Times*. Herndon, VA: Alban Institute.

The Holy Bible (1978). II Corinthians. Grand Rapids, MI: Zondervan.

CHAPTER TEN

Leaders and groups in traumatized and traumatizing organizations: a matter of everyday survival

Gerhard Wilke

Introduction

Current organizational structures and behaviour patterns are marked by a high degree of disturbance and signify that leaders, their teams, and institutions are caught in a cycle of endless transition. The effect of the repeated reconfiguration of teams, departmental structures, and leadership arrangements has produced symptoms of failed dependency and cumulative trauma. The absence of reliable structures, the piercing of holding environments, and the regular removal of authority figures causes organizations and their members to regress to more primitive forms of defence against their increasing sense of existential insecurity. The pressure to globalize, modernize, and change in order to prevent extinction has produced organizations where the fear of redundancy and marginalization, rather than the primary task, are uppermost in the minds of leaders and employees. It is not surprising that the attendant defences against the fear of not surviving are also visible in most teams. On stage and in role, leaders present a "false self", and off stage, in a coaching session, for example, reveal their "true self" (Winnicott, 1986). Groups work in dependency or compliant mode in a public forum, and reveal their true feelings when they meet over coffee or have a gossip in the corridors. What has become obvious is that the tension between the private self in what social anthropologists call a "sacred" and private space, and the public self in a "profane" and unsafe place, has become unbearable. The role conflict causes increasing numbers of high performing leaders and team members to take refuge in the sick role.

I want to explore the traumatizing effects on organizations and groups of the frequent change of leader, the transitional nature of organizational structures and the deconstruction of hierarchies. I draw on the evidence gathered in an ethnographic and group analytic research project on leadership transitions. The full results were published in *Living Leadership: A Practical Guide for Ordinary Heroes* (Binney, Wilke, & Williams, 2009). As one of the tasks of an analytic consultant is to explore new ways in which to sustain hope, I will also try to show a way out of the current dilemma of groups and their leaders paralysing each other, lest more authentic and truthful dialogue in public should threaten their job security, their sense of identification, their need for belonging, and the future of the whole organization.

The research method

The research group investigated the frequent changes of leadership and the response of executive teams to repeated experiences of loss and reattachment. We hoped to find out what practical strategies ordinary hero leaders used to cope with an uncertain management context and transitory holding structures. We focused on the leadership issue because it is cast in the role of a magic wand in current debates about organizational dilemmas and, in our judgement, leadership changes signify a critical event that ritually dramatizes the culture of an organization and says something about the values and norms of the society in which it is embedded. Through the fate of the leader, the up-and-down side of the current form of modernization is revealed. We hoped to find an alternative to the currently dominant paradigm of thinking of leaders in terms of hero worship and transformation, by observing how leaders and groups co-operate with, or sabotage, each other when under great pressure.

I was personally attracted to this research project because I had been disturbed in my work as an organizational consultant by the increased call for transformational leaders in a context of organizational modernization. The ritualistic demand for leadership as the answer to all the current ills in organizations had echoes of the 1930s, when very disturbing and complex social and economic problems were reduced to a millennarian belief in the magical power of leaders over the obedient and blindly believing mass. At the time I joined the research group, the current dynamic in organizations and around leadership felt to me like a kind of re-enactment of the perverted forms of modernization, communication, control, and leadership that had triumphed within the communist and fascist systems. The search for transforming heroes who had the propensity to divide people into those who are with us and those who are against us seemed to signify that our times were out of joint. I saw the search for such leaders as a symptom of, rather than the answer to, the "disembedding" of social structures and authority relationships that Giddens (1999) has described as typical of globalization. I wanted to test this hypothesis and understand what survival value the primitive defence mechanism of merging with the organization as the mother, and the need to over-identify with the leader as the messiah, had for the individual leader, the team, and the organization. The research team was drawn from people with diverse backgrounds and disciplines to encourage the sharing of alternative views and the effective challenging of pre-existing ideas. The group contained people with backgrounds in strategic consulting, organizational development and expertise in psychotherapy. The work we did differed from most management research projects in that we lived like anthropologists alongside leaders and their organizations for one day a month.

Our research took four years to complete and was carried out in three phases:

1. The first phase involved over forty interviews with company chairmen, chief executives, human resources directors, and senior head-hunters across Europe. The purpose was to hear the issues as perceived by the key players and map out the ground we needed to cover. We also wanted to get a sense of the taboo areas in the organizations and identify what made each unique and singular. In this initial process of engagement, while retaining a critical distance, we also looked for and found volunteers who would expose themselves and their teams to a qualitative research

project that required of them to review the way they worked with each other and how they avoided doing so.

2. The centrepiece of the work was a set of eight case studies. We accompanied new executives, general managers, and heads of function (and the people around them) for the two years following their appointment. Our primary work was accompanying the leaders, observing them in role, taking time in between to exchange views on important meetings and discussing key decisions, strategies, actions, and behaviours. We talked to a range of people across the organization to get a view of the culture and how the whole system worked.

3. Psychoanalytic and group analytic techniques were used in the research process in the following way: the monthly day with our case study leader started with a process of free association. We asked the leader to imagine the day ahead by anticipating critical incidents and exploring how such events are usually tackled and perhaps used to make things work. The day ended with an observation of a normal business meeting with the leader and the executive group. When the agenda of the meeting had finished, we invited the whole group to reflect with us on how they had worked, defended against the task, and faced up to, or avoided, difficult issues. In between the meetings that we observed, we reflected with the leader on how the group had worked and what role he or she, as a leader, played in the different phases of the group process during the meeting. This was done to get a better understanding of a leader's way of thinking and how it helped or hindered the process of dealing with the dual task of maintaining operational performance and adapting to permanent organizational change.

4. We checked our findings with many hundreds of managers and leaders in meetings, workshops, and conferences across the world. We were struck by how the themes of getting connected with the people they depended on for delivery, getting real with themselves and their people and bosses about limits and what was do-able in a given period of time, getting help by overcoming the shame of asking for it and legitimizing a dialogue about interdependence, and, last but not least, working on and off the table with their groups and bosses to avoid group-think and unreal expectations, resonated with very diverse groups.

People repeatedly said, "You have told us nothing new, but you describe what actually happens, without fear of the consequences. This tells us that we are not mad and do not just have a distorted view of reality when we try to talk about do-ability and raise objections to unrealistic targets."

The research process mirrored the complexity, confusion, and uncertainty in the world of organizational consultants and academics about the meaning of what has happened and what is going on in current organizations. I will, therefore, limit myself to building up an impressionistic picture of the context in which leaders and groups interact and try to maintain some hope and self-confidence in the face of a struggle for organizational survival, repeated demands for higher performance, more flexible ways of working, and compliance with externally designed and validated work processes.

Evidence of cumulative trauma

A work situation or task can be traumatizing when the demands made on an individual or group exceed their capacity to meet it. Trauma theory tends to distinguish three types of trauma:

1. People can be traumatized by natural catastrophes, such as the 2009 earthquake in Italy.
2. People can be traumatized by being abused by family members, attacked by an external group, or by being within a totalitarian system.
3. People who repeatedly experience being overburdened by demands that lie beyond their capacity to cope can be cumulatively traumatized.

During the research, I witnessed cumulative traumatization in relation to leaders, their teams, and organizations. While writing this text, I discovered that I was unable to think coherently about traumatizing events in current organizations. Try as I might, I could only have thoughts about one observed pattern of behaviour at a time; I could not string the thoughts together and build up an integrated storyline. Thinking involves making connections, and traumatizing processes destroy the capacity to think and connect, unless a "containing" object can be found. What enabled me to move on was the recognition that it was not just my own inadequacy that produced incoherent text, but that I had become a "container", a "carrier" for the "encapsulated" secrets and taboos of the organizations we observed. It was also important that I shared my shame of being able only to sketch out isolated jigsaw pieces and my failure to convey the full picture. I got out of the entrapment of the one-to-one relationship with the blank page by seeking help with thinking things through. In so doing, I found a third object that facilitated a transition from a state of having one thought at a time to a state of thinking in a connected way. It is this difficulty of thinking and working in a connected way that we encountered over and over again, which made me conclude that we were witnessing cumulative trauma in current organizations, headed up by people we called "survivor leaders" and organized into groups that displaced the symptoms of transgenerational transference.

Insecure attachment, serial disruption, and incomplete mourning

Irrespective of the business that people were in, or the service they offered, we observed the following patterns in private and public sector organizations: they all seemed to be in a state of permanent transition because one reorganization followed the next, and before one merger or takeover had been worked through, a new one started. Just as an attachment process between the group and the new substitute parent had begun, a new leader took over and the old one was sidelined, symbolically assassinated, or retired. Instead of reaping the benefit of secure attachments between leader and group, the organization unconsciously seemed to collect incomplete mourning processes that demanded attention with each new transition. The people who repeatedly dealt with these situations lacked an understanding of the dynamics of re-enactment, transgenerational transference, and unexpressed survivor guilt. I recently asked a middle manager in a very large company, "Who do you report to?" He answered, "Very good question. I'll get back to you in a fortnight with the answer. Only, by then, our management structure might have changed again."

This exchange demonstrates what has become the norm; when teams or organizations encounter difficulties, the cry goes up that it must be a leadership or restructuring issue. If things are not working out as they are supposed to, it is the leader's fault and the solution is to get a new one. Before the leader meets the people, he/she is charged with rearranging people into yet another structure. It is as if organizations have adopted the behaviour of IKEA customers; they chuck out and replace things when they feel like it. The catalogue promotes the illusion of unlimited choice and the desirability of constantly rearranging the domestic world that you inhabit and that mirrors your projected self-ideal. People are not furniture, they have feelings, and puncturing their sense of security has consequences for their level of engagement and motivation. When the old leader leaves and the new one takes over, and the team is "re-engineered", traumatizing psychological processes, generally denied and made socially unconscious, take hold of the group and surface during the next transition or crisis.

After a few of these leadership transition cycles, those left behind in the rearranged organization began unconsciously to see themselves as the only reliable guardians of continuity, but they also developed symptoms of survivor guilt. Team members had learnt to see all leaders as transient figures, and the group itself took over the responsibility for the survival of the organization and retained a focus on the task. The bosses, in their eyes, treated the organization as a self-serving sweetshop. It could be argued that their perception was confirmed by the credit crunch and the banking crisis. In the organizations that we observed "work groups" felt treated as an object and its members were cast in the role of naughty children by a series of "missionary leaders". The result of these repeated developmental breaks in the evolution of an organization's holding culture was that its ordinary members and middle managers turned their repressed aggression not against the "substitute parents" who have failed them, but against themselves. They ended up feeling that they, not the top bosses, had toppled the leader. "Serial disruptions" produced signs, within the group matrix, of the transgenerational transmission of incomplete mourning processes, of unexpressed shame and guilt, and the fear of annihilation, persecution, and fragmentation.

In moments of crisis, the lack of secure attachment between leader and group was repeatedly exposed, but dealt with only rarely, when it felt safe enough. When things were tense and should have been spoken about openly, the groups tended to go into compliance mode. They identified with the aggressor, the leader who embodied and personified the system that exposed them repeatedly to the helpless feelings associated with tasks they could not complete in the way envisaged in the handbooks and templates. The propensity to shut up and comply seemed to be reinforced by the unprocessed guilt feelings that can be found in victims of trauma. Survivors of trauma tend to identify with the aggressor to the point where the real guilt of the perpetrator is turned into the guilt feelings of the victim. They are driven to keep the persecuting object alive, as it has become introjected and has taken hold of them as a persecuting superego. The counter-intuitive dynamic at work is that the loss of the persecuting object will leave the sufferer with no object to relate to at all. This defence mechanism takes us into the psychology of perversion, survival, and creativity explored by Chasseguet-Smirgel (1985). She wrote, "Perversion and perverse behaviour are particularly present at those times in the history of mankind which precede or accompany major social and political upheavals".

Permanent transitions

Although transition is a normal part of human life and essential to the renewal of organizations, the speed and frequency of transition now seems counter-productive and traumatizing to those who live through the process over and over again. It is as if an individual or family has to move house, change job, or face the death of a close relative every few months. Most management writers, including those who consult with a psychoanalytic frame of mind, argue that endless transitions are an inherent part of the organizational world in the postmodern age. "Change is the only constant and the past is no guide to the future", is the prevalent ideological battle-cry. I feel strongly that this perspective denies the cumulative trauma, tangible in organizations, and ignores the fact that continuity and stability are equally vital. Indeed, the working through of the effects of the cumulative trauma in organizations will, from an analytical viewpoint, require secure enough containers for the externalization of the encapsulated pain and repressed memories. As an anthropologist, I would argue that transitions remain disturbances, and have a traumatizing effect when they are not visibly followed by a relatively stable state, at least for the length of time required for one leader and group to attach securely to each other. In the research, we found that this process takes between eighteen and twenty-four months, not the "First hundred days" advocated by most management books as a norm for the make-or-break period for incoming leaders. Erikson (1950) tried, in his work on the human life cycle, to show that we need time and space to develop the appropriate emotional capabilities for each stage of life. To accomplish the move from one stage to the next, we enter periods of confusing and disorientating transitions, such as adolescence or middle age, transitional periods which social anthropologists have called "liminal time", when social roles, social norms, and values are open, for a limited period, to revision and redefinition. The purpose of the transition is to destabilize, adapt, and restabilize our sense of "I" and "we" to altered internal and external circumstances. What holds for the individual career path can be applied metaphorically to organizations, as they seem to have developed a culture where the identity of each member becomes a permanent reconstruction site. If permanent transitions are seen as the only existential state of being in an organization, we can conclude that the prevailing management ideology about change being the only certainty in life is a rationalization, defending against the recognition that the organization is traumatized, and operates according to the laws of the social unconscious, not rational methods of planning and a coherent division of labour.

Permanent transitions remind the members of an organization of their mortality, vulnerability, and lack of control. It is these subjects for thought that must be made taboo and socially unconscious if the ideal of permanent improvement is to be maintained. This results in most people forgetting the pain associated with progress in order to go on living, delegating the task of remembrance and the processing of the psychological fall-out to "chosen" individuals. These tend to be people who cannot and will not forget in moments of crisis and have a propensity to volunteer for the role of the "historian", the "psychologist", the "alternative leader", or the "court fool". As at carnival time, which is a classic period of transition and a world turned upside-down, they put on their group mask, slip into the role of medium between past, present, and future, and, like a soothsayer or a shaman, remind the group of the hidden truths of the world they all inhabit.

"I" and "we" identity

Volkan (2004) has shown that an individual's mature functioning depends on the integration of a sense of "I" and "we". In periods of stability, most of us relate consciously to our sense of "me" and "us", and take the identification with the "we" for granted. In times of crisis, we seek cover under the large group tent of our belonging group, which lends us a sense of security and identity, and we sacrifice our sense of "I" on the altar of a merged "we". In such situations, we experience a time collapse, and treat past, present, and future as one. We call for, and submit to, charismatic leaders who refer to the group's chosen trauma and mobilize everyone in the belonging group to fight off external threats, and seek comfort in each other's mindless sense of followership. Volkan's theory is a reworking of Freud's book, *Group Psychology and the Analysis of the Ego*, where the old master analysed why people went enthusiastically and with a sense of knowing blindness into the First World War and their probable death (Freud, 1921c). Volkan shows that the leader can make a difference and direct the crowd in such a way that it remains a defensive and benign mass, busy trying to repair the leaky large group tent through its own efforts. The leader who chose such a path in recent times was Mandela. The leader who pursued the malignant path of integrating the insecure group through hatred of the enemy was Milošević. He used the "chosen trauma" of the Serbs, which is associated with a loss of pride and the experience of being shamed in the past, to whip up hatred against those who were perceived as having caused the denigration and pollution of the idealized sense of "I" and "we". In the first case, leader and group can find a way back to dialogue, identity integration, and exchange with outsider groups; in the second scenario, leader and mass merge and turn their aggressive energy on to external enemies and pursue a course where the integration of the "I" and "we" identity depends on the defeat of the enemy.

Applied to current organizations, this theory helps us justify the need for a leader in a group and explains why leading a group or manipulating it can have such a profound effect on the level of "civilization" and "de-civilization" (Elias, 1974). The research produced evidence of Volkan's claim that groups rush under the large group tent of their "idealized" organization in order to give themselves a sense of being part of something bigger and more powerful than their helpless selves. Group members tended to split the organization into the good company and the bad team, as this helped them cope with their inner feeling of impotent rage in the face of the endless transitions imposed by their local leader. The idealization of the organization also allowed them to formulate rationalizations to explain why things were better in the past, are unbearable at present, and will improve in the future. Group members developed stories that cast the CEO in the role of the lone hero who has a good vision, but is surrounded by wicked bureaucrats who distort the strategy and the truth. These self-soothing stories kept hope alive and protected group members from having to confront their collusion with the process of permanent transition, in spite of their wish to maintain the status quo.

What is self-destructive about the idealization of the organization and denigration of the local team and leader is that it deprives the cumulatively traumatized group of a holding container in which it could, when it has attached securely to a leader, act out its fear of retraumatization. In a denigrated and unsafe group, painful experiences associated with cumulative trauma cannot be remembered and will have to be acted out, split off, and projected into enemies or scapegoats. The leader is turned into the object of messianic hope or the scapegoat of the mob, while the group becomes an object of fear for the leader. When this happens, the next change of leader, the next restructuring process, and the next negative holding experience is pre-programmed. When the "I" and "we" are integrated in a mature position, people can form a cohesive group that tolerates difference and is able to connect with other groups within the overall system, without fear of touching and without the need to defend its territory. In this way of thinking, an organization can function as a system where the whole is greater than the sum of its parts. In a situation of permanent transition, as we found, the odds are stacked against this degree of civilized exchange. The ability to imagine what holds the whole system together and what it takes to co-operate across boundaries to co-ordinate production and the delivery of services was impaired. The speed of the changes was such that chaos seemed to rule and it was difficult to tell who was in which role, what the reporting lines were, and who, if anybody, had a clear picture of the overall goal of the collective effort.

It would be misleading to conclude that the lack of clarity was simply the result of the leader's missing competence or the group's resistance. The chaos was inherent in the situation. Uncertainty ruled in the private and public sectors. Attempts to make everything clear in the longer term were more a flight from a difficult reality than a workable method of dealing with it. The "primary task" of the leader in this context was to name the confusion, step back from the formal meeting agenda, and open up a transitional and "potential space" (Winnicott, 2002) in order to clarify the next set of tasks, the constraints of the context, and the resources and options in the group. Only by addressing what Hirschhorn (1997) has called the "primary risk" of survival could the "primary task" of delivery be faced. What follows from this is a different way of looking at leadership. Leading happens and is located between people; leaders are in the middle rather than on top and groups are located and suspended in a web of interdependent matrices. According to Huffington and colleagues (2004), the psychological contract between the leader and the group and its members has changed fundamentally, due to the levelling of hierarchies, the creation of open space offices, the practice of hot-desking, and the introduction of "matrix organizations", where reporting lines cross vertical and lateral boundaries. No one has a secure sense of place and position any more, and the leader gets caught between the demands that the bosses make and the demands that the individuals in the team make. In the absence of clear roles and a secure and containing hierarchy, the leader currently personifies and embodies the structure and the task of the whole organization. The issue in this context is not so much leadership, but whether a leader can muster enough trust and "I" and "we" integration in the group to legitimize his/her authority in the eyes of the followers. Why? Because leading and being led has the appearance of a permanent group process. Having or not having this capacity to work with the group, through it, and in it seems to be the difference between survival and retraumatization in an ever-changing context. This suggests to me that we need to reframe the leadership problem in terms of the legitimation of authority. The way things get done, strategic change is implemented, and organizational cultures are adapted is fundamentally linked to the question of who has the authority to lead and who legitimizes the need for a "first among equals" position.

Collapse of social structures into a permanent group process

Hopper argues in his work on the social unconscious that institutions within society that function like a permanent group process do so because their members are exposed to failed dependency at the hands of overly intrusive or absent organisational leaders. They experience severe helplessness due to existential insecurity and are permanently overburdened by the tasks the organization imposes on them. In such situations the difference between what Bion (1961) calls the work group, and what sociologists have described as the social system, disappears. The formal, external, and objective social structure collapses into the subjective experience of a group process. The need for security, safety, belonging, and recognition is personified and located in group members who have a valance to enact roles that signify these feelings. People who unconsciously hold the task for the group to feel guilty, to be ashamed, to show resistance and aggression enact these qualities when their expression is needed in the group process to defend against the shared fear of annihilation and fragmentation. This existential fear is generated by the loss of a social holding structure and the need to go on surviving. Leading personalities emerge from time to time within the group to embody what is hated, feared, and longed for in order to re-enact the shared trauma of being in a survival scenario. The group is attracted to re-experiencing aspects of the cumulative trauma of feeling abused or overburdened, hoping that this time they can punish the leader who is again exposing them to so much helplessness, or learn to live with the pain.

The research revealed such interaction patterns in current organizations. All the leaders we observed, together with members of their groups, had repeatedly been asked to leave their posts, been redeployed to new ones, or applied to their current post to escape a previous situation that they had found intolerable. The leaders were full of painful experiences of having been abandoned by their groups when their own survival was at stake, reminding us of the fact that over the life cycle it is also the children who can fail their dependent parents. What was striking is how the feelings associated with these traumatic, rather than positive, experiences stopped the leaders from using the group to share the burden of responsibility and power. The groups were frightened of trusting their current leader because they had been involved in abandoning or assassinating a previous one. The leaders perceived the group as dangerous, untamed, and wild, and were weary of having open and frank exchanges in the round. Controversial issues that could have integrated the group were taken out of meetings and dealt with in one-to-one conversations that excluded the group and denigrated its potential to help. What people feared, the fragmentation and repeated re-engineering of their work group, was unconsciously re-enacted.

The permanent transitions and repeated exposure to organizational re-engineering burdened the groups with serial experiences of failed dependency and incomplete mourning, signifying a process of transition. It was not surprising that group members in this context felt as if their organizational parents had abandoned them and they, like the leaders, suffered from a fear of contact, lest they should be caught up in uncontrollable events and risk self-destruction. Leader and group defended against their fear of being made to feel absolutely helpless by being compliant and inauthentic in public meetings and angry and passionate in private gatherings. Business that would have been done by a mature work group in public was done in corridors, in the toilets, or over coffee. Meetings with the whole group and the leader resembled a ritualistic gathering of non-believers, attending church on a fixed day and time. These gatherings functioned to ratify what had been decided outside the room, and enacted the degree of alienation and mistrust between the participants. It was a strange kind of inversion of structure and group process, as the structured meeting resembled a pathological group process and the encounters in the informal organization were a reminder that the spontaneous group process was in touch with the primary task of the organization. In private, group members clearly saw the need to integrate the formal and informal communication channels. They also repeatedly revealed that they were in touch with the need to work together and face up to the unfinished emotional business in the organization. Current psychoanalytic theory assumes that in traumatized individuals and groups, the boundary between structure and process, between individual and group, and between inside and outside world collapses, and that the regime of external suffering and exposure to helplessness takes over each group member's mind. We saw that it was true in official meetings, but not when people gossiped and talked openly. In these "liminal" moments between meetings, people revealed that they could hold on to how human beings relate, talk, and work together without being permanently in the grip of their trauma. The hope of reconnecting the formal and inauthentic world of structured meetings, and the informal and authentic world of gossip, emerged in situations of crisis and during unforeseen and critical incidents. It needed a trigger event and the presence of a "linking object" (Volkan, 2002), embodied by the leader or a fearless group member, to reconnect social structure and group process.

Re-enactment, hope, and repair

The organizations and their members seemed, like trauma patients, irresistibly attracted to repeating the scenes in which they felt overwhelmed, and even the top managers treated them like a natural catastrophe: something that happened to them, not linked to their own actions. What alerted me to this dynamic was a sense that people were not simply victims of events, but actively involved in bringing painful experiences of loss, helplessness, and powerlessness upon themselves. They were attracted to a dynamic that was painful and disturbing, but seemed familiar and reassuring. Those caught up in these experiences repressed the feelings associated with the events so deeply that they could not be remembered and talked about. There seemed to be a socially unconscious need to re-experience the trauma of being overwhelmed and abandoned by the organizational parents in the hope that the renewed experience of the pain and loss could be translated into words and integrated into the mind as something normal. The fantasy was that a ritualized repetition of something threatening, such as a leadership change and a reconfiguration of the organizational structure, could magically conjure up an authority figure or a parental couple that would fix the group and its accumulated trauma. In Denmark, the health system has made it a legal requirement that a pair lead a hospital. We noticed that, in stressful moments, the groups sought to give birth to a rescuing leader as father and a less manic and more depressive organization as mother. If only this coupling could be maintained for a while, the dependent people seemed to believe, they would re-experience a containing relationship, internalize it, and use it to feel more held in their place of work and secure within their adult self-ideal. By being able to internalize a repeated experience of security and basic trust in the external environment, people hoped that they would recover the ability to grow up as fast as was expected of them. In the absence of this environmental mothering (Winnicott, 1963), they seemed to fear a repetition of the trauma of too much change in too little time, leaving them feeling abandoned and bereft again.

Despite the simmering rage that they were left with and which had nowhere to go and was too painful to keep in mind, people soon displayed their propensity to be in the victim position again. What was that about? On the negative side, it seemed to be connected with the attempt to master and control the pain of the cumulative trauma by volunteering to live through it once more. On the positive side, the re-enactment was a search for a holding and containing object and a better attachment experience. What group members were unconsciously looking for was a situation in which they could start a process of recovery by externalizing the inner object representation of the traumatizing interactions and have an experience of being held. What can be achieved was demonstrated by one of our case study leaders. Faced with unrealistic targets from the top, in danger of yet another mini trauma, she realized that simply imposing the stretch targets would not work. She explained the situation to the group in the meeting, and then said, "Let's not rush into doing things too quickly, despite the pressure. Let's step back from the relentless demands to do more. I want to know where each of you stands and what possible resources you can free up. If we don't tell each other about the strain we are under, we will just add to everyone's pressure. I need to know how I can best back you, and how you can make sure that we don't lose credibility with the rest of the organization."

Critical incidents, on and off the table

We observed that unforeseen and "critical incidents" facilitated a re-pairing experience and restored hope. Crisis moments and how they were experienced in the relationship between leader and group turned out to be the key to making things work, legitimizing authority and establishing sufficient trust in the organization. Critical incidents and their joint mastery either deepened the level of exchange and engagement between group and leader, or widened the communication gap and heightened levels of mutual distrust. Under pressure, when everyone was tempted to act rather than think, group and leader tested each other's authenticity and trustworthiness. A good enough leader was able to intervene in a crisis meeting in such a way that the capacity to imagine what the others were thinking and feeling was maintained. They could do that if they understood that they needed to work "on and off the table", and realized that each team that meets is a work group on the table and a basic assumption group, or worse, under it. What we found is that the leader is ideally and practically needed to hold the frame of the meeting and bring what is off the table and blocks progress into the dialogue on the table. If the meeting was not contained, the whole group, out of a feeling of helplessness and abandonment, needed to find a scapegoat and regressed into "us and them" thinking. In that situation, the leader either colluded with seeking attention in the victim position or became a cut-off and isolated figure who completed the meeting in a robotic and bureaucratic way. Both scenarios left everyone feeling that they had survived the meeting, working alongside each other, but not together.

On a significant number of occasions, we observed that it was a "leading group member" who named the elephant in the room and got the meeting unstuck. In this sense, Volkan's thesis that the leader's interventions decide whether a group follows a malign or benign path needs to be reframed. The leaders we observed were often caught in their dual role as being the eldest sibling in their own group and the youngest or middle sibling in the management group. The imagined leader above, who had the power over organizational life and death, shaped many of the meetings, despite being absent in body and mind. What follows from this, theoretically, is that we need to bear in mind the complex relationship between individual, group, organization and context when we try to understand how organizations work. It would be helpful to let go of thinking in dyadic terms and adopt a group view. In a Winnicottian sense, there is neither a leader nor a follower, but only a relationship between them. Seen from a group analytic perspective, leadership is shared and moves between leader and group within the matrix of a team and within the foundation matrix of the whole organization, consisting of interdependent sub-groups. The whole system and its parts are suspended within a societal context that constrains what is and is not do-able at any moment in time. What enabled leader and group to move out of a paranoid–schizoid position into a depressive one was a focus on do-ability, reality testing, and the acceptance of interdependence.

In each of our case studies, a critical incident and how the leader and the group handled it shifted the energy flow. It was the experience of facing up to a difficult situation together that created the environmental conditions for more trustful and committed ways of co-operating. In the book, we call this process getting connected, getting real, and getting help, by which we mean working with what is, rather than what ought to be, and making it legitimate to ask for and offer help. A leader or group who could make the best of a situation, go with the flow of the meeting, and work on the rational and emotional level could motivate each other to release bottled up creative energy. Having this experience together made the pain of the cumulative trauma a little more tolerable and facilitated a process of stepping back from the fight/flight scenarios and the pull of omnipotent, charismatic solutions as a way of dealing with the disturbing and traumatizing context of permanent organizational change.

Conclusions

I have tried to show that the way organizations work now is cumulatively traumatizing for groups and their leaders. At the surface level of conscious planning and control, the holding structures in organizations have been deconstructed in the service of modernization and people work in a context of permanent transitions and uncertainty. The organization of work appears to have taken on the form of a constant group process rather than an ordered social structure. At the unconscious level, leaders, followers, and interdependent groups reconstruct and evolve emotional and psychological holding structures through their interactions in critical moments. These mental structures mirror an upside-down world and can, when internalized, contain the anxiety induced by the absence of reliable organizational parents by pairing the primary task of the organization with the primary risk of survival. When the interdependence of the primary risk and primary task can be held in the mind of a leader, a group, and a whole organization, the fateful attraction of the re-enactment of the cumulative trauma of repeated exposure to failed dependency can be resisted and a work-group mentality retained. The accomplishment of this developmental step, rests on "good enough" authority figures that have character, the capacity for attachment, and the courage to resist flights of fancy and "us and them" thinking. Ideally, the leader of a group performs this function, but, in a context of permanent transition co-operation, performance and survival have become a group task. It is time to separate from the magical thinking associated with the currently fashionable idea that it is all up to the one and only leader and a compliant and malleable band of dedicated followers. What is needed, and what we found works, is the emergence of authority figures during critical incidents who can work, as one of our case study leaders called it, on and off the table (simultaneously with the work-and-basic-assumption group); someone who engages with the group's anxiety about the nature of the task and the uncertainty provoked by the context by modelling responsible organizational parenting and by giving directions and taking due care of the group dynamic when the leader or no one else is able, in the moment, to enact the role of the authority figure. This shift from depending on one leader to the emergence of an authority figure at the right moment in the group requires a change of mind, focusing no longer on the individual saviour and locating the hope for the successful completion of the task in the group and its considerable resources and expertise.

References

Binney, G., Wilke, G., & Williams, C. (2009). *Living Leadership: A Practical Guide for Ordinary Heroes.* Harlow: Financial Times/Prentice Hall.

Bion, W. R. (1961). *Experiences in Groups and Other Papers.* London: Tavistock.

Chasseguet-Smirgel, J. (1985). *Creativity and Perversion.* London: Free Association Books.

Elias, N. (1974). *Die Gesellschaft der Individuen.* Frankfurt: Suhrkamp Wissenschaft.

Erikson, E. H. (1950). *Identity and the Life Cycle.* New York: International Universities Press.

Freud, S. (1921c). *Group Psychology and the Analysis of the Ego. S.E., 18*: 67–143. London: Hogarth.

Giddens, A. (1999). *Runaway World: How Globalisation is Reshaping our Lives.* London: Profile Books.

Hirschhorn, L. (1997). *Reworking Authority: Leading and Following in Post-Modern Organizations.* Cambridge, MA: MIT Press.

Huffington, C., Armstrong, D., Halton, W., Hoyle, L., & Pooley, J. (2004). *Working Below the Surface: The Emotional Life of Contemporary Organizations*. London: Karnac.

Volkan, V. (2004). *Blind Trust: Large Groups and Their Leaders in Times of Crisis and Terror*. Charlottesville: Pitchstone.

Volkan, V. D. (2002). Varieties of transgenerational transmission. In: V. Volkan, G. Ast, & F. W. Greer Jnr (Eds.), *The Third Reich in the Unconscious* (pp. 4–6). New York: Brunner-Routledge.

Winnicott, D. W. (1963). The development of the capacity for concern. In: C. Winnicott, R. Shepherd, & M. Davis (Eds.). *Deprivation and Delinquency* (pp. 100–105). London: Tavistock.

Winnicott, D. W. (1986). *Home Is Where We Start From*. Harmondsworth: Penguin.

Winnicott, D. W. (2002). *Playing and Reality*. London: Routledge.

CHAPTER ELEVEN

Organizations in traumatized societies: the Israeli case*[1]

Orit Nuttman-Shwartz and Haim Weinberg

Introduction

The fear of annihilation is manifest in patterns of incohesion in which aggregation oscillates with massification, and social and cultural forms of encapsulation are commonplace. This can be understood in terms of Incohesion: Aggregation/Massification as the fourth basic assumption in the unconscious life of social systems, including organizations and their wider societies (Hopper, 2003a,b). Israel is a traumatized and traumatizing society. Its people and its culture are virtually saturated with memories of traumatic events, which go back for centuries, and which have unconsciously affected the mentality and actions of Jewish and non-Jewish citizens alike. Current fears of annihilation are linked with those fears experienced by previous generations. Thus, organizations in Israel tend to be characterized by (ba) I:A/M in terms of both their own dynamic matrices and the foundation matrix of their contextual society.

---

*A previous version of this chapter was published in 2008, in *Organisational and Social Dynamics (OPUS)*, 8(2): 138–153..

Aspects of trauma in the history of the Jewish people as seen in Israeli society

The state of Israel was conceived and born as a national home for the Jewish people, and has faced ongoing struggles since it was established. Centuries of disasters and persecution in the Diaspora have left their traces in the "collective memory" of the Jewish people. These processes can be understood in terms of their "social unconscious" (Hopper, 2003a,b, 2007; Hopper & Weinberg, 2011; Weinberg, 2007).

Associations and connections with "primordial" social trauma are ubiquitous in Israel. Every act of terror revives the fear that the survival of the Jewish people is threatened. A series of past events is shadowed by this fear: for example, the destruction of the Second Temple, the exile from Spain in 1492, and the Holocaust, or Shoah.

In this context, the Holocaust is especially important because it has played a central role in moulding the new identity of a strong people who protect themselves from a hostile outside world, and who lean heavily on their military power. The Holocaust is a "chosen trauma", a shared mental representation of a massive trauma experienced by the ancestors of the group members, the echoes of which keep the existential threat alive in the national consciousness (Volkan, 1999). This helps to ward off potential complacency about continuing threats.

The image of the weak and victimized Jew associated with the Holocaust must be contrasted with the image of the Israeli *Sabra*, a heroic character who stands against all pressures, and who has adopted enlightened and humanistic social values (Almog, 1997; Gretz, 1995). This new image has been used to create a unified social identity for immigrants to Israel as well as an idealized fantasy for Jewish communities dispersed throughout the world. These two overpowering but opposing images are available for splitting, disavowal, and projection into the ubiquitous "other", as illustrated in the following clinical vignette.

> In a group session, the participants brought up memories and associations from their parental homes, and examined how those memories influenced their development. One of the group members, a woman, became very emotional. She wanted to tell her story, but her throat was clogged, and she almost choked as tears filled her eyes. The group was patient and

waited until her emotional storm passed. When she was able to talk, she recalled an encounter with her father a few years before, when he had come to visit her new house. She met him on the main road, and they walked through a peaceful Arab village in order to reach the Jewish village where she lived (in the Galilee). Her father became restless, and suggested that they bypass the Arab village. Suddenly, she felt a wave of rage towards him and shouted, "Why do you have to project your fears from the Diaspora on to me? I don't want to be influenced by this grovelling attitude of yours."

Clearly, the life experience of Jewish Israelis is shaped by their collective memories of traumatization within the social unconscious of Israeli society. Jewish Israelis have tended to see themselves as either compassionate victims or as heroic victors. Other possibilities and combinations have been too difficult to contemplate.

The chosen trauma of the Holocaust and the "chosen glory" of the *Sabra* have, however, been weakened as collective defences against the fear of annihilation. Attempts to rule another "people", that is, the Palestinians, has taken its toll. Since the eruption of the second Intifada in October 2000, violent political conflict has escalated dramatically, and existential anxieties, threats, and paranoia have dominated the public scene. Concerns about security have taken priority over questions of human rights. The more Israelis try to defend themselves against threats of terror, the more insensitive to injustice they become. The price of this growing insensitivity has manifested itself in callousness towards neighbours, especially the poor and the weak. Increased diversity among population groups has generated instability and insecurity. Increased economic and social inequalities are associated with discrimination against minorities, new immigrants, and foreign workers (Laufer & Harel, 2003; Mor-Barak, Nuttman-Shwartz, & Findler, 2005).

The same trends are evident in responses to the Qassam war at the south-western border of Israel. Whereas some areas of Israel, especially those near the Gaza Strip, have been exposed to daily terror attacks over the past seven years, the rest of the country has continued to live as if nothing was happening, with no protests, no demonstrations, and only minor expressions of identification (Nuttman-Shwartz, 2007). Most residents of Israel would seem to have dissociated themselves from the ongoing threat. They have failed to acknowledge the implications of living in such a dangerous place. It is reported that the residents of the northern region of Israel have felt ignored and unappreciated, despite their having been bombarded with Katyusha rockets.

Following the Second Lebanon War in July 2006, and for the first time since the state of Israel was established, Israelis felt that they had not "won", and that they were helpless in the struggle against well-organized guerrilla fighters. Regardless of the objective facts, self-doubts regarding the country's resilience crept into the public discourse. This even led to the establishment of a Committee of Inquiry, appointed to investigate who was responsible for the poor outcome of the war.

Israel as a traumatized society

In the *Diagnostic and Statistical Manual of Mental Disorders IV* (*DSM-IV*) a traumatic event is defined as one involving "actual or threatened death or serious injury, or other threat to one's physical integrity" (American Psychiatric Association, 1994, p. 424). Such threats can be to life and to physical integrity, or they can involve injury, loss of close and beloved people, and loss of one's self-image and values. A traumatic event disrupts normal life and upsets the relationship between the traumatized people and their surrounding environment. As a result, fear of the unknown and a sense of helplessness ensue (Weinberg, Nuttman-Shwartz, & Gilmore, 2005).

Many group analysts have argued (Hopper, 2003b; Scheidlinger, 1968; Volkan, 2002; Weinberg, 2006; Weinberg & Nuttman-Shwartz, 2006) that such traumas lead to regression, not only in individuals, but also in their social systems. "Societal (large group) regression" occurs after a society has faced a massive trauma, and this functions to maintain or restore the shared social identity among members of the society (Volkan, 2002). Such regression occurs when the majority of people who belong to that society share a variety of anxieties and defences against them. Group members lose their individuality, rally blindly behind the leader, become divided into "good" and "bad" segments within the society, create a sharp division between "us" and "them" *vis-à-vis* "enemy" groups, use extensive introjective and projective mechanisms extensively, and show extreme swings in their "public mood".

On this basis, Israel can be considered to be a traumatized society, not only historically, but also currently. Daily life in Israel is always under the shadow of possible war, terror attacks, and other situations that are either life threatening or endanger the well-being of Israeli citizens. "Normal life" in Israel involves continuous stress, and persistent threats to physical and psychological integrity. Moreover, Israel evinces many signs of societal regression, especially in connection with the intolerance of internal differences. For example, left-wing Israelis consider the Jewish settlers who inhabit territories in the West Bank to be the enemies of peace, whereas people on the right wing call the left-wingers criminals and friends of terrorists. The assassination of Prime Minister Rabin is an extreme example of where this polarization can lead (Schneider, 2002). The public mood in Israel changes dramatically from depression and feelings of helplessness after terror attacks to euphoria and manic feelings after victories or successful military actions (Hadari, 2002). The prevailing mood of Israeli society swings like a pendulum from hyper-vigilance to numbing of responsiveness, which is typical of PTSD (Herman, 1992). On the one hand, many Israeli citizens overreact to the threat of suicide bombings: for example, mothers are anxious whenever their children go out, or people avoid shopping malls and restaurants; on the other, many continue to follow the routine of their daily lives, seemingly indifferent to the horrifying scenes of terrorism on television and in newspapers.[2]

There can be little doubt that Israel is a traumatized society, and that Israeli citizens share in common both a history of trauma and the daily experience of it.

Organizations in Israel as a traumatized society

By definition, organizations have structure, hierarchy, and leadership, as well as definite roles, rules, clear boundaries, and communication procedures. An organization is not a large group, but a particular kind of social formation whose members identify with its goals, maintain its boundaries, and respect its norms (McDougal, 1920). Organizations rely on their histories and traditions, and emphasize their own continuity. In abstract terms, the organization is the opposite of a chaotic crowd. However, under certain conditions, for example, when the traumatic experience of failed dependency has occurred within the organization and/or its societal context, the organization is likely to regress. This can be seen in the blurring of boundaries, a desire for fusion, the use of archaic defence mechanisms such as projection, splitting, and projective identification. Thus, just as societies can become more like organizations, organizations can become more like groups, and groups can become more like individuals. "There is a constant dialectic tension between the organization, which offers 'order', and the large group, which is a boiling caldron of chaos" (Triest, 2003, p. 173).

As Hopper has argued (2003b), Bion's (1961) theory of basic assumptions and the personifications of them can be applied to traumatized organizations because they have become like large groups. Moreover, they are especially likely to manifest the dynamics of the fourth basic assumption of Incohesion: Aggregation/Massification or (ba) I: A/M. In aggregation, people feel alienated from one another and indifferent and hostile to one another, and tend to withdraw from relationships; in the extreme forms of aggregation, contra-groups develop and oppose one another. In contrast, in massification, people feel a sense of interpersonal merger, deny their differences, and culti-vate an illusion of togetherness and sameness. For example, it would seem that, in response to trauma, Israel often becomes like a large group (Hopper, 1975), swinging between periods of heated conflict between sub-groups and contra-groups (e.g., those who are right-wing *vs.* those who are left-wing, Ashkenazi *vs.* Sephardi Jews, and religious *vs.* secular Jews), and between a sense of "all is lost" and the "centre will not hold" and an unquestioned illusion of consensus, total cohesion, and solidarity. (Unfortunately, aggregation would seem to prevail during times of peace, and massification during times of war and terror.)

With respect to organizations, at least two overarching processes are involved: the experience of the population at large, and the expe-rience of the members of the particular organizations in question. These two processes are always interrelated. The first process brings together certain aspects of the historical and the contemporary contexts of the society, reviving memories, anxieties, and defences that are harboured in its social unconscious. No matter how bureaucra-tized an organization might become, and no matter how rigidly its boundaries are structured, the society is bound to get "under the skin" of it, so to speak. The second process involves the direct enactments of the basic assumptions in the unconscious life of an organization in response to traumatic events within it. Thus, following traumatogenic processes of loss, damage, and massive disruption associated with the fear of annihilation, organizations in Israel are especially likely to evince the dynamics of the basic assumption of Incohesion: Aggregation/Massification.

Empirical vignettes of organizations in Israel, with special reference to the basic assumption of Incohesion: Aggregation/Massification

The first vignette: organizational responses to accidents and deaths

An industrial factory, situated in the central region of Israel, employs 250 workers and ten managers. In July 1997, hydrogen gas exploded in a production device, killing two employees, one of whom was a manager. There was a steep rise in the anxiety level of all of the workers and managers in the organization. The workers formed a group that was seemingly cohesive, in which they repeatedly discussed this unfortunate event, and reconstructed their whereabouts at the time of the accident. Strict safety norms and regulations, as well as higher levels of control, were enforced and maintained by the workers and managers. None the less, the managers avoided taking other responsibilities related to the work at the factory, and preferred to involve their superiors in virtually all aspects of decision making, no matter how mundane the issues were. They delayed the completion of tasks, and tensions developed between managers and workers at all levels of the organizational hierarchy. Essentially, the groups became pseudo-cohesive rather than genuinely cohesive, as seen, for example, in an excessively high number of apparently ritualized memorial events. In other words, they became characterized by massification. Groups characterized by massification are not manageable, because role differentiation and specialization cannot be maintained.

About half a year later, another accident occurred, killing another worker. The second accident was also caused by the ignition and explosion of hydrogen. However, the workers and managers did not respond to the second event in the same way that they had responded to the first. In the second event, the executive management threatened that if another fatal accident occurred, they would close the factory. Everyone felt a sense of existential and financial danger, and an atmosphere of fear, suspicion, and paranoia prevailed. No one wanted to fill the dead worker's position, and an outside contractor was brought in to finish the job. In the search for a scapegoat, the workers directed their anger at the manager of the factory, who had planned the system fifteen years earlier, and held him responsible for the accidents. Eventually, the manager had a heart attack and resigned. Although the factory invested a large sum of money in buying new safety equipment, no memorial events were held following the death associated with the second accident. Although the second accident led to many changes in the management, these changes focused on formulating written regulations and instructions, and did not relate to any dimension of interpersonal relations at the factory.

The responses to these two accidents can be described in terms of aggregation and massification. On the one hand, everyone looked out for himself, and there was a widespread sense of "me-ness", as reflected in constant splitting between the management and workers, as well as within the management and among groups of workers; on the other, there was a widespread sense of "we-ness", as reflected in scapegoating and in the investment of considerable intellectual and emotional energy in following impersonal regulations (Lawrence, Bain, & Gould, 1996).

This case study shows how a traumatized organization and the traumatized society in which it is embedded are always intertwined. Overreaction to dramatic events, which is analogous to the startle response in PTSD, and to hypersensitive responses to trauma more generally (Herman, 1992), is actually a characteristic of Israeli society as-a-whole, and a characteristic of the management style of the organizations within it. The preoccupation with memorial ceremonies and with perpetuating the memory of the deceased is commonplace and ritualized (Hopper, 2003b). In this organization, the capacity to mourn became limited after the second accident, just as the capacity to mourn in Israeli society became constricted after the massive trauma of the Holocaust. In Israel, "men do not cry"; they do not display emotions such as fear and weakness in the attempt to cope with danger. Moreover, even though Israeli men are more exposed than women to terror attacks, women have reported more psychological symptoms following these attacks (Bleich, Gelkopf, & Solomon, 2003). As is the case in the wider society, the organization split into sub-groups and contra-groups, emphasizing conflicts among them, on the one hand, and/or attempted superficial and temporary unification in the face of a severe threat, on the other. In order to survive, people ignored the fear, minimized communication around the trauma, and continued living "as if there is no war" both outside and inside the organization. As pressures to survive minimized the capacity for the thoughtful and reflective elaboration of the trauma, discussions about responsibility and leadership were stunted. Both in their society as-a-whole and in their organizations, Israelis fall back on the worn-out slogan "strong army—strong people—strong leadership".

Second vignette: recurring trauma in the Israeli Institute of Group Analysis

The establishment in 2001 of the Israeli Institute of Group Analysis (IIGA) can be traced back to the late 1960s, when S. H. Foulkes visited Israel and presented his work to colleagues, some of whom had already become interested in psychoanalytic group therapy and in group analysis specifically. In 1978, the well-known psychiatrist Shamai Davidson, the Director of Shalvata, an important mental hospital in Israel, invited a team of British group analysts to visit the hospital and to demonstrate the value of group analysis as a clinical project. (The members of the visiting team were Vivienne Cohen, Arnon Ben-Tovim, Earl Hopper, Lionel Kreeger, Malcolm Pines, and Meg Sharpe.) Later, in 1991, following several visits from other colleagues in London, a block training Foundation Course in group analysis was started.

In 1995, a Diploma Course was initiated. However, a year later, this course was interrupted suddenly and traumatically, causing considerable damage to the forty-four participants, who were senior mental health professionals and group therapists. Massive splitting occurred among the Israeli participants in the course, as well as among the British staff members, and between the Israeli participants and the staff members. This led to projections, projective and introjective identifications, and, eventually, to the disintegration of the group of participants and the staff group. Among the many factors that might account for this traumatic event are the historical relations between Israel and Britain (Hadar & Ofer, 2001). These processes are now part of the social unconscious in the dynamic matrix of the Israeli Institute of Group Analysis, and they continue to be manifest on many levels of it. The development of group analysis in Israel has been punctuated by interruptions, crises, and traumas, more than is usually the case for such organizations in Israel during the past several decades. Although the IIGA was established for the purpose of healing past wounds and helping the people involved in its training courses overcome their own traumatic experiences, in the interest of helping them to be of help to others, the shadow of excessive and traumatic splitting has remained in the culture of the institution. This has dictated a very cautious style of managing conflicts, even more than is typical of all training organizations. For example, after the Diploma Course was reconvened with a new staff team from Britain and elsewhere in Europe, the participants in the large group training sessions did not engage in authentic and committed elaboration of the previous trauma. Decision-making processes have continued to be fraught.

Nevertheless, in 2003 the Diploma Course finished successfully. However, a year before the course ended, the IIGA started a new Diploma Course for senior therapists. One of the reasons for this seemingly hasty decision was IIGA's desire to become a "normal" organization, the majority of whose members had not experienced organizational trauma of the kind described. However, from its inception, the new Diploma Course evoked uneasiness and restlessness among its participants and staff. For example, in the first sessions of the large group, participants expressed fears relating to potential competition and loss of privileges.

During that period of time, the board of the IIGA formulated a draft of the bylaws of the Institute, which were brought before a general assembly for discussion and evaluation. One of the important items on the agenda was the issue of determining who would be eligible for a full diploma and title of "Group Analyst". The social workers on the new Diploma Course wanted the Board to recognize that, on the basis of their previous training, they had been leading groups, and, therefore, that it should be recognized that they had fulfilled some of the requirements for certification. However, the Board wanted to apply the Institute's formal requirements to all of the students. This conflict involved vociferous struggles, and generated a sense of vulnerability and a fear of fragmentation. Many participants, including members of the Board, devoted time and effort in order to try to solve the conflict. They offered a compromise proposal. However, the social workers felt that this came too late. In any case, they were already too hurt to accept a solution. Thus, following this long, difficult, and highly emotional process, history repeated itself: a stormy meeting led to severe splitting, and some of the social workers left the Institute, feeling traumatized and rejected. The Board felt hurt that their efforts and authority were not recognized.

This unfortunate event can be seen as a re-enactment of the original organizational trauma, in which the "victims" of the first traumatically interrupted Course had, in turn, "victimized" the social workers who participated in the second Course. From the point of view of the board members who had made several efforts to create a dialogue, it can be interpreted as an expression of ingratitude, and as based on a misinterpretation of their benevolent intentions. Many additional and alternative explanations for what occurred are possible. No one explanation is sufficient and all are a matter of interpretation. For example, the response of the original "victims" can be understood in terms of an "identification with the aggressor". Certainly, this is evident in Israeli society. Identification with the aggressor is one way of explaining why Jews who were victims of the Holocaust have become aggressors who are insensitive to the suffering of another people (the Palestinians). In fact, Israelis and Palestinians both feel victimized and perceive the "other" as doing injustice to them.

Such processes can be seen as a kind of group transference of an unconsciously perceived situation from its broader context to the present context of the organization (Hopper, 2007). It can be argued that in terms of the social unconscious of the Jewish people, the hasty decision to start a second Diploma Course on the basis of the "rational" argument that it was necessary to create an organization whose membership had not been traumatized by difficult administrative decisions and experiences, involved a repetition of the story in the Bible that the Jewish people were obliged to wander through the desert for forty years in order that all memories and other traces of slavery in Egypt were eradicated from their culture. (The Bible story seems to have neglected the power of the social unconscious and collective memories in it.) Similarly, in terms of the social unconscious of Israeli society, many aspects of this vignette involved the repetition of the painful experiences associated with waves of immigration and related disputes concerning the legitimate entitlement to limited resources. This can itself be understood as a societal version of sibling rivalry.

Further discussion and conclusion

The State of Israel was established in the wake of the Holocaust, largely because it became self evident that the Jewish people needed a safe haven from the atrocities in Europe and elsewhere in the world. Many of the survivors tried to overcome their traumatic experiences by suppressing and repressing their memories, avoiding any discussions of them, and ignoring the death camp prisoner numbers tattooed on their wrists. Native-born Israelis joined this conspiracy of silence. For years, the memories of the Holocaust and its deep impact on the survivors remained unspoken and not worked through. In the initial period following the establishment of the Israeli State, during the 1950s and 1960s, there was no public discussion about the Holocaust. The memories were still too painful, and there was an element of shame about being so helpless and not being able to resist the massacre. Thus, the prevailing atmosphere of denial and the evasion of discussion about what really happened left the survivors feeling isolated and misunderstood. They were not able to mourn their losses, and focused on surviving without touching their painful memories. In some cases, this response resulted in nightmares, which were sometimes reflected in hidden guilt feelings, and mostly projected into the children of the Holocaust survivors, the so-called "second generation". This is the natural platform for the emergence of a chosen trauma in a nation's memory that cannot be elaborated or worked through (Volkan, 1997). In this context, the oscillation between processes of aggregation and massification in the basic assumption of Incohesion continue to characterize Israel as a traumatized society (Doron & Lebel, 2003; Nuttman-Shwartz, Lictentriet, & Rubin, 2004). This basic assumption also characterizes the unconscious life of traumatized organizations. These vignettes of traumatized organizations within the context of a traumatized society suggest that the only way for organizations to free themselves from enacting their traumatic experiences is through attempts by their members to work through the trauma that they have experienced within the context of their organizations. True dialogue under conditions of trauma is extremely difficult, if not impossible. We are reminded of the repeated efforts to bring the leaders of the "two" sides of the conflicts in the Middle East to various negotiating tables in a way that might lead to reconciliation between Israelis and Palestinians. Actually, as long as such reconciliation processes do not occur, the danger of the repetition of previous trauma remains explosively omnipresent. These processes are beyond specific individual persons. They reflect the foundation matrix of the wider society and the dynamic matrices of the organizations within it. It is hardly surprising that, in such circumstances, the basic assumption of Incohesion: Aggregation/Massification is ubiquitous.

Editorial note

The publication of *Trauma and Organizations* was delayed at more or less the last minute by objections raised by colleagues in Israel to the proofed copy of this chapter, which was distributed by the authors of it to some of the participants in a conference in Israel concerning "transparency" and "responsibility" in the governance of organizations. Colleagues who were members of the board of IIGA during the period of time of the second Diploma Course took strong exception to the authors' account of the difficulties associated with the resignation of some of the social workers who were students on the Course. These colleagues insisted that the authors rewrite their account of this event, and that before it was published in *Trauma and Organizations*, this new account be approved by all of them. After several attempts to reach agreement, the approved material was sent to me. However, I have taken it upon myself to redraft this material, and to re-edit the chapter as a whole. I decided not to delay the publication of the book any longer through the time consuming process of seeking further agreements concerning what is, in effect, my own final draft. Although it is important not to engage in self-indulgent interpretations of complex events in order to support any particular theory of them, I do understand this unhappy event as yet another illustration of processes of equivalence. Clearly, unresolved anxieties associated with the traumatic experience were manifest in the authorial, editorial, and actual publication process. It is difficult not to understand these processes as enactments of a barely encapsulated event within the dynamic matrix of the IIGA and within the foundation matrix of Israel as a whole, if not of the Jewish people. I doubt that this publication is the end of the matter, but I hope that the processes of working through the traumatogenic experience will continue. As I outlined in my Foreword to this book, this sorry but illustrative tale is entirely typical of working with and within traumatogenic processes, especially, but not only, in the context of traumatized organizations in their traumatized societies, such as Israel, Northern Ireland, and elsewhere.

Notes

1. We would like to thank Dr Earl Hopper for his helpful comments on many previous drafts of this chapter, and for encouraging us to consider what we call the Israeli "social unconscious", and especially what it means to live in a traumatized and traumatizing society.

2. This splitting and oscillation enable Israelis to continue living in the face of ongoing existential threats. In fact, some recent research has shown that in the shadow of massive and continuous national and individual traumas, Israelis have largely adapted to the situation without substantial mental health consequences, and they have sought to cope with terrorism and its ongoing threats in various ways (Bleich, Gelkopf, & Solomon, 2003; Nuttman-Shwartz & Dekel, 2009; Yanay, David, & Shayit, 2004). Moreover, the sense of belonging to the community and to the country has increased, and this has served as a protective shield for people living under ongoing threat (Nuttman-Shwartz & Dekel, 2010). Many of the studies of the long term impact of exposure to terror on Israeli society show that Israeli society is fairly resistant to stress and terror; although symptoms of anxiety, tension, and stress are evident, they appear to be low in intensity and do not really typify PTSD (Bleich, Gelkopf, Melamed, & Solomon, 2006; Dekel & Nuttman Shwartz, 2009; Gelkopf, Solomon, Berger, & Bleich, 2008). However, the ongoing stress of terrorist attacks has undermined the citizens' sense of security and confidence in the state, which is supposed to protect them and ensure their safety. This is true for people who were not directly injured or who were not even personally acquainted with victims of terror.

References

Almog, O. (1997). *The Sabra: Profile*. Tel Aviv: Afikim Library, Am Oved (in Hebrew).

American Psychiatric Association (1994). *Diagnostic and Statistical Manual of Mental Disorders* (4th edn). Washington, DC: American Psychiatric Association.

Bion, W. R. (1961). *Experiences in Groups and Other Papers*. London: Tavistock.

Bleich, A., Gelkopf, M., & Solomon, Z. (2003). Exposure to terrorism, stress-related mental health symptoms, and coping behaviors among a nationally representative sample in Israel. *Journal of the American Medical Association, 290*: 612–620.

Bleich, A., Gelkopf, M., Melamed, Y., & Solomon, Z. (2006). Mental health and resiliency following 44 months of terrorism: a survey of an Israeli national representative sample, *BMC Medicine, 4*: 21. Accessed 1 June 2008 at www.pubmedcentral.nih.gov/articlerender.fcgiartid=1560155.

Dekel, R., & Nuttman Shwartz, O. (2009). PTSD and PTG following Qassam attacks: correlations and contributors among development town and kibbutz residents. *Health and Social Work, 34*: 87–96.

Doron, G., & Lebel, U. (2003). *Politics of Bereavement*. Tel Aviv: Hakibbutz Hameuchad (in Hebrew).

Gelkopf, M., Solomon, Z., Berger, R., & Bleich, A. (2008). The mental health impact of terrorism in Israel: a repeat cross-sectional study of Arabs and Jews. *Acta Psychiatric Scandinavia, 117*: 369–380.

Gretz, N. (1995). *Captive of a Dream: National Myths in Israeli Culture*. Tel Aviv: Am Oved (in Hebrew).

Hadar, B., & Ofer, G. (2001). The social unconscious reflected in politics, organizations and groups: a case of overseas group analysis training. *Group Analysis, 34*: 375–385.

Hadari, Y. (2002). *Messiah Riding on a Tank: Israeli Public Thinking between Sinai War and Yom Kippur War: 1955–1975*. Jerusalem: Shalom Hartman Institute (in Hebrew).

Herman, L. J. (1992). *Trauma and Recovery*. New York: Basic Books.

Hopper, E. (1975). A sociological view of large groups. In: L. Kreeger (Ed.), *The Large Group Dynamics and Therapy*. London: Constable [reprinted London: Karnac, 1994, and in Hopper, E. (2003) *The Social Unconscious: Selected Papers*. London: Jessica Kingsley].

Hopper, E. (2003a). *The Social Unconscious: Selected Papers*. London: Jessica Kingsley.

Hopper, E. (2003b). *Traumatic Experience in the Unconscious Life of Groups*. London: Jessica Kingsley.

Hopper, E. (2007). Theoretical and conceptual notes concerning transference and countertransference processes in groups and by groups, and the social unconscious: Part III. *Group Analysis, 40*: 285–300.

Hopper, E., & Weinberg, H. (Eds.) (2011). *The Social Unconcious in Persons, Groups, and Societies, Volume 1: Mainly Theory*. London: Karnac.

Laufer, A., & Harel, Y. (2003). Correlation between school perception and pupil involvement in bulling physical fights and weapon carrying. *Megamot: Behavioral Science Journal, 42*: 437–459 (in Hebrew).

Lawrence, W. G., Bain, A., & Gould, L. (1996). The fifth basic assumption. *Free Associations, 6*(37): 28–55.

McDougal, W. (1920). *The Group Mind*. New York: Putnam.

Mor-Barak, M., Nuttman-Shwartz, O., & Findler L. (2005). The inclusive workplace as response to labor force diversity in Israel. *Work, Society and Law, 11*: 305–322 (in Hebrew).

Nuttman-Shwartz, O. (2007). When life is no longer taken for granted. *Eretz Ahcheret, 42*, 48–52, (in Hebrew).

Nuttman-Shwartz, O., & Dekel, R. (2009). Ways of coping and sense of belonging to the college in the face of a persistent security threat. *Journal of Traumatic Stress, 22*: 667–670.

Nuttman-Shwartz, O., & Dekel, R. (2010). Periphery under fire. In: A. Sason (Ed.), *Sderot Book* (pp. 259–264). Tel Aviv: Makom (in Hebrew).

Nuttman-Shwartz, O., Lictentriet, R., & Rubin S., S. (2004). Recognizing and including "civilian bereavement" within the consensus of the Israeli society's bereavements: a position paper. The Sderot Conference on Society, October, 2004, Sderot, Israel (in Hebrew).

Scheidlinger, S. (1968). The concept of regression in group psychotherapy. *International Journal of Group Psychotherapy, 18*: 3–20.

Schneider, S. (2002). Fundamentalism and paranoia in groups and society. *Group, 26*: 17–28.

Triest, J. (2003). The large group and the organisation. In: S. Schneider & H. Weinberg (Eds.), *The Large Group Re-visited: The Herd, Primal Horde, Crowds and Masses* (pp. 157–168). London: Jessica Kingsley.

Volkan, V. D. (1997). *Bloodlines from Ethnic Pride to Ethnic Terrorism*. New York: Farrar Straus & Giroux.

Volkan, V. D. (1999). Psychoanalysis and diplomacy: Part I. Individual and large group identity. *Journal of Applied Psychoanalytic Studies, 1*: 29–55.

Volkan, V. D. (2002). September 11th and societal regression. *Group Analysis, 35*: 456–483.

Weinberg, H. (2006). Regression in the group revisited. *Group*, *30*: 1–17.

Weinberg, H. (2007). So what is this social unconscious anyway? *Group Analysis*, *40*: 307–322.

Weinberg, H., & Nuttman-Shwartz, O. (2006). Group work and therapy in Israel: mirroring a regressed–traumatised society. *Organisational and Social Dynamics*, *OPUS*, *6*: 95–110.

Weinberg, H., Nuttman-Shwartz, O., & Gilmore, M. (2005). Trauma groups: an overview. *Group Analysis*, *38*: 189–204.

Yanay, U., David, E., & Shayit, K. (2004). Perceptions of personal safety in Jerusalem neighborhoods. *Hevra Verevaha* [Society and Welfare], *24*: 201–218 (in Hebrew).

CHAPTER TWELVE

Two perspectives on a trauma in a training group: the systems-centred approach and the theory of incohesion*

Susan P. Gantt and Earl Hopper

Introduction

Along with Yvonne Agazarian, we were interested in exploring our respective theoretical approaches: the theory of living human systems (TLHS) and its systems-centred training (SCT) (Agazarian, 1997), and group analysis and psychoanalysis (e.g., Hopper, 2003, 2009). Therefore, we made a tentative plan for Earl to observe an SCT group that was meeting as part of a three-day SCT training event in London. Unfortunately, we did not confirm our plans, and Susan did not inform the group that Earl would be observing it. Thus, the group was completely unprepared for Earl's arrival. None the less, our regrettable slip offered us a chance to consider this traumatic experience from our two different perspectives.

To this end, we will first summarize the TLHS and SCT. We will then illustrate the traumatogenic process within the group, drawing

---

*Previous versions of this chapter were published as "Two perspectives on a trauma in a training group: the systems-centred approach and the theory of incohesion: Part I." *Group Analysis*, 41(1): 92–106, March 2008; and Part II, *Group Analysis*, 41(2): 123–139, June 2008.

on retrospective descriptions of their experience by the members of the group. This will be discussed from each of the two theoretical perspectives. We conclude with an acknowledgement of some of the main differences in the two approaches, with a view to further possible lines of integration and application, especially to work with trauma in organizations.

A theory of living human systems and its systems-centred therapy

SCT was developed from TLSH, a central axiom of which is that living human systems are characterized by a hierarchy of isomorphic systems that are energy-organizing, goal-directed, and self-correcting (Agazarian, 1997). *Hierarchy* defines a system as consisting always of a set of three nested sub-systems, with the middle sub-system both existing in the context of another system, and being the context for another system. For a group, the set of three systems are the group-as-a-whole, the sub-group system which exists in the context of the group-as-a-whole, and the role system which exists in the context of the sub-group system. Each one of these systems is isomorphic with the other two. *Isomorphy* means that each of the three nested systems are similar in structure and function. Structure is defined by boundaries which can be permeable or impermeable to information. Borrowing from Miller (1978), SCT defines the energy of living human systems as information. Function defines how systems survive, develop, and transform through discriminating and integrating differences. Thus, in SCT, the role, sub-group, and group-as-a-whole systems will be similar in how open or closed their boundaries are to information/energy and how information/energy is discriminated and integrated within each system. The SCT practice developed from this theory is then applied to systems as small as a person, a couple, or a "small" group, or as large as a "large" group, organization, or even a nation.

In practice, SCT focuses on developing the "system context" in which people can change. SCT assumes that the system context is the strongest influence on human behaviour and, therefore, SCT deliberately builds the system context that supports exploration and change. Thus, SCT develops the systems-centred hierarchy within a group that potentiates development in each of the system contexts, that is, the group-as-a-whole, the sub-groups, and the roles.

Functional sub-grouping

Building an SCT group begins by introducing the method of functional sub-grouping (Agazarian, 1997). Functional sub-grouping is a conflict resolution method that contains the group conflicts in separate sub-groups until the conflict can be discriminated and integrated in the group-as-a-whole. Functional sub-grouping implements the theoretical definition of function (discriminating and integrating differences).

In functional sub-grouping, members learn to ask, "Anybody else?" after each member makes a contribution to the group. This behaviour creates a group norm for joining with others to explore similarities. Members of one sub-group contain their side of the group conflict and explore it together in a climate of similarity, and in "roving" eye contact with each other. When there is a pause, then the members of the "other" sub-group who hold the other side of the conflict explore together, also in a climate of similarity. As each sub-group works in turn in the security and containment of a climate of similarity, members first discover the differences within their own sub-group, and then the similarities in what was initially different between their own sub-groups and other sub-groups. This enables an integration of the two sides of the conflict in the group-as-a-whole. Functional sub-grouping helps to dissolve the rigid boundaries that characterize stereotyped sub-groups, or what Hopper calls "contra-groups", which might be dysfunctional for the cohesion and development of the system.

Weakening the restraining forces in the phases
of system development

SCT also works from the hypothesis that weakening the restraining forces is a more efficient method of change than strengthening driving forces (Lewin, 1951). Weakening restraining forces releases the driving forces available in the system. In addition, building on the work of Bennis and Shephard (1956), SCT has delineated three major phases of system development: authority, intimacy, and integration or work (Agazarian, 1994, 1999). The authority phase is dominated by issues of power and control; the intimacy phase focuses on the separation–individuation conflicts that make intimate relating challenging; and the integration or work phase is concerned with the ongoing work of bringing knowledge into context. SCT defines each phase of system development as a system context, and identifies a predictable force-field of driving and restraining forces that operationally define each phase of system development.

SCT explicitly weakens the restraining forces that are specific to each phase of system development. The force-field for each phase then serves as a map for guiding intervention strategies by weakening the phase-relevant restraining forces, which releases the driving forces to development. In this way, the change interventions are paced to the system's phase context. Both sides of the conflicts in each phase can then be discriminated and integrated in the service of system development, using the conflict resolution method of functional sub-grouping (Agazarian, 1994, 2003).

Roles and plans of system development

Building on the work of role theorists in sociology and social psychology, for example, Mead (1934), and in the field of family therapy, for example, Minuchin (1974), Agazarian conceptualized a role as a bridge construct between the individual and the group (Agazarian & Peters, 1981). A role was conceptualized as playing the same function in both the person and the group. A role is a sub-system with relatively impermeable boundaries containing information that is unable to be integrated by persons in other roles in the larger system context. Roles involve characteristic ways of thinking, perceiving, and feeling, and particular emotional regulation strategies, attitudes, and beliefs, and even posture and gestures (Agazarian & Gantt, 2004).

In developing a systems-centred perspective on roles, SCT has introduced a framework that can be applied at all levels of living human systems. For example, roles are conceptualized as systems or sub-systems, both within the context of a person-as-a-system and within the context of a group-as-a-system. Thus, roles can be described in terms of their system properties: for example, how permeable are the role boundaries to information, how easily is new information integrated within the role system, what is the larger context in which the role exists, and what is the goal to which the role relates?

SCT also discriminates between functional roles and personalized roles in terms of properties of the systems in which they are embedded.

Functional roles have appropriately permeable boundaries in order to facilitate the integration of differences, and relate to the goal and current system context (Gantt, 2005). Personalized roles relate to a past context at the expense of the present context and its goals, have relatively impermeable boundaries, fixed and redundant discriminations, and rarely integrate differences, with the consequence of inhibited development. Similarly, stereotyped roles relate to implicit group goals, and are usually related to a personalized habitual role as well.

SCT links roles to phases of system development (Agazarian, 1994). Each of the phases is likely to spawn particular roles that can be either functional or stereotypical. For example, with respect to stereotypic roles: the authority phase stimulates roles of helper and identified patient, scapegoat and scapegoater, victim and bully, dominant and submissive, the intimacy phase, the roles of alienated or despairing or merged and blissful, and the integration phase, the stereotypic roles of self-absorbed or task-absorbed (Agazarian & Gantt, 2004). These stereotypic roles are characterized by relatively impermeable boundaries and contain the conflicts and information that the group system has not yet integrated in each of its phases. Each phase of system development must resolve the developmental conflicts inherent in the phase in order to develop into a working system. When stereotypic roles become fixated, they contain system conflicts at the expense of system development.

When stereotypic roles can be "reclaimed" by the group, and the projections into the role undone and explored in functional sub-groups, the information contained within the stereotyped role can be discriminated and integrated. Thus, when stereotyped roles can be explored in functional sub-grouping, they can serve as a pathway for group development rather than fixating group development.

SCT identifies predictable triggers to the stereotypic roles as frustration in the authority phase, misattunements in the intimacy phase, and uncertainty in the integration phase. Further, Agazarian has hypothesized that the dominant–submissive role locks identified by SCT are an authority phase response to a failed care-giving–care-seeking interaction (McCluskey, 2002), building on Heard & Lake (1997). The roles characteristic of the intimacy phase, in which the conflicts relate to issues of separation–individuation and of closeness and distance, are linked to early attachment issues (Bowlby, 1982).

More recently, Agazarian and Gantt (Agazarian, 2003, Agazarian & Gantt, 2004; Ladden, Gantt, Rude, & Agazarian, 2007) have suggested that roles might influence the maintenance of symptoms in generalized anxiety disorder and other psychological disorders. Misattunements in a group system often stimulate stereotyped and personalized roles. Specifically, the enchanted or merged role relates to anxious attachments, and the alienated role to avoidant attachments.

The group and its trauma

We will now present empirical material concerning the event which, in retrospect, we have defined as traumatic. The SCT training group had been working for two and a half days, and was in the last afternoon of a three-day experiential workshop on exploring roles. This group was composed of members at an intermediate level in SCT training. They had mastered the basics of developing and taking membership in an SCT group, including centring into themselves and their primary experience, using functional sub-grouping to contain and explore group conflicts, and had competence in modifying cognitive defences of anxiety, somatic defences of tension, and discharge defences of depression and outrage against retaliatory impulses. The focus of the workshop was the exploration of old, stereotyped, personalized roles elicited in the group context.

With one hour of "small group" work remaining, the observer, Earl Hopper, entered the room and the system (although it could be argued that, in so far as he was somewhere in Susan's and Yvonne's minds, he had already done so!). The leader and the group were taken by surprise. The leader, Susan, recovered enough to orientate the group to the plan that she and Earl had made for him to observe, and to tell the group that she had "forgotten" to let them know about this. Not surprisingly, therefore, the interruption violated the structure of the group. Simultaneously, the observer's behaviour violated the SCT norms of observing. These violations precipitated an "authority issue" with the leader. In fact, the group explored some of its ensuing paranoia and hatred toward the leadership. However, when this subsided, Susan suggested to the group that they explore the impact of the unexpected interruption in the context of roles, which was the focus of the workshop, by taking note of what roles and role solutions were stimulated by the leader's failing to prepare them for this intrusion by the unexpected observer. The group duly obliged their leader's request.

What happened from the perspective of the participants

Within a few weeks, Susan wrote to each of the participants asking them to write briefly about their memory of the group session. Within a month of the session, they sent their reports to Susan, which we include verbatim below. Although this verbatim material shows some diversity of views and themes, taken together it indicates a collective group response to a traumatic event following a failure in leadership and the unexpected break in structure and norms.

The first member

I saw an elderly man come into the room. I assumed that he was in the wrong place and on realizing this, would leave. As it became apparent that he was coming further into the room, I expected Susan or Tim (pseudonym) would address him, either ask where he was trying to find or ask him to leave the room. Tim was an advanced trainee who was working in a "containing role". [Referring to an SCT leadership training role in which a member works authentically to join and support sub-groups in the service of the overall development of the group-as-a-whole instead of in the service of his or her personal learning or growth.] However, he came further into the room, and I became increasingly surprised that neither Susan nor Tim appeared to be dealing with the interruption. I think that, as he headed for a seat on the far side of the room and had some verbal exchange with Susan about where he should be, she announced that she had forgotten to tell the group that we would be having an observer.

It seemed extraordinary that having an observer could be forgotten and I do not think I really believed that this was what had happened. I felt really angry and assumed that Yvonne [the workshop director and leader to the other training group in the adjoining room] had set this up. I thought she thought that as a (whole) group we had not dealt with the authority issue and had set up the interruption in order to provoke a reaction. I think one of the other members started talking in a furious fashion about some previous contact she had had with Earl, but I think I was probably constructing my own view of what was happening at the time.

My response to "being set up" was one of defiance, thinking "don't think you can make me do what you want me to." This made me not want to verbalize my feeling about the leader (Yvonne).

The mystery man sat behind me and I couldn't see him. I realize now that I had no curiosity about who he was (I didn't know him). Perhaps also because he was out of my line of vision I could in some way "wipe him out". (I had used this expression about the member taking on the container role in a group on the previous day. On that occasion I had been able to wipe him out by keeping him out of my line of vision.)

It was rather more difficult to keep the mystery man out of my vision as I became gradually aware that he was making noises, and leaning forward on his chair, and, intermittently, I could see him in my peripheral vision. This aroused the thought that he was not conducting himself in a manner appropriate to an observer.

The group was disrupted by his entrance. It seemed that we had all been shocked and gone into our person role, but gradually we were able to move back into the member role. There was strong support and agreement from the group that we should do this and it really helped. As we took up the member role, we were able to explore the experience. Finally I think the group felt satisfied that we had been able to return to the goal of the work, that is, to explore roles.

A second member

I don't recall having spoken yet in this group when a man walked into the room. I remember having an impulse to get up and speak to him, but, knowing I was not the leader, I looked to Susan. I then looked back at him and heard another member say Earl Hopper's name. I had not recognized him before this, even though I had met him. I also knew about a difficult personal meeting another member had had with Earl in another context and how difficult it had been.

Susan then said that he was coming to observe us, and I remember thinking how composed Susan looked as she told us that she had forgotten to tell us. I also felt shocked and incredulous, but did not feel angry. I was aware of my care-taking impulse in relation to Susan.

The group now felt incredibly chaotic and raucous, with all the attention shifted from the group and the "hold" of the leader to the outside of the group on to Earl. As if we had turned inside out. This was made easier by him eating a biscuit, as well as leaning forward into the group, as it seemed, at times, he was having difficulty hearing.

After some time of the group out-raging, I said, from my container role, that we needed to vector our energy back across the boundary to the work we had started at the beginning of the session. I reminded the group that we had been begun again, to look at the fork between adaptive and maladaptive roles, and we needed to return to that using this to do so. I also asked the group if everyone was centred, and said that we needed to go inside of ourselves for our experience. I felt the group responded and there was some shift. Attention was still towards Earl, but it felt as if the experience was more in the group and inside of ourselves than out of the group.

The group continued to explore their experience, with Earl and Susan as "trigger" to go into role. We sub-grouped more strongly now, and as the energy came into the group, Susan became the target for the authority issue that had been triggered. This was worked with a bit, but time was a constraint also. It felt as if I left the group with unfinished business.

I am still surprised that the group brought in surprises and learnings and satisfactions, as well as dissatisfactions, including myself. [Referring to the usual SCT structure used in the last ten minutes of the group for reviewing the work of the group.]

Third participant

What I remember is the door opening and thinking he's got the wrong room and in a minute Susan will say something. This was quickly followed by my feeling of shock as I recognized Earl Hopper and thinking surely he can't be coming into this group. The group sense of shock and disruption as he came in. Exploring our bewilderment and then anger in sub-groups. Knowing that my shock came partly from a previous encounter with Earl Hopper and trying to keep my focus on the present. Finding the eye contact very helpful, particularly with two members. Having to work hard at staying focused on our goal of exploring roles and not be drawn into watching Earl Hopper. Feeling angry with the fact that he ate biscuits, rocked on his chair, picked his nose. Thinking he hasn't got the faintest idea of how to be an observer—and saying so to Susan at the end, suggesting it was her responsibility to coach him in his role. Realizing this was a great opportunity to explore not going into my "rabbit in the headlights role". Feeling slightly hysterical and laughing with others at the absurdity of the situation. Images of powerful people and statues (Boudicca sticks out). Expressing our anger towards Susan. Taking charge of ourselves and our goal and a sense of Susan only being in the background. Very strong sense of the sub-grouping supporting us and the group supporting its members. Feeling at the end that we had sat in the fire and come out transformed and stronger.

The fourth member

After some deliberation, I have discovered that I need more information in order to make a decision about participating in the research. I have found it difficult to reply to your e-mail which I realised has concerned two issues. Firstly, when I thought about the group session and writing about my experiences, I realised I did not feel able to write about the group without consent from everyone who participated. Secondly, I have an idea that unresolved feelings concerning Earl Hopper may be clouding my ability to make a decision about participating in the research. Although, I learned a great deal from the last session, perhaps around recognising and containing strong and deep emotions triggered by the arrival of Earl Hopper, somehow this felt different to the work the group had previously been doing. I felt the impact of Earl Hopper in the last group session changed the course of the group's development and impacted on the work of the group. I was left with a feeling of dissatisfaction and frustration that our last session had been affected in this way. Perhaps more time would have resolved the issue, however due to time constraints the group work of unfinished business and ending was different. I have an inkling that these unresolved feelings, particularly towards Earl Hopper, are impacting on my ability to make an informed decision about participating in the research. I have an impulse to ignore these feelings and just participate (in a compliant role), however if I am able to use my new found awareness of roles, I would like to learn from my emotional knowledge and consider a different solution to the problem. Therefore, I would like to know more about the research before agreeing to participate and in order to make an informed decision! Finally, I would also like to mention that the three day training was a deeply powerful experience for me and it was a pleasure and a privilege to take part and to work with you and the others in the group. [Subsequent permission was given for the inclusion of this material.]

Fifth participant

When Earl entered the room I had mostly curiosity. I did become more self-conscious. However, it was more excitement than anxiety. Actually, I was excited to "show off". As I worked in the group, I started to perceive differences between myself and the group members who were having a more aversive response. I tried to stay empathic by thinking about how I could feel if "triggered" by someone who came into the group unannounced.

As I write this, I realize that I became much more self-conscious, started to lose a systems perspective, went into my head, and became somewhat alienated from the group. I then had the impulse to: (1) join a sub-group even if I was not resonating with a sub-group; and (2) target the visitor whom I started to judge (e.g., What a jerk. Look at his posture. The guy is totally defensive. He thinks he is better than us, etc.). However, I am not sure of the chronology of events. Bottom line is that I did not have a strong reaction that I was aware of, judged myself, made inauthentic attempts to join a sub-group versus staying with the fact that I really was not too sure about what my experience was, then admitting to the sub-group that I was not really in it. All of that opposed to staying curious about my reaction and keeping a systems perspective in mind.

Sixth member

The work we did in the group exploring the roles we go into was extremely valuable and I feel it has shifted something in myself. In particular, I am amazed by the physical experiences and how functional sub-grouping helped to build on it and contain it; the physical/apprehensive experience and the cognitive understanding of a role has really given me a sense of "identity" of the roles (or at least one!) I have. This makes it much easer to understand it from all perspectives and begin to make changes. Because of the work we did in the first two days, it was possible to contain the energy in the group, during a very difficult moment when E. Hopper came into the room. I imagine it would have had quite a destructive effect on a non-SCT group! Again, I was amazed at how we remained focused, supported each other in the sub-groups, kept the energy inside the group and had some fun too.

Seventh member

I remember the group had a slow beginning. The group took some time to work out the aims and goals of the group session. There was a distraction around the position of one member's chair. The group managed the turbulence and brought energy across the boundaries into the here and now with the aim of continuing the work of the group and the work of unfinished business. Goals included "exploring triggers and the pull to role" and "exploration of what is avoided and missed by going into role and/or the cost of the role." One subgroup was exploring the impulse to stay in role and hold on to anger and not wanting to give up the role.

The door opened and an unfamiliar person came into the room. This person, who I thought was lost, walked over to the tea and biscuits and began to eat. He walked through into the other room and then quickly returned, pulling up a chair and continuing to eat. He stayed for the duration of the rest of the group occasionally swinging on his chair.

The group leader told us she had forgotten to let the group know, or to ask the group, about the observer joining the group for the afternoon. Reactions that followed included shock, upset, disappointment, anger and some hysteria. The leader asked if the group wanted to continue to work on roles and use this incident to continue to explore responses and reactions in sub-groups. I felt outraged. Both with the observer and the group leader. I felt cross, defiant, disempowered, childlike. The group had the work of integrating this new piece of information and new presence and re-establishing the boundaries. The group was, amazingly, gradually, slowly, able to explore and process the reactions and emotions, and I guess the retaliatory impulse, and continue the work of the group. This was made possible through subgrouping around experience and drawing attention back to the goals and making choices about how to continue working in the group. The group member in the container role and the group leader facilitated this process. Overall, the experience was hugely empowering and I learnt a great deal about the power of choice.

Discussion of the group and its trauma

From the SCT view: Susan

From the SCT point of view, the group's responses provide a rich description of the phase dynamics that were provoked by the traumatic event, starting with an authority phase, moving to the intimacy phase, and then to the recovery of work functioning, in this case facilitated by my own leadership. First, anger, outrage, and paranoia emerged—if not erupted. These were all part of the group's authority issue toward the group leader(s) (and the observer) and an inevitable response in any living human system to an unexpected break in structure and norms. Second, the break in structure provoked a break in security, which precipitated the old, familiar, personalized and stereotyped roles that members and groups use to organize in the face of anxiety and insecurity. This level of experience speaks to the underlying issues in the intimacy phase that are related to separation–individuation dynamics. As one member said, he had to cope with the sense that the group was "turned inside out". Very early role adaptations, which manage survival and the experience of annihilation anxiety in response to the sense of falling apart, re-emerged, and, thus, could be explored. SCT sees this intimacy phase work as developing the containment necessary for the exploration of actual experience of "falling apart" in order that the experience can become more integrated and less encapsulated in a survival role.

It was a testament to the group's overall development that it was, in fact, able to continue working in co-operation with the leader's direction. In their exploration, group members identified many of the pulls to old roles, with some recognition of how these roles helped them manage their personal responses, albeit stereotypically. Although the pull to the old roles signalled the degree of disruption in security that the group was experiencing, the group worked to re-establish its identity and security. Over time, members returned to their membership roles, and were able to centre into their personal experience and bring this into a sub-group in the service of exploration and development. This enabled the group to re-establish a sense of structure and security, as seen in the increase in its cohesion, which enabled the recovery of work group functioning.

Several members of the group identified their expectations that the leader would manage and remedy the unexpected interruption. Thus, the traumatic event for the group was not only that the interruption and intrusion occurred, but also, and perhaps more importantly, that the leader failed to protect the group from this intrusion, and then failed to extrude the intruder from the group. One member described this clearly. The paranoia surfaced: "It seemed extraordinary that having an observer could be forgotten, and I don't think I really believed that this was what had happened. I felt really angry and assumed that Yvonne [the workshop director and leader in the other training group] had set this up."

Another member recognized his care-taking impulse in response to the leader, but then focused on his own leadership behaviour in the group, with little sense of Susan's leadership: "I was aware of my care-taking impulse in relation to Susan . . .".

Participants identified several possible roles, some of which were enacted, but others were discussed and explored: a defiant role, a paranoid victim role, a rescuer role, a "rabbit in the headlights" role, a show-off role, an egoistic role, and a targeting role ("them versus us"). Other roles can be inferred from the group's behaviour and/or from their own write-ups: for example, a taking charge role, the one-up role, an outraged role, etc. Each of the roles would have a personal history for the members who felt or enacted them, and simultaneously represent an attempt at group adaptation to the trauma precipitated by failed dependency.

At the level of the group-as-a-whole, each of these roles offered a container for part of the group's reaction and attempted to remedy the break in security. Eventually, participants sought sub-group affiliations. Each of the sub-groups also played a role in the work of the group-as-a-whole to stabilize and repair itself. The constellation of roles and sub-groups then represented the group's adaptation to the traumatic event.

These roles represented a mixture of the experience of both the authority phase and the intimacy phase. Many of the participants remembered an impulse to turn to the leader to manage and solve the problem of the intruder, only to discover that the leader had, in fact, introduced the problem. Several of these members were then able to explore roles in relation to the leader. This introduced a much greater complexity to the group and spawned the level of response related to the deeper issues of dependency and security that SCT identifies as characteristic of the intimacy phase.

SCT would expect that when dependency has failed, the earlier role solutions with strong roots to the attachment system dynamics would become manifest in an attempt to stabilize the group. One member reported the impulse to disappear down the rabbit hole into herself and her body (a "withdrawing role"), and another member to the role of "being different" and recognizing that he did not introduce the difference as the basis for another functional sub-group. Both roles are related to avoidance, or to what SCT terms the disenchantment roles in intimacy (what Hopper calls "aggregation"). However, several members reported their sense of the group bonding together and supporting each other, as seen in their insistence that this trauma would have been destructive to a "non-SCT" group, which reflected the emergence of enchantment (what Hopper calls "massification") in response to the aggregation of primal attachments. In effect, at the intimacy level, in which the main issues are those of early attachment and separation–individuation, the group produced two sub-groups, one in which the members held the disenchantment roles and one in which the members held enchantment roles.

The focus in SCT is on re-establishing the group system in support of the exploration of the response to the break in security. Stabilizing with functional sub-grouping increases the potential for both survival and development, attempting to provide a secure containment for exploring (through discriminating and integrating the experience) the annihilation anxiety that was managed through the role encapsulations and oscillations. Thus, with functional sub-grouping, the oscillations can be organized in the service of development instead of defence and fixation.

Although, for most part, I managed the challenges presented to the leader and to the group by holding the SCT structure and group norms for the exploration of such experience, in retrospect additional work would have been useful. The role solutions that the group was holding might have been reframed in a way that enabled the group to explore the two kinds of intimacy roles in the two functional sub-groups, that is, those holding the enchantment roles and those holding the disenchantment roles. This would have maximized the opportunity for repair to the group-as-a-whole, and, isomorphically, a repair in each member. Functional sub-grouping would be used to shift the group from an enactment to an exploration, thus, enabling group security to be re-established and simultaneously potentiating the developmental process of discriminating and integrating the information.

In sum, from an SCT perspective, this group trauma provoked the emergence of roles with roots to basic attachment styles related to the intimacy phase dynamics characterized by separation–individuation issues. It is here that Earl Hopper's understanding of the annihilation anxiety and incohesion is enormously useful in deepening the way in which SCT understands the intimacy phase of system development and its defining processes and developmental challenges.

The (ba) I:A/M view: Earl

The dynamics of what SCT calls the authority phase are associated with unconscious Oedipal dynamics. I was experienced as a paternal, sexual, phallic intruder into the individual children of the "mother" group and its "maternal leader", the maternal body of the group and of its maternal leader, and into the "mind" of the group and its maternal leader. Mother failed to protect her children from the sexual father. The children were also exposed to a primal scene experience in which they had to cope with their sudden awareness that their leaders, Susan and Yvonne, had relationships with Earl that allowed this to have been arranged "behind the scenes", so to say. Thus, Susan and Yvonne were perceived as having colluded with the perpetration of Oedipal trauma and primal scene trauma with all its related confusions.

The dynamics of what SCT calls the intimacy phase are associated with the unconscious dynamics of separation and individuation. Here, we are less concerned with the myth of Oedipus and more concerned with the myth of Osirus concerning personal fragmentation and social cohesion. In this connection, the empirical material illustrates, in order: intrusion, broken boundaries, and failed dependency (Oedipus), and the fear of annihilation and its vicissitudes involving psychic fission and fragmentation oscillating with psychic fusion and confusion, group aggregation oscillating with group massification (Osirus). The material also illustrates the development of roles associated with aggregation and massification, role suction, personifications of roles by people who have developed crustacean and/or amoeboid defensive personality organization, and the patterns of their aggressive feelings and aggression. The personification of aggregation was seen in terms of crustacean/lone wolf functioning: for example, in one member's reflection, "I became much more self-conscious, started to lose a systems perspective, went into my head, and became somewhat alienated from the group." The personification of massification was seen in amoeboid/morale boosting functioning, for example, in another member's singing the praises of SCT and the skills that it provided.

The projection of extreme incompetence on to me as the observer, who was defined as being outside the SCT framework, was essential to the development and maintenance of the massification process. I broke SCT rules about how to conduct an observation. To say the least, I was unwelcome! I was perceived as ill mannered, with dirty habits, and as self-soothing—if not masturbatory (rocking in his chair). In other words, I was denigrated, virtually demonized as a dirty old man who interrupted the relationships of the members of the group with a variety of their maternal objects. However, this was not only a matter of a paternal and phallic intrusion of an Oedipal scenario, but also a matter of my having interrupted illusions of enchantment and perfect security. Not only was it essential to impress the "observer" with a marvellous "scenario", it was also necessary for the group to see itself in this way. Individual participants who showed any sign of not falling in with the exceedingly positive self-image of the group were scapegoated. Obviously, scapegoating is essential to the development and maintenance of the massification process. (It is beyond the scope of this chapter to discuss the ways that groups perceive scapegoats in terms of their relationships to the leader of the group.)

It is very important to focus on unconscious meanings of communications. The group's evaluations of Susan and of me involved idealization and denigration. Without wishing to be self-protective, I would suggest that in reality I was not all *that* horrible, and Susan and Yvonne all that marvellous—despite their failures. Actually, many of the participants in SCT Courses continue to seek my advice concerning their own personal psychoanalytical and group analytical therapy. Although Susan and Yvonne's "oversight" was "forgotten" fairly quickly, I would suggest that it was encapsulated in the service of maintaining the enchanted massification of the SCT "movement". (It would also be well worth considering what my countertransference might tell us about what I was witnessing and what might have been projected into me, but this, too, is beyond the scope of the present paper.)

Clearly, the group worked very hard in order to recover their work group functioning, which they did achieve by the end of the session. None the less, this recovery was also associated with massification processes. In the same way that all basic assumptions can be functional for particular kinds of work group activity (e.g., during times of war, the fight/flight basic assumption serves the work group processes required by the military and by a citizenry mobilized for war), massification serves the development and maintenance of morale.

Susan

Hopper's understanding of the oscillating role defences that manage annihilation anxiety is extremely useful for SCT. In the intimacy phase work so essential in working with trauma, SCT emphasizes containing the pull to the role oscillation in functional sub-grouping. As each set of roles is contained and then explored in turn, the information encapsulated by the role and related to the annihilation anxiety therein can be discriminated and integrated, thereby potentiating system development rather than the fixation of oscillation (Agazarian, 2003). SCT acknowledges the value of Hopper's hypotheses concerning the fear of annihilation aroused in intimacy conflicts, and his elaborations of the oscillating role defences through which these experiences are managed. However, whereas SCT emphasizes system dynamics, basic assumption theory emphasizes the psychodynamics, or, to put this another way, whereas SCT begins with the dynamics of the most comprehensive system and its sub-systems, basic assumption theory begins with psychodynamics of the members of the system. Of course, Hopper's version of basic assumption theory conceptualizes persons as members of the system with its own dynamics, and SCT fully recognizes that members of systems have psychodynamics. Yet, rather than focusing on either psychodynamics or social system dynamics, SCT conceptualizes such dynamics as isomorphic at all levels of reality, including the organization, the group, the person, and the organism. SCT focuses on building the system that can explore whatever dynamics emerge, so the information/energy can be discriminated and integrated in the service of system development at all system levels.

It seems relevant that, in writing this chapter, I have found myself wanting to protect the group from pathologizing interpretations of their responses to this traumatic event, especially in so far as such pathologizing interpretations might be experienced as another intrusive traumatic event. Yet, I do not think my impulse is purely personal, in that it is here that the differences in the emphasis on psychodynamics and system dynamics are most pronounced. From a systems perspective, framing human dynamics in terms of psychopathology risks increasing the personalization of the group responses in a way that closes the boundaries to exploration rather than opens them. Looking at a system solution in context detoxifies the understanding of the group solutions and the personalized solutions, and creates a system for exploration that enhances the potential for development.

Earl

Isomorphy is a matter of degree, and cannot, or at least should not, be assumed. The basic assumption of Incohesion is much more relevant to the understanding of the fear of annihilation that is characteristic of what has been termed the intimacy phase than it is to the understanding of Oedipal anxieties that are characteristic of what has been called the authority phase. Failed dependency is not only a matter of an incestuous event coupled with the sense that mother has turned a blind eye, but also a matter of the experience of profound helplessness and fear of annihilation that follow from actual damage, abandonment, and loss, which are the main ingredients of a traumatogenic process which involves ruptures in the safety shield. The mergers of massification are not about removing the father as much as they are about becoming part of the mind and body of mother, which are assumed to be the location of perfect safety and harmony, although this is obviously a matter of emphasis and focus.

With regard to the recovery of work-group functioning, it is important to recognize that the responses to traumatized people and their groupings by significant others are very important in determining the severity of both short- and longer-term sequelae of traumatic experience. Susan's behaviour, and, in turn, the behaviour of most of the individuals in the group, facilitated the return to work-group functioning. Their behaviour reflected the skills that they had developed in the context of SCT. However, I believe that I would have achieved the same outcomes, but on the basis of clarification, holding, containing, and, ultimately, interpretation of the unconscious aspects of traumatic experience. I hope that these experiences would be metabolized in a way that enabled the participants in the group to feel, think, and behave in more "mature" ways, not only in the group, but also in other contexts.

I take issue with Susan's belief that basic assumption theory and interventions based on it serve to "pathologize" a particular set of group dynamics and its personification by particular individuals, unless she believes that anxiety and burdensome defences against it are always an indication of "pathology". Of course, under certain circumstances, adults are likely to experience Oedipal anxieties and psychotic anxieties. However, this is a matter of degree. Some people are likely to experience such anxieties more intensely and more regularly than do others, and at inappropriate times and places. I would also ask to what in the world does "trauma" refer, if not to "pathology"?

Yet, I do not think about groups or social systems in terms of pathology. For example, when I work as a consultant to organizations to which I refer metaphorically as "traumatized", "wounded", or "broken", and less metaphorically as "disrupted", I think about these organizations as "pathogenic", in that they have become structured in ways that cause their personnel to feel anxious, which is a natural, normal, and healthy response to danger. I often work in organizations and in countries in which high levels of anxiety are statistically normal. So, too, is (ba) I:A/M. In fact, this basic assumption might, at times, be functional in that it is necessary for the mobilization of work-group functioning. Without (ba) I:AM, groups might fall apart much more quickly and totally than they so often do. Of course, group psychotherapy, or, rather, psychotherapy for people in groups, differs from working with groups and other kinds of social system for the purposes of training or helping to clarify matters with a view to changing the system itself, for example, organizational development or community social work. However, in working as a group analyst and as a consultant, I have experienced some amazingly hopeful and creative attempts to make use of traumatic experience and to improve matters.

In conclusion

This kind of dialogue is an important step in using diverse theoretical understandings for enriching organizational consultancy, especially with respect to the development of leadership in the service of the restoration of work-group functioning. We share a strong commitment to theory as essential in guiding practice. The understanding of anni-hilation anxiety and traumatogenic processes in terms of the theory of incohesion has deepened the SCT understanding of the dynamics of the intimacy phase; and the techniques and skills offered by SCT for building more effective and efficient social systems supplement the psychoanalytical and group analytical understanding of basic assumption processes and their personifications. Understanding alone is not enough for the restoration of work group functioning; it is also necessary to develop theoretically informed interventions into management processes.

References

Agazarian, Y. M. (1994). The phases of development and the systems-centered group. In M. Pines & V. Schermer (Eds.), *Ring of Fire: Primitive Object Relations and Affect in Group Psychotherapy* (pp. 36–85). London: Routledge, Chapman & Hall.

Agazarian, Y. M. (1997). *Systems-centered Therapy for Groups*. New York: Guilford Press.

Agazarian, Y. M. (1999). Phases of development in the systems-centered group. *Small Group Research, 30*(1): 82–107.

Agazarian, Y. M. (2003). Book review of Hopper, E., *Traumatic Experience in the Unconscious Life of Groups*. *Systems-Centered Training News, 11*(1): 3–4.

Agazarian, Y. M., & Gantt, S. P. (2004). Working with roles in systems-centered groups. Paper presented to the American Psychological Association Annual Convention, Honolulu, August.

Agazarian, Y. M., & Peters, R. (1981). *The Visible and Invisible Group*. London: Routledge & Kegan Paul. Reprinted in paperback, London: Karnac, 1987.

Bennis, W. G., & Shephard, H. A. (1956). A theory of group development. *Human Relations, 9*(4), 415–437.

Bowlby, J. (1982). *Attachment* (2nd edn). New York: Basic Books.

Gantt, S. P. (2005). Functional role-taking in organizations and work groups. *The Group Psychologist, 15*(5): 15.

Heard, B., & Lake, D. (1997). *The Challenge of Attachment for Caregiving*. London: Routledge, Chapman & Hall.

Hopper, E. (2003). *Traumatic Experience in the Unconscious Life of Groups*. London: Jessica Kingsley.

Hopper, E. (2009). Building bridges between psychoanalysis and group analysis in theory and clinical practice. *Group Analysis*, *42*(4): 406–425.

Ladden, L., Gantt, S. P., Rude S., & Agazarian, Y. M. (2007). Systems-centered therapy: a protocol for treating generalized anxiety disorder. *Journal of Contemporary Psychotherapy*, *37*(2): 61–70.

Lewin, K. (1951). *Field Theory in Social Science*. New York: Harper & Row.

McCluskey, U. (2002). The dynamics of attachment and systems-centered group psychotherapy. *Group Dynamics*, *6*: 131–142.

Mead, G. H. (1934). *Mind, Self and Society*, C. W. Morris (Ed.). Chicago, IL: University of Chicago Press.

Miller, J. G. (1978). *Living Systems*. New York: McGraw-Hill.

Minuchin, S. (1974). *Families and Family Therapy*. Cambridge, MA: Harvard University Press.

CHAPTER THIRTEEN

Building individual resilience and organizational hardiness: addressing post-trauma worker's block*

Jeffrey Kleinberg

The trauma of 9/11 shook everyone, but most bounced back and returned to pre-trauma levels of functioning. Others did not, and the ripple effects of the terror attacks may be seen in significant numbers of people whose work morale and performance did not return to their pre-9/11 levels. Briefly, they have been struggling with what I am labelling, "worker's block" (WB), and their degree of disengagement is a function of the target of the attacks, their personal resilience and the hardiness of the organizations for which they work. My purpose here is to alert organizational specialists, managers, and governmental leaders to the potential impact of community trauma on short- and long-term worker productivity and emotional problems. Designing and implementing structures that could build individual resilience and organizational hardiness would promote recovery and might very well prevent personal and economic collapse in the wake of future tragedies.

I will describe contributing factors to WB, a dysfunctional state that stems from a blend of individual and organizational deficits. WB

---

*This paper is an expanded, integrated and updated version of three of my previously published articles (Kleinberg, 2000, 2005, 2007).

embodies a post-trauma condition that can be dissected and treated by psychotherapists and organizational specialists. Looking to the future, I will propose ways to fortify resiliency and hardiness by applying our knowledge of individual, group, and organizational dynamics. I will incorporate the concept of emotional intelligence and consider post-trauma hopelessness in my discussion of individual resiliency and its deficits; further, I shall identify basic assumption group defences and related dysfunctional patterns that need to be resolved to enhance organizational hardiness.

My observations of impaired work lives were initially and largely drawn from psychotherapy with adults and confirmed by colleagues in places struck by natural and man-made disasters. Assistance to organizations deeply affected by terror attacks in Turkey, Israel, and India, as well as to those struck by natural disasters in China, Rome, and in the Gulf Coast region of the USA revealed many concerns about worker morale and productivity. But the identification of WB started shortly after the two hijacked planes destroyed the World Trade Center.

On the 12 September 2001, I hesitantly returned to my practice in New York City as a psychologist–psychoanalyst. The previous day's events had traumatized individuals and the organizations in which they were working. What I did not realize at the time, but soon discovered, was that a sample of the people I was counselling had significantly changed their view of work and the workplace. Rapidly disengaging from their jobs, feeling betrayed by employers who failed to protect them or help them grieve, workers were suffering. Employees did not realize what was happening to them, and very few employers seemed to recognize the psychological damage that had been done to their workforce. I came to identify an emergent post traumatic stress reaction: worker's block (WB), a rapid emotional, attitudinal, and relational disengagement from the job that might not be classifiable as an illness, but is powerful enough to create a personal and a corporate crisis. Hope for a safe and rewarding professional future fades as the individual sees that his employer is unstable. Hope that he or she will recover diminishes as the community trauma exacerbates personal vulnerability.

Reports from the workplace confirm the presence of continuing post-trauma job problems. For example, Bill Santiago (Mercer, 2002, p. 12), a corporate recruiter for the Jewish Home and Hospital (JHH) in New York City, observed, "Post-9/11 had a horrible effect on morale. Everyone pulled together for the emergency, but weeks later there was a lot of lingering depression. People would be talking about their families and just burst out crying". Similarly, Jocelyn Perez (Mercer, 2002, p. 12), a nurse administrator at Bellevue Hospital, stated, "We saw the initial impact 3–4 weeks later, as absenteeism went up and staff members were having more conflict with each other".

Studies of sleep patterns before and after 9/11/01 represent additional sources of work impairment. According to the Associated Press (Recer, 2002), as transmitted by CBS News:

> A poll conducted by the National Sleep Foundation found the death and destruction of the terrorist attacks caused about 69 percent of Americans to have some insomnia during the period immediately after Sept. 11. A survey a year earlier found only 51 percent experiencing insomnia.
>
> James Walsh, president of the foundation and a sleep researcher at St. Luke's Hospital Sleep Medicine & Research Center in Chesterfield, Mo., said Sept. 11 affected the sleep poll figures for all of 2001 and suggests a generalized increase in sleeplessness. "Last year's figure was 51 percent for insomnia, and this year it is 58 percent for the entire year," said Walsh. "All the terrorist activities are one of the major stresses in our lives now."

Pervasive sleep disturbances are bound to lead to fatigue, which, in turn, interferes with morale, performance, and collegiality.

In a similar vein, the American Psychological Association issued a series of alerts, compiled by Gurwith, Silovsky, Schultz, Kees, and Burlingame (2002), informing members about post-trauma work problems that were likely to be faced by teachers, including excessive worrying, discomfort over intense emotions, decreased concentration, and difficulty in developing lesson plans. While no study of teacher impairment arising from 9/11 has been reported, it is safe to assume that those who actually experienced these anticipated reactions would be suffering from WB.

There are few studies of the long-term impact of trauma on workers' attitudes and performance. One exception is the study conducted by Wagner and his associates (1998), who found that the rate of absenteeism and early retirement among German fire-fighters was linked to their failure to cope effectively with occupational stress. Another exception is the six-month follow-up of survivors of the 1995 Oklahoma City bombing of a federal office. North and colleagues (1999) found that 53% of those with PTSD reported dissatisfaction with their work performance, 78% of those suffering from PTSD plus another psychiatric disorder, such as depression, were similarly dissatisfied, and that more than 30% of those survivors with a non-PTSD diagnosis or no diagnosis at all expressed a negative view of their work performance.

Whether distance from the Ground Zero might be linked to the observed frequency of WB is not yet clear. While Ryan, West, & Carr (2003) found little change in worker attitudes towards their job following 9/11, their large sample of respondents to an online survey did not reside in New York City or Washington, DC. In a nation-wide survey, Silver, Holman, McIntosh, Poulin, and Gil-Rivas (2002) concluded, "The psychological effects of a major national trauma are not limited to those who experience it directly, and the degree of response is not predicted simply by objective measures of exposure to or loss from trauma" (p. 1235). This finding corroborated the conclusions of a national study conducted days after the terror strikes by Schuster and colleagues (2001). They warned, "Even clinicians who practice in regions that are far from the recent attacks should be prepared to assist people with trauma-related symptoms of stress" (p. 1507).

In fact, we are still seeing some after-effects of terror strikes on patients' vocational attitudes and performance. Galea and colleagues (2002), after studying the psychological disturbances arising in New York City within two months of the terror attacks, and considering prior research, stated,

> Severe lasting psychological effects are generally seen after disasters causing extensive loss of life, property damage, and widespread financial strain and after disasters that are intentionally caused. These elements were all present in the September 11 attacks, suggesting that the psychological sequelae in New York City are substantial and will be long lasting. (p. 982)

WB might persist despite the passage of time.

The factors that contribute to WB

The factors that contribute to the development of WB can be categorized in terms of stressor, organizational hardiness, and personal resilience, and the interaction among them. I will now consider each set of factors in turn.

The stressor

At 8:41 a.m. on 9/11/01, most were either at work, or travelling to work. Work suddenly was no longer a refuge from other areas of life, a proving ground for fulfilling ambition, or a means to upward mobility. That morning, our expectations for work were changed forever.

Work roles are central to identity formation. The terrorists might have been trying to strike a blow at our economy, but they also effectively disrupted a salient life structure. If our ego-ideal, Freud's construct explaining our selection of life goals and the kind of person we want to become, is dominated by our ambition and achievements, then any career setbacks we experience will shake our self-esteem and confidence. 9/11, therefore, hit many hard because it attacked one of the key determinants of how we value ourselves.

What makes it so hard to get a handle on the extent and severity of WB is the malaise it creates: who has the energy to probe what is going on? The victim feels tired, and seemingly does not really care. Hopelessness might also set in. In a post-trauma time period, very few have the desire to look too deeply at what is happening to others and to themselves. And if the employing organization tends to deny such problems, no one may be aware that the ripple effect can bring down morale and performance and threaten staff mental health.

The calamities of 9/11 were unusual in their penetration of US space, their devastating effects, and the ongoing threats they created to the world of work. The assault on American territory revealed that there was much less security at work than many had imagined. For many, presumed security from early childhood was also called into question.

Work is difficult in unsafe settings. Insecurity bred of economic instability and threats of physical harm cut into productivity and creativity. Fear inhibits collegiality. Concerns over the adequacy of leadership mounted in the days following 9/11.

Many could not get images of the terror attacks out of their mind. Childhood fears of annihilation might have been stirred up, magnifying the damage. Office buildings were targets. The news coverage stressed that businesses were destroyed, employees killed, and commerce disrupted. Workers far from Ground Zero could identify with their counterparts at the damaged firms and personally felt the ripple effects of the rapid business decline in the ensuing months.

Of utmost significance here is the ongoing nature of the crisis. "We're waiting for the next shoe to drop," became the watchword. For some, an ambulance siren, a car backfiring, or a low-flying plane triggered a near-panic attack. (The 2009 photographic mission of an air force plane flying low over the Statue of Liberty re-terrorized many financial service workers.) Since the potential for further trauma never passes, ongoing threats produce peritraumatic stress.

Faced with unrelenting stress, the worker finds it difficult to plan ahead. The focus instead is on one day at a time, or, as one patient said, "one nanosecond at time." Fear of additional attacks pushes many into a protective stance—home is more important than the office, and family members are more important than colleagues or clients.

Peritraumatic stress is also likely to lead to increasing disharmony between management and staff. Workers no longer believe assurances from authority that the worst is over and that steps have been taken to prevent further problems. "We shouldn't have trusted them before; why should we believe them now?" asked one man, who, before 9/11, felt secure in the job. In the New York City Fire Department, rescue workers directed their anger at the commissioner, Thomas Von Essen. At an internationally televised benefits concert, the fire-fighters booed him, even though he was considered a national symbol for heroism. According to the *New York Times* of 9 November 2001,

> He has been called a 'goon' by union leaders he once worked with side by side. . . . Now, he said he is counting the days until he leaves the greatest job he will ever have had. 'I can't stand that I am counting the days, either.' (Dwyer, 2001)

Dissension, including unwarranted suspicion of others, discussed below, exacerbates attitudinal and behavioural problems on the job.

A recent study of 1,939 residents of the New York metropolitan area (Goode, 2003, p. 1) pointed to the cumulative effects of stressors that occurred subsequent to 9/11/01:

> Among New Yorkers who suffered from post-traumatic stress disorder after Sept. 11, 2001, those who have lost family members, lost jobs or experienced other stress since the attack are the most likely to still be having symptoms, researchers have found. . . . [P]eople who had experienced two stressful events since the Sept. 11 attack, like divorce or the death of a family member, were 47 times as likely to have persistent symptoms as those who had the symptoms several months earlier but had not faced such stress. Those who had gone through only one stressful event were 4.5 times as likely to have continuing symptoms.

Thus, the calamitous nature of the strike, a revelation of how vulnerable we really were, the direct attack on commerce, fears of further terrorism, and the cumulative effects of subsequent personal crises all contributed significantly to the emergence of WB. (I observed similar responses to the Gulf Coast hurricane of 2005, and the earthquake of 2008 in China.)

Organizational hardiness

The organization, itself, is the second variable that contributes to the magnitude of a widespread job crisis. Organizations, like the people who staff them, can be hit with trauma. History, culture, and hardiness influence the degree of regression that organizations experience. An enterprise that has a history of prior trauma, never integrated, a culture that does not value emotional expression, empathy, and teamwork, and lacks the command and control mechanisms to manage the effects of trauma, is vulnerable to regression. Structures that enable the organization to function in ordinary times weaken under peritraumatic strain. One can only imagine what Red Cross staffers experienced at work when their CEO, Bernadine Healy, became involved in a major fight with her Board over many unresolved issues before and immediately after 9/11. "'We're all afraid for our jobs,' one senior official . . . wrote in an e-mail message that ended up circulating widely through the Red Cross's quite gossipy e-mail system" (Sontag, p. 4). Organizational leadership might be unable or unwilling to recognize the nature and causes of substantial worker disengagement.

Peritraumatic stress challenges the organization's tension regulation systems. They are stretched beyond their capacity, and tension cannot be diffused or channelled into safe and productive outlets. Organizational structures (decision making, communications, and personnel) threaten to collapse. Cohesion diminishes rapidly and morale evaporates, while the cohesion of the organization deteriorates. Individual narcissism emerges, as the worker turns to others of congruent and or complementary personality styles and levels of regression to form defensive sub-groups. The unconscious fantasy is that the sub-groups will protect its constituents from destruction. In the face of trauma, structures of organizations that are highly vulnerable to regression begin to collapse. In catastrophic circumstances, the condition of organizations worsens as structures deteriorate and counterproductive sub-groups begin to form in an attempt to manage heightened levels of anxiety. As happened in many enterprises after 9/11, worker distrust caused many to detach from their usual affiliate groups, including those that were segments of the official bureaucracy.

Organizations that had inadequate tension regulation systems experienced more than instability; staff members were provoked into high states of personal anxiety. In a recapitulation of early childhood fears, workers were faced with calamitous prospects: loss of life, loss of safety nets (comparable to maternal holding), loss of self, etc. These losses are rooted in our earliest years, before the development of autonomous, self-preservative capacities. Regression places us in danger, and, in desperation, the individual is drawn to groups that seem to offer safe harbour.

When the unconscious motive for forming or joining a sub-group is primarily safety, a basic assumption group emerges. As conceptualized by Bion (1961), the assumptions (or organizing strategies) driving such groups reflect the safety-seeking motivation of its members and their unspoken agreement to sacrifice the organization's mission in the interest of coping with seemingly overwhelming anxiety. The defensive groupings described by Bion include those that are flight/fight dependency and pairing. Hopper (2001a) has identified a fourth basic assumption that emerges when the very survival of the social system is threatened: Incohesion: Aggregation/Massification.

Sub-grouping isolates the individual worker and magnifies his vulnerabilities. An incohesive organization does not allow the secure expression of feelings regarding the trauma, makes one feel unsafe, and promotes WB. This defensive position is an unhealthy response to strain: it alienates the worker from the work, and is contagious.

Paranoid ideation sweeps through an organization that lacks sufficient hardiness to absorb and respond effectively to acute peritraumatic stress. As Jacques (1976) and Kernberg (1998) observed, a faulty organizational structure serves as the breeding ground for persecutory anxiety. Individuals and sub-groups seek to "uncover" enemies within and from without.

The degree to which the worker's company is hardy, protects the minimally resilient worker. Hopper (2001b, 2004, personal communication) suggests that

> an absence of organizational hardiness might be understood in terms of basic assumption processes generally and Incohesion: Aggregation/ Massification in particular. . . . A high rate of 'worker's block' definitely leads to aggregation, and once aggregation gets established or crystallised it contributes to an increased rate of worker's block. Massification, a major element of which is the development of pseudo-morale, is a very clear cut defensive response to states of aggregation, and this may even be seen in a number of executives of various kinds running around 'listening' but never 'hearing'. I think that 'hardiness' can be understood as a property of a relatively mature work group.

> The organization that assumes the group defence of aggregation is unable to respond adaptively to a trauma: collaboration, support, mutual understanding are absent as staff, seemingly "connected," are rather cut-off from one another. Role differentiation is so firm as to make cooperation difficult. Shared beliefs are absent. Individuals are disconnected and subgroups are so firmly boundaried (or "encapsulated") that collective thinking and action become impossible. This organization may be paralyzed in the face of trauma; the fear of personal and organizational fission and fragmentation invokes this counterproductive basic assumption defense. Problem-solving deteriorates as managers, afraid they will lose their jobs, or their lives, communicate through euphemism and bureaucratise, or may not communicate at all. (Hopper, 2001a, p. 153)

Sub-groups within an organization that adopt a massification defence might be seen as working in concert, thanks to seemingly porous role differentiation and high morale, but this is an illusion. Without having to dig too deeply, the observer will note undermining, "accidental" mistakes, attacks directed outwardly to competitive agencies, and a general climate of tension and suspiciousness. Humour is absent. Sub-group members may be defending against fear of fusion that escalates in the face of trauma. Problem solving suffers as managers become bogged down by largely irrelevant details: for example, in continually debating the meaning of certain rules, the big picture is lost.

In my clinical and organizational work, I have identified seven organizational attributes that manage tension and, thus, contribute to hardiness. When they are absent or in short supply in the face of terror, these deficiencies threaten to harm already at-risk workers.

1. *Self-reflective systems* enable the organization to identify disruptive as well as facilitative forces having an impact upon it. Parallel processes in various internal and external groups are noted and are employed to further the understanding of what the group is experiencing. Insights might be disseminated to workers to help them understand their emotional state and relations with others. For example, a week after 9/11, executives in a large public agency initiated a discussion about how its few Moslem staffers were faring. There was concern that those associated in any way to the attackers were subject to scapegoating. Without the capacity to self-reflect accurately, organizations might focus on inconsequential threats and fail to perceive significant dynamic forces impeding their re-stabilization.

2. *Intact institutional memory* allows the organization to learn from past experiences of coping with trauma and to identify past catastrophes that might not have been worked through that add to the organization's vulnerability. Hope can be instilled in the staff through recalling past successes in addressing severe problems. Without recalling and understanding its trauma history, organizational leadership might have no choice but to adopt a trial-and-error approach to crisis management.

3. *A collaborative style* enables individual workers and their departments to consensually validate what is occurring and dismiss unsubstantiated rumours. An authoritarian leadership style might result in a sense of fragmentation, and a "we-*vs.*-they" climate.

4. *An organizational culture* that values professional development and stresses preparedness and initiative serves to reward creative

problem solving. Norms, values, and attitudes are conveyed to new workers and reinforced everyday in recurring interpersonal transactions. Fostering morale and co-operation as well as a democratic style of leadership contributes to a hardy organization. Alternatively, cultures that take "safe" approaches to a crisis while disregarding the welfare of individuals will block the emergence of informal leaders to help in a crisis. One mental health agency could not quickly mobilize its staff after 9/11 because it seemed too risky to one's professional status should the effort fail.

5. *Leadership* that is self-aware and confident mobilizes the workforce and stabilizes the organization in the wake of a trauma. Lacking confidence in organizational leadership, staff hope vanishes. Weak leaders who have little sense of their strengths, limitations, and impact on others might leave employees feeling directionless and alienated from management.

6. *Networking* with sister organizations in a crisis allows for sharing of information and resources and avoids confusing traditional competitors with the enemy.

7. *Boundary elasticity* allows managers in an emergency to put aside traditional ways of relating to subordinates so that the workforce can share ideas and feel heard. The traditional organizational hierarchy can be reinstituted after the crisis subsides. Without this flexibility, the organization remains rigid and unable to build cohesion. According to Hopper (2004, personal communication):

> Boundary issues within the context of traumatised organisations need to be considered, in 'regressed' organisations. Normal organisational processes are likely to be weakened and people are likely to relate to one another more comprehensively than they would when the organisation is functioning in a more healthy/mature/effective manner.

These correlates of hardiness need to be assessed as the consultant enters the client system. A recommendation, for example, was made to one agency that staff representing all levels of the hierarchy meet together to build cohesion. These exchanges provided important information to the leadership about steps that would have to be taken to restore confidence and stability among the workforce. The consultants, skilled at group dynamics and mental health, were able to work empathically with the executive team that also had been traumatized to integrate and utilize the data arriving from throughout the company and the industry.

Personal resilience

When difficulties arise, the self employs mechanisms aimed at regulating tension and selecting and implementing strategic behavioural responses that are to address the crisis. If the event is extreme, beyond that which would or could be anticipated in the ordinary course of events, the ability of individuals to weather the storm varies. Some are able to handle the stress, and restabilize; others have much more difficulty doing that. The former are seen as resilient, the latter as vulnerable. The degree of resilience correlates with the potential for developing WB.

Frederickson, Tugade, Waugh, and Larkin (2003) describe psychological resilience as "a relatively stable personality characteristic characterized by the ability to bounce back from negative experience and by flexible adaptation to the ever-changing demands of life" (p. 367). Frederickson and his associates cite the capacity to experience "positive emotions", such as humour, creative exploration, relaxation, and optimistic thinking, as one of the basic adaptational systems associated with resilience. They studied how college students coped with 9/11. Utilizing data collected prior to and after the terror attacks, the researchers found that subjects able to evoke positive emotions were able to cope with the attacks more effectively than their peers who could not. Frederickson and his colleagues concluded, "We saw that amidst the emotional turmoil generated by the September 11th terrorist attacks, subtle and fleeting experiences of gratitude, interest, love, and other positive emotions appeared to hold depressive symptoms at bay and fuel post-crisis growth" (p. 374).

In my clinical and consultative work, I have examined contributors to individual resilience that, when limited, make the individual vulnerable to WB. Resilience seems to be an aspect of emotional intelligence (EQ), and is supported by hope.

Mayer and Salovey (1997, p. 5) see the vulnerable individual as lacking "the ability to perceive emotions, to access and generate emotions so as to assist thought, to understand emotions and emotional knowledge, and to reflectively regulate emotions so as to promote emotional and intellectual growth". They further detail the skills that comprise this ability. Their third domain, "Understanding and analysing emotions; employing emotional knowledge", is described as the ability to "interpret meanings that emotions convey regarding relationships" (p. 10). When one suffers a loss, he or she is likely to feel sad. Insight about the observed feeling would guide emotional response to trauma.

The EQ abilities to self-reflect and deduce accurately one's emotional state (Goleman, 1998) and design a correlated strategy for coping with high levels of tension result in a resilient approach to trauma. Without an envelope of hope, however, the individual is unable to function during and after a trauma, and is likely to experience WB.

Hope is optimism embedded in a general belief system that things will work out. It springs eternal in that, without hope, the self is dying. Hope is interpersonal; it is the product of mutual sustenance through collaboration, feedback loops, and a sense that we are all in it together. Hope is derived from action towards a goal that can be achieved through significant effort. The uphill climb seems worth the effort. The goal is achievable with varying degrees of struggle. Persistence towards a meaningful end carries the effort forward. Self-actualization is a motivating force that shapes efforts to overcome obstacles; thus, hope springs *internal*, but is fuelled by what happens in a social context—in relations with individuals and groups.

What is the developmental course of hope? Mitchell (1999) argues against the earlier classical drive theory view that the infant's hope is regressive and pathogenically unrealistic. Instead, he sees hope as a positive force that stems from the care-giver's fulfilment of the newborn's needs. Building on Erikson's focus on the trust and the faith that flow from the satisfaction of early needs, Winnicott's belief that hope represents a "self-healing return to the point where psychological growth was suspended", and Kohut's notion that hope is expressed in the patient's groping towards self-cure by trying to extract from others what was missing early in his development, Mitchell (1999, p. 221) suggests that there is "a dialectical relationship between the static and familiar and the longing for something fuller and more rewarding". He adds that traumas might have produced hopes that are now mostly irrelevant to current needs, and that a revision of our thinking about hope is needed.

Hope can also be destroyed by unrelenting external circumstances that threaten the self. Social system dysfunctions, such as discrimination or structural unemployment, are such threats. Organizations that breed suspicion and fragmentation create tension that can overwhelm the self and instil an expectation of defeat. Terrorism undercuts safety, jeopardizes feelings of being protected, destroys hopefulness, and contributes to worker disaffection. After trauma, the restoration and reshaping of hope occurs in a context of interpersonal validation and empathic support through individuals and groups. In response to Mitchell's argument, and drawing on Rycroft's view that where there is "life" there is hope, and vice versa, Hopper (2001b) adds that hope can be defined as the exercise of the transcendent imagination, leading to attempts to make things better both for oneself and for others, including the next generation. Snyder (2000) have investigated the process of hope formation and restoration and hold that hope is a function of self-efficacy and perceived pathways, the extent to which the individual believes he or she can solve the problem being confronted and the degree to which possible solutions can be identified. The most hopeful person is the one who believes that he or she has the power to meet the problem effectively and sees a specific way to do it.

Beyond the individual's hope are the group counterparts to self efficacy and pathways. Group efficacy refers to the group belief that it can overcome a crisis, and that working as a team can be more productive than are individuals working alone. Group pathways are seen as the degree to which the members perceive the capacity of the group to generate promising ways of dealing with the presenting problem. In an organization, then, group efficacy and group pathways interact with self efficacy and self pathways to either promote or impede hope.

Hopefulness is seen in formulation of personal hardiness (their term for individual resilience), which flows from three related beliefs concerning the interaction between self and world: commitment, control, and challenge:

Persons strong in the sense of commitment expect to be able to make whatever they are doing seem interesting and worthwhile through their resourcefulness (instead of feeling bored and empty). Those strong in a sense of control believe that they can influence the direction and outcome of what is going on around them through their own efforts (as opposed to feeling like the victims of circumstance).

Finally, persons high in a sense of challenge believe that their lives are most fulfilled when they are growing and developing through learning from experience rather than wishing for easy comfort and security.

According to Maddi, Kahn, and Maddi (1998), resilience hinges on the gathering of constructive social support. Citing research by Kobasa and Puccetti (1983), Maddi concludes that a highly resilient person seeks out those who would facilitate coping, whereas the vulnerable person is likely to search for those who would provide mere comfort, thus undermining efforts to manage more effectively.

The resilient and hopeful individual is able to respond to trauma and avoid WB by means of the following:

Absorbing primary shock. In the immediate aftermath of trauma, the resilient individual recognizes that he/she is in shock, what the symptoms are, that he/she is in a self-protective mode, and, thus, sees shock as part of a process, and can work his/her way out of it. A limited capacity to absorb the initial shock wave leaves the person overwhelmed by the trauma and paralysed. A flight/fight response to the emergency might then follow.

Managing secondary reactions. Assuming that the individual can develop at least a minimal emotional distance from the first shockwave, the resilient person can view the wish to flee or fight as an instinctive, and not necessarily as a rational, response. He is able to interrupt the automatic sequence between the triggering event and the flight/fight response. Someone with a deficit in resilience might find himself unable to stop an emergency response in order to rationally examine alternatives.

Evaluating realistically the nature of the threat. The resilient person can collect data on the nature of trauma by scanning internal and external environments. She can integrate data by incorporating memories for comparison and utilizing the views of credible others about the trauma. Someone with limited resilience will probably colour the estimates with residue from unresolved traumas of the past. Panic will feed on itself and the person will continue to make increasingly poor judgements about her situation.

Modifying one's emotional state. The resilient individual is able to regulate his tension state by calming down to the point where he can make some rational and self-affirming decisions. Utilizing his connections with others—and being able to deepen them through empathy—

could help him cope. An ability to ask for and receive support aids the person in managing his emotions. Using relaxation techniques could be helpful as well. Controlling his emotional state will allow him to assess his circumstances realistically and begin to formulate a plan. Lacking resilience, an individual might remain unable to function and have to become over-reliant on others. Unfortunately, they might not have his interests at heart. A fragile person might be more subject to panic observed in others, as fear becomes a contagion, further causing deterioration.

Planning a response to the trauma. The resilient individual is able to identify self-affirming goals that will enhance her safety and security and those of her family, friends, and colleagues. She is able to develop alternative strategies available for reaching these self-affirming goals, predict probable consequences of the options, and select the most feasible and constructive. The resilient person can then review the chosen strategy for possible unconscious contamination and related pitfalls. The individual with a resilience deficit cannot see the forest for the trees, and might be overwhelmed with anxiety that choices made are destructive.

Implementing a plan. The resilient individual is able to implement the best possible strategy, all the while monitoring progress. He can make mid-course corrections as conditions change or expectations do not hold up. He is able to sustain motivation, work collaboratively with others, and watch for indications that the group or organizational task is getting sidetracked and take the appropriate action to refocus the effort. A person not so resilient cannot act expeditiously, might get bogged down in conflict with others, and ultimately surrender to the wishes of others.

Reviewing and learning from the experience. The resilient individual is able to evaluate her response to the trauma, identify mistakes made, and search for possible unconscious determinants that had been previously ignored or not sufficiently weighed. Ultimately, she can assess her ability to manage trauma and look for ways to strengthen deficits. The person lacking sufficient resilience cannot gain sufficient emotional distance to conduct an objective self-assessment. She might be destined to repeat the same mistakes the next time trauma strikes.

Resilience in the face of peritraumatic stress might evoke malignant responses ranging from minor and temporary to major and lasting. On the job, WB arises when resilience is impaired. In summary, an individual strained by trauma, lacking resilience, and employed by an organization lacking hardiness is likely to suffer WB.

Proposed interventions

I will now outline several programmes for addressing the actual or potential problem of WB in the context of work roles in organizations that can themselves be conceptualized as traumatized.

Addressing the problem of WB requires interventions at the levels of the individual and the organization. Equally important, however, is the need to take both preventative and remedial measures. At the individual level, the preventative goal is to strengthen resilience; at the organizational level of intervention, the goal is to enhance hardiness. After the trauma, the strategy at the individual level is to identify and address WB that is spotted in some, while responding to others who might be suffering from PTSD; the goal in the overall enterprise is to restore stability and build up hardiness in the face of future attacks.

Intervention at the individual level

For the individual suffering from WB, a supportive group needs to focus on issues that help one understand what has contributed to the post-trauma emotional disengagement from work. Members would be encouraged to discuss how the unexpected has seemingly derailed progress towards long-held goals. The extent to which the current disaster resonates with past unresolved or unintegrated crises needs to be examined, since old emotional scars can make the worker more susceptible to new stressors. As the group member increases her understanding of the role of the defective organization in exacerbating the post-trauma effects, she sees that her stress reaction is not entirely her fault. Colleagues would probably be able to share their disappointment in their own supervisors. The failure of management to protect her or respond effectively to the trauma could be worked on in the group as transference re-enacted with the group leader. Members might be encouraged to speak with their superiors about deficient organizational structures and mechanisms for protecting and aiding the workforce.

In a safe group climate, the individual suffering from WB might gain insight into the factors that have contributed to, and the widespread occurrence of, stress reactions in the workplace. However, insight alone is not enough to overcome WB; the individual needs to strengthen coping skills for managing persistent stress. Participation in a theme centred group enables the better prepared to lend their experience to the more vulnerable. Klein and Schermer (2000) offer many group approaches to address the needs of individuals suffering in the aftermath of trauma.

It is important to apply what we have learned about EQ (Kleinberg, 2000). The group serves as a laboratory for identifying deficits in the capacity to manage one's emotions in the group and, presumably, on the job. I have found it useful to have the group thoroughly analyse discordant episodes that arise. Hopefulness can be enhanced through interventions that encourage group members to share the effective ways that they have handled adversity in the past. As Yalom (1970) points out, hope—a curative factor—is instilled when members can demonstrate to one another that problems can be addressed, and that history suggests that hope is warranted. Such exchanges can create mentoring bonds within the group to reactivate hope through mutual support and encouragement.

Maddi, Kahn, and Maddi (1998) developed training for workers dealing with ordinary amounts of work stress. Both EQ and hopefulness seem to be themes of this resilience training.

An optimal mixed-model, group approach to resilience training would help to overcome barriers to achieving resilience and provide a real-time learning experience in self-reflection, emotional management (including tension regulation and empathy), cognitive restructuring, and in planning and implementing responses based on the introspection and realistic appraisal of external data. Strengthening positive emotional responses to acute levels of stress would enable workers, according to Frederickson (1998, 2001), to "broaden one's thought–action repertoire, expanding the range of cognitions and behaviors that come to mind". This "broaden-and-build" theory of positive emotions assumes that broadened mindsets enable the increasingly resilient individual to build physical, intellectual, and social resources. Then staff would be prepared for trauma and be less vulnerable to WB.

Interventions at the organizational level

At the organizational level, proposals for inoculation against further organizational breakdown include group reviews of case studies, efforts to strengthen organizational hardiness, and establishing plans that focus on the emotional needs of staff at the time of acute stress, and not just on ways to get the computers up and running again.

A stepwise consideration of past responses to trauma would identify the relationship between mistakes made under stress and the continued impact of hidden past unresolved issues, or still existing organizational deficits. An organizational consultant could deepen the retrospective by examining the unconscious residue from prior traumas that might impede the company's recovery from the present crisis. Such reviews can add to staff beliefs that the organizational leaders are taking charge, and chaos is being reined in. To further strengthen hope, mentoring programmes can be established. In addition, leadership can stimulate hope by what they say (they need to examine and discuss among themselves their own feelings of hope and hopelessness) and how much faith they express in the power of individuals, sub-groups, and the organization-as-a-whole to deal with the current crisis.

Pathways can be developed in a group context using brainstorming and other techniques to stimulate creativity. Sufficient attention would need to be paid to emerging resistances or basic assumption dynamics. These solution-finding meetings would include coaching in defining problems, developing optional solutions and preparing for contingencies.

To build organizational hardiness, enterprises need to assess existing mechanisms for tension regulation, identify and work through past, unprocessed trauma, as well as encourage the development of a culture that rewards transparent communication and consensus building. Training of executives, supervisors, and line staff would focus on group dynamics, collaborative decision making, tension regulation, strengthening internal structures for emotional communication and support, sensitizing management to the need for openness, and aiding staffers struggling with stress and an uncertain future.

If the organization commits to minimizing the psychological risk to its workforce from future disasters, management in collaboration with staff at all levels needs to develop a plan, assign responsibility, allocate resources, and perhaps hire consultants with a group perspective. Any tendency to avoid these issues must be addressed, since group denial is a possible roadblock to post-trauma organizational development. Leadership is key to preparation, and, as the American Psychological Association Task Force on Workshop Violence recommended (2003) on its website at the two-year anniversary of 9/11: "Organizations must offer leaders at all levels access to training, development opportunities and resources to facilitate leadership actions".

Interventions at the individual and organizational levels to identify and address WB must be evaluated and the results shared internally and with sister enterprises. Dissemination conferences can further the effort to orientate organizations to the problems of the workforce in times of acute stress.

Conclusion

The 9/11 terror attacks on the workplace caused many personnel to experience a rapid emotional disengagement from their job, termed here, "worker's block". Workers who do not "qualify" for a diagnosis of PTSD might still be suffering silently on the job. Mental health professionals, human resource personnel, and executives need to combine their efforts to understand and respond to real and imagined threats to worker mental health and the economy posed by future community trauma. In this chapter, I have explored the relative contributions of peritraumatic strain, individual resilience, and organizational hardiness to WB, and presented several preventative and remedial proposals

References

American Psychological Association (2003). Responses to workplace violence post 9/11—What can organizations do? Accessed at www. apa.org/pubinfo/post911workplace.html.
Bion, W. R. (1961). *Experience in Groups*. London: Routledge.
Dwyer, J. (2001). Fire commissioner to leave confused, unhappy, unloved. *New York Times*, November 9th, online edition, p. 1.

Frederickson, B. (1998). What good are positive emotions. *Rev. Gen. Psych.*, 2(3): 300–319.

Frederickson, B. (2001). The role of positive emotions in positive psychology. *Am. Psychologist*, 56(3): 218–226.

Frederickson, B. L., Tugade, M. M., Waugh, C. E., & Larkin, G. R. (2003). What good are positive emotions in a crisis? A prospective study of resilience and emotions following the terrorist attacks on the United States on September 11, 2001. *Journal of Personality and Social Psychology*, 83(2): 365–376.

Galea, S., Ahern, J., Resnick, H., Kilpatrick, D., Bucuvalas, M., Gold, J., & Vlahov, D. (2002). Psychological sequelae of the September 11 terrorist attacks in New York City. *New England Journal of Medicine*, 346(13): 982–987.

Goleman, D. (1998). *Working with Emotional Intelligence*. New York: Bantam.

Gurwith, R., Silovsky, J., Schultz, S., Kees, M. & Burlingame, S. (2002). Reactions and guidelines for children following trauma/disaster. American Psychological Association. Accessed September 8 2002 at: www.apa.org.

Hopper, E. (2001a). Difficult patient in group analysis: the personification of (ba): I:A/M. *GROUP*, 25(3): 139–172.

Hopper, E. (2001b). On the nature of hope in psychoanalysis and group analysis. *British Journal of Psychotherapy*, 18(2): 205–226. Reprinted in Hopper, E. (2003), *The Social Unconscious: Selected Papers*. London: Jessica Kingsley.

Jaques, E. (1976). *A General Theory of Bureaucracy*. New York: Halsted.

Kernberg, O. (1998). *Ideology, Conflict, and Leadership in Groups and Organizations*. New Haven, CT: Yale University Press.

Klein, R. H., & Schermer, V. L. (2000). *Group Psychotherapy for Psychological Trauma*. New York: Guilford Press.

Kleinberg, J. L. (2000). Beyond emotional intelligence at work: adding insight to injury through group psychotherapy. *Group*, 24(4): 261–278.

Kleinberg, J. L. (2005). On the job after 9/11: looking at worker's block through a group lens. *Journal of Group-Analytic Psychotherapy*, 38(2): 203–218.

Kleinberg, J. L. (2007). Restoring hope through posttrauma groups. *Group*, 31(4): 293–308.

Kobasa, S. C., & Puccetti, M. C. (1983). Personality and social resources in stress resistance. *Journal of Personality and Social Psychology*, 45(4): 839–850.

Maddi, S. R., Kahn, S., & Maddi, K. L. (1998). The effectiveness of hardiness training. *Consulting Psychology Journal: Practice and Research, 50,* 78–86.

Mayer, J. D., & Salovey, P. (1997). What is emotional intelligence? In: P. Salovey & D. Sluyter (Eds.), *Emotional Development and Emotional Intelligence: Implications for Educators* (pp. 3–31). New York: Basic Books.

Mercer, T. A. (2002). Never forget: the emotional fallout of Sept. 11 remains a major clinical concern in New York. *Advance for Nurses,* 2(16): 10–14.

Mitchell, S. H. (1999). *Hope and Dread in Psychoanalysis.* New York: Basic Books.

North, C., Nixon, S., Shariat, S., Mallonee, S., McMillen, J., Spitznagel, E., & Smith, E. (1999). Psychiatric disorders among survivors of the Oklahoma City bombing. *Journal of the American Medical Association,* 282(8): 755–762.

Recer, P. (2002). Losing sleep over Sept. 11. Accessed September 7, 2002 at: www.cbsnews.com/stories/2002/04/02/health/main505151.shtml.

Ryan, A., West, B., & Carr, J. (2003). Effects of terrorist attacks of 9/11/01 on employee attitudes. *Journal of Applied Psychology, 88*(4): 647–659.

Schuster, M., Bradley, D., Jaycox, L., Collins, R., Marshall, G., Elliott, M., Zhou, M., Kanouse, D., Morrison, J., & Berry, S. (2001). A national survey of stress reactions after the September 11, 2001, terrorist attacks. *New England Journal of Medicine, 345*(29): 1507–1512.

Silver, R. C., Holman, E. A., McIntosh, D. N., Poulin, M., & Gil-Rivas, V. (2002). Nationwide longitudinal study of psychological responses to September 11, *Journal of the American Medical Association, 288*(10): 1235–1244.

Snyder, C. (2000). *Handbook of Hope: Theory, Measures, and Applications.* MA: Academic Press.

Sontag, D. (2001). What brought Bernadine Healy down? *New York Times Magazine,* December 23rd, online edition.

Wagner, D., Heinrichs, M., & Ehlert, U. (1998). Prevalence of symptoms of posttraumatic stress disorder in German professional firefighters. *American Journal of Psychiatry, 155*(12): 1727–1732.

Yalom, I. D. (1970). *The Theory and Practice of Group Psychotherapy.* New York: Basic Books.

INDEX

abuse, xxviii, 49, 68, 111–112,
114–118, 120, 123, 140, 160, 164,
199, 207
sexual, xx, 67, 93, 111, 113, 115–116,
118–119, 121–122
Adlam, J., xxv, 152, 154, 157, 163–164,
169, 171
Agazarian, Y. M., xxvii, 233–240, 246,
248–250, 253–254
aggression, xxv, xli, 19, 31, 39, 41, 50,
89–90, 93–94, 96–99, 101–102,
104, 107, 109, 119, 156, 163, 174,
176, 178, 185, 201–202, 204, 207,
225, 248
Ahern, J., 258, 275
Alford, C. F., xl, xlix, 104, 109
Almog, O., 216, 229
Ambrosini, P., 5–6, 21
American Group Psychotherapy
Association (AGPA), xxiii
American Psychiatric Association,
218, 229
American Psychological Association,
257, 274
anger, xli, 61–62, 99, 147, 163, 167,
183, 192, 208, 222, 239–242,
244–245, 260
anxiety
abandonment, 181–182, 191
annihilation, 177–178, 245, 247, 250,
253
psychotic, xxxvi–xxxvii, 93, 133,
177, 252

survival, 143, 147, 174, 193
Armstrong, D., xxxii, xlix, 7, 20–21,
160, 170, 206, 214
attachment, xxxiv, 15, 39, 68, 114, 196,
200–201, 210, 212, 237–238,
246–247
Atwal, A., 144, 147

Bain, A., xxxv, l, 40, 44, 222, 230
Bakan, J., 46, 63
Baker, L., 69, 87
Bakker, A. B., 145, 149
Barr, C. S., 68, 86
Barratt, R., 133, 135–136, 148
Barton, R., 146, 148
Bateman, A., 70–71, 86
Bauman, Z., 153, 170
Becker, M. L., 68, 86
behaviour, xxviii, 7, 19, 31, 47–48, 50,
66, 68, 74, 76, 84–86, 90, 97, 118,
130, 135, 140–141, 162, 165, 184,
193, 195, 198–199, 201–202,
234–235, 238, 246, 251, 260, 266,
272
Bennis, W. G., 235, 253
Benvenuto, S., 49, 63
Berger, P. L., 175, 193
Berger, R., 228–229
Berke, J., 134, 148
Berry, S., 258, 276
Billow, R. M., 152, 155, 170
Bindman, J., 142, 148
Binney, G., 196, 213

Bion, W. R., xviii, xxix, xxxi–xxxiii, xxxv, xxxix, xlix, l, 6, 21, 40, 43, 133–134, 144, 147–148, 153–154, 169, 170, 177, 194, 207, 213, 220, 229, 262, 274
Blackman, N., 113, 125
Bleich, A., 223, 228–229
Bollas, C., 193–194
Bordia, P., 4, 21
Bowlby, J., 237, 253
Bradley, D., 258, 276
Brenner, I., xlviii–xlix
Brooke, R., 152, 170
Brooker, C., 144, 150
Brown, C. G., 180, 194
Buber, M., xlviii–xlix
Bucuvalas, M., 258, 275
Burlingame, S., 257, 275
Burns, T., 144, 148

Caldwell, K., 144, 147
Campbell, I. C., 67–68, 86
Carr, J., 258, 276
Champoux, M., 68, 86
Chasseguet-Smirgel, J., 49, 62–63, 202, 213
clinical vignettes, 65–66, 71, 116, 216, 221, 223, 226
    Alice, 71–72
    Belinda, 72
    Betty, 72
    Catherine, 72–74
    Susie, 116–117, 124
    X, 117–123
Coleridge, S. T., xlvii–xlviii
Collins, R., 258, 276
Coltart, N., 71, 86
community care, 130–131, 139–146
Connan, F., 67–68, 86
containment, xxvi, xxxv, xli, xlv, 5, 9, 29, 36–37, 50, 60, 76, 85, 93, 102–104, 112–113, 118, 133, 143, 162, 174, 176, 188–189, 200, 202, 205–206, 209–212, 235, 237–247, 250–251
Cooper, A., 151, 170

Cottis, T., xxv, 113–114, 125
Craib, I., 147–148

David, E., 228, 231
Davies, C., 145, 148
Davies, R., 136–137, 148
death, xx, xxxiii, xxxvi, 29, 113, 115–116, 120, 183, 202, 204, 211, 218, 221–222, 226, 257, 261, 267
DeClerck, P., 153, 170
Dekel, R., 228–230
De Mare, P., xxxix, xlix
denial, 3, 5, 9, 11, 17, 29–30, 43, 47–51, 57–58, 61–62, 114, 139, 226, 274
denigration, xxvi, xxxii, xl, 7, 76, 83, 113–114, 139, 143, 189, 204–205, 208, 249
dependency, xxvi, xxxii, xlii, xlvi–xlvii, 40, 43, 51, 55, 90, 93, 95, 153, 159, 162–163, 177–181, 185–186, 188–189, 192, 195, 246, 262
    failed, xvii–xviii, xx–xxi, xxiv, xxvii, xxxvi, xlvii, 29, 41, 45–46, 62, 89, 93–94, 99, 115, 195, 207–208, 212, 220, 246, 248, 251
    inter-, 27, 92, 95, 198, 206, 211–212
depression, xvii, xxxii, 24, 51, 61, 68, 82, 91, 147, 157, 176, 181, 209, 211, 219, 238, 257–258, 266
Difonzo, N., 4, 21
Dluhy, M., xxii, xxx
Doron, G., 226, 229
Downing, L., 62, 64
Dunphy, D. C., 6, 21
Dupont, J., 147–148
Dwyer, J., 260, 274

eating disorder(s), xxi, xxiv–xxv, 66–67, 69, 71, 73, 75, 83–86, 156–157, 162
    anorexia nervosa (AN), 66–67, 69, 72–73, 75–76, 83–84, 86, 152
Ehlert, U., 257, 276
Eisler, I., 69, 86
Elias, N., 204, 213

Elliott, M., 258, 276
emotional intelligence (EQ), 256,
   266–267, 272
envy, xix, xxxii–xxxiii, xlvi, 8, 19, 29,
   35, 39, 41, 43, 46, 51–52, 55,
   71–73, 93, 96, 98, 100–101, 105,
   109, 113, 160
Erikson, E. H., 203, 213, 267
Esterhuyzen, A., 113, 125
experience(s) *see also*: traumatic
   life, 68, 122, 157, 217
   painful, 85, 205, 207, 209, 226

fantasy, xlii, 4–6, 8, 14, 18–19, 39, 116,
   119–121, 133, 177–179, 181,
   184–185, 189, 191–193, 209, 216,
   262
fight/flight, xxxii, 40, 95, 153, 177,
   212, 249
Findler, L., 217, 230
Fonagy, P., 70–71, 86–87
Forster, L., 144, 148
Foster, A., 131, 148, 151, 161, 170
Foucault, M., 153, 155, 170
Foulkes, H., xviii, xxix, xxxiii, xxxix,
   223
Fowles, J., xxii, xxix
fragmentation, xxxvi–xxxviii, 40–41,
   43, 71, 75, 85, 92–94, 98, 105, 123,
   138–139, 143–144, 146, 158,
   163–164, 201, 207–208, 225, 248,
   263–264, 268
Francis, D. D., 68, 87
Frederickson, B. L., 266, 272, 275
Freud, A., xl, xlix
Freud, S., xxix, 6, 21, 35, 62–63, 147,
   204, 213, 259

Gabbard, G. O., xix, xxviii, xxix, 28,
   42–43, 159, 163–164, 167, 170
Gabriel, Y., xxviii, xxix
Galea, S., 258, 275
Galford, R., xx, xxix
Gantt, S. P., xxvii, 62, 66, 87, 233,
   236–242, 244, 246, 248–250,
   253–254

Garland, C., 164, 170
Gelkopf, M., 223, 228–229
Giddens, A., 197, 213
Gilligan, J., 153, 158, 165, 170
Gilmore, M., 218, 231
Gil-Rivas, V., 258, 276
Girard, R., 99, 103, 105, 109
Glasser, M., 155, 170
Gluyas, R., 62–63
Goffman, E., 131–132, 148
Gold, J., 258, 275
Goldman, D., 68, 86
Goleman, D., 267, 275
Gould, L. J., xxxv, l, 40, 44, 222, 230
Gouldner, A. W., 193–194
Gretz, N., 216, 229
guilt, xix, 36, 93, 99, 101–102, 120,
   124, 142, 191, 200–202, 207, 226
Gurian, E., xxii, xxix
Gurwith, R., 257, 275

Hadar, B., 224, 229
Hadari, Y., 219, 229
Halton, W., 206, 214
Harel, Y., 217, 230
Harker, J., 145, 150
hate, xxxvii, 48, 60, 73, 98–101, 104,
   113, 152, 158–159, 167, 184, 204,
   207, 238
Health Commission, 131, 148
Heard, B., 237, 253
Heinrichs, M., 257, 276
Herman, L. J., 219, 222, 229
Higgins, N., 142, 148
Higley, J. D., 68, 86
Hills, B., 144, 148
Hinshelwood, R. D., xxv, 133–134,
   137, 140, 147–149
Hirschhorn, L., 206, 213
Hochschild, A., 129, 149
Hollins, S., 113, 125
Holman, E. A., 258, 276
Holocaust, xviii, 216–217, 222, 225–226
Holy Bible, The, 173, 175, 194, 225
Hopper, E., xvii–xx, xxvii–xxviii,
   xxix–xxxii, xxxviii–xl, xlv, xlvii,

xlix–l, 5, 18, 21, 29–32, 40–45,
    49–50, 63, 66–67, 71, 73, 75, 82,
    84, 87, 89, 93–95, 97, 99, 102–104,
    106–109, 111–112, 114–115, 120,
    125, 144, 147, 149, 151, 162, 164,
    169–170, 174–175, 177–178, 194,
    207, 215–216, 218, 220, 222–223,
    225, 228–230, 233, 235, 238–243,
    247–248, 250–251, 253–254,
    262–263, 265, 268, 275
Hormann, S., xxviii, xxx
Horwitz, L., 20, 103, 109
Hoyle, L., 206, 214
Huffington, C., 206, 214
Hyde, P., xx, xxx
hypothalamic–pituitary–adrenal
    (HPA) axis, 68–69, 71

Incohesion:
    Aggregation/Massification ((ba)
    I:A/M), xviii, xxiii–xxiv, xxvii,
    xxxi, xxxiii, xxxvii, xli, xliv–xlv,
    40–41, 66–67, 75–76, 79, 85, 89,
    94, 111–112, 177, 215, 220–221,
    227, 248, 252, 262–263
institutionalization, xliv, 130–132,
    135, 138, 140–142, 145, 156, 159
intervention, xliv, 36, 111, 135,
    151–152, 190, 211, 236, 252–253,
    271–274
introjective identification(s), xxii,
    xxxvii, xliii, 103, 114, 152, 193,
    223
Israel, xviii, xx, xxvi, 215–228, 256
Israeli Institute of Group Analysis
    (IIGA), 223–225, 227–228
Itzkowitz, N., 117, 126

Jackson, S. E., 130, 145, 149
Janssen, P. M. P., 145, 149
Jaques, E., 263, 275
Jaycox, L., 258, 276
Jewish people, xlviii, 216, 219,
    225–226, 228
Jones, A., 145, 149
Jonge, J. D., 145, 149

Kafka, F., 168, 170
Kahn, S., 269, 272, 276
Kanouse, D., 258, 276
Karterud, S., 7, 21
Katzman, M., 67–68, 86
Kees, M., 257, 275
Kernberg, O. F., xxxix, 3, 9, 19–22,
    37–38, 40, 44, 263, 275
Khaleelee, O., 45, 63
Khan, W. A., xxviii, xxx
Kilpatrick, D., 258, 275
Klein, M., xxix, xxxii–xxxiii, xlvi, 147
Klein, R. H., 272, 275
Kleinberg, J. L., xxvii, 255, 272, 275
Klimova, H., xliii, l
Knowlson, J., 133, 149
Kobasa, S. C., 269, 275
Kohut, H., 7, 22, 267
Kreeger, L., xxi, xxx, xlvi, l, 223

Lacan, J., 62–63
Ladden, L., 238, 254
Lake, D., 237, 253
Laplanche, J., 35, 44
Larkin, G. R., 266, 275
Lasch, C., 46, 63
Laufer, A., 217, 230
Lawrence, W. G., xxii, xxix–xxxi,
    xxxv, xlvii, l, 40, 44, 222, 230
leadership
    change, xxiv, 196, 209
    couple, 23, 29–31, 36–41
    good, 37, 41, 84
    mature, 37–38
    organizational, xxvi, 46, 207, 261,
        264–265, 273
    pastoral, 173–176, 179–181, 185,
        189, 191
    strong, 112, 223
    succession(s), 190, 192
    team, 26, 29, 35, 37–38
Lebel, U., 226, 229
Leff, J., 131, 149
Lesch, K. P., 68, 86
Lester, E., xxviii, xxix
Lévi-Strauss, C., 153, 170

Lewin, K., 235, 254
Lictentriet, R., 226, 230
life *see also*: unconscious
  congregational, 181–182, 185
  daily, 27, 93, 115, 219
  early, 67–68, 157
  family, 72, 117, 176, 179
  human, 202–203
  organizational, 3, 37, 45, 52, 165,
    174, 177, 211
Lightman, S. L., 67–68, 86
Lloyd, H., 144, 148
Long, S. D., xxiv, xliii, l, 30, 44–47,
    49–50, 62–64
Lousada, J., 151, 170

Maddi, K. L., 269, 272, 276
Maddi, S. R., 269, 272, 276
Main, T. H., 129, 132–135, 138, 140,
    149, 153, 170
Mallonee, S., 258, 276
Marshall, G., 258, 276
Martin, D., 130–133, 149
Maslach, C., 130, 145, 149
massification, xvii, xxv–xxvi, xxxv,
    xxxviii–xxxix, xli–xlii, xliv–xlvii,
    5, 18, 41, 50, 71, 75, 78–80, 82, 85,
    89–90, 93–94, 97–100, 102–105,
    107, 118, 147, 164, 177–178, 191,
    215, 220–222, 226, 247–251, 263
Mayer, J. D., 266, 276
McCluskey, U., 237, 254
McDougal, W., 219, 230
McIntosh, D. N., 258, 276
McMillen, J., 258, 276
Mead, G. H., 236, 254
Meaney, M. J., 68, 87
Melamed, Y., 228–229
Menzies, I., 135, 139–140, 147, 149
Menzies-Lyth, I. E. P., xxxi, l, 113,
    125
Mercer, T. A., 256–257, 276
Middle East, 89–91, 94, 99, 102, 106,
    227
Miller, E. J., xlvii, l, 45, 51, 63
Miller, J. G., 234, 254

Minuchin, S., 69, 236, 254
mirroring, xxii, xxxviii, xliv, 30–31,
    36, 38, 89, 113–114, 120, 151,
    157–158, 160, 164–165, 185, 199,
    201, 212
Mitchell, S. H., 267–268, 276
Mojović, M., xxviii, xxx, xliii, l, 160,
    171
Mor-Barak, M., 217, 230
Morrison, J., 258, 276
Motz, A., 118, 125
mourning, xx, xxvi, xliii, 18, 56, 61,
    79, 106–107, 112–113, 120–122,
    124, 222, 226
  incomplete, 200–201, 208
myth(s)/mythology, xl, 6, 37, 248

narcissism, xxiv, xxxv, xxxvii, 5, 8–9,
    18–20, 30, 37, 39, 46, 57, 61–62,
    104–105, 143, 145, 169, 181, 189,
    193, 262
Navia, L., 157, 171
Neill, C., 112, 118, 125
Neuhaus, R. J., 175, 193
Newman, T. K., 68, 86
Newton, J., 49, 64
Nicholls, D., 67, 87
Nitsun, M., 28, 44
Nixon, S., 258, 276
Nobus, D., 62, 64
Norman, I. J., 144–145, 148, 150
North, C., 258, 276
Nunn, K., 85, 87
Nuttman-Shwartz, O., xxvi, 217–218,
    226, 228–231

objective/objectivity, 21, 105, 135,
    140, 167, 207, 218, 258, 270
O'Driscoll, D., 113, 125
Oedipal ideas, 101, 248–249, 251–252
Ofer, G., 224, 229
oil
  companies, 89, 91–92, 94, 99, 103,
    107–108
  embargo, 90, 94, 99
  industry, 94, 100, 107

organization(al) *see also*: life,
    perverse, trauma, unconscious
    (life of)
    culture, 50, 206, 264
    hospital, 25, 34, 37
    identity, xxiv, 6–7, 9–10, 17–18, 20
    in-the-mind, 7, 9, 17–18
    process(es), xxiv, 33, 35, 265
    structure, xxv, 42, 52, 116, 123, 132,
        175, 195–196, 209, 262–263, 271
outrage, 14, 80, 104, 142, 173, 183,
    238, 244–246
Owen, W., 158–159, 171
Oxford English Dictionary, 47, 64

Pajaczkowska, C., 62, 64
Palestinian(s), 217, 225, 227
paranoia/paranoid, 3, 9, 14, 17–21,
    37, 83, 124, 138, 177, 217, 222,
    238, 245–246, 263
    rumours, 3–4, 18–19
paranoiagenesis, xxiii–xxiv, 3, 19–20
paranoid–schizoid position, xvii, 147,
    211
Parker, C. C., 68, 86
Peck, E., 145, 150
Perera, S. B., 103, 105, 110
peritraumatic stress, 260–263, 270, 274
perverse
    dynamics, 47–48, 50, 61–62
    organization, 46–48
    process, xxiv, 56, 58, 61
    state(s) of mind, 30, 48–50, 61
perversion, xxxvii, xliii, 45–50, 55, 62,
    202
Petch, E., 142, 150
Peters, R., 236, 253
Pines, M., 42, 44, 223
Pontalis, J. B., 35, 44
Poole, A. D., 145, 150
Pooley, J., 206, 214
post-traumatic stress disorder (PTSD),
    219, 222, 228, 258, 261, 271, 274
Poulin, M., 258, 276
Power, M., 142, 150
Procci, W. R., 120, 125

projection, xliii, 4–6, 16, 18–19, 31, 36,
    40–41, 90, 98–102, 113, 116, 124,
    139, 144, 152, 154, 159–162, 169,
    193, 201, 205, 216–218, 220, 223,
    226, 237, 249
projective identification, xxii, xxxvii,
    xliii, 5, 9, 17, 103, 113–114, 152,
    162, 189, 192–193, 220, 223
Puccetti, M. C., 269, 275

Queens Road Church, 173, 178–182,
    185–186, 188–189, 192–193
    Mrs Harris, 180–184, 188, 190, 192
    Reverend Gregory, 180–185,
        189–190, 192
    Reverend Mansfield, 182
    Reverend Naismith, 182–185,
        188–189
    Sunday School, 183, 187, 190

rage, 74, 101–102, 104–105, 117,
    119–122, 174, 178, 205, 210, 217,
    241
Recer, P., 257, 276
Rediger, G. L., 174, 194
Redl, F., xxxix, 82, 87, 103, 110
regulation, 12, 26, 55–56, 68–69, 71,
    90, 98, 122, 179, 181, 221–222,
    236, 266
    tension, 262, 266, 269, 272–273
Resnick, H., 258, 275
Rey, H., 155, 171
risk management, 96, 142, 146
Roberts, V., 134, 150–151, 161, 170
Rosenbaum, B., xxiv, 166
Rosenfeld, H. A., xxxvii, l
Rosman, B. L., 69, 87
Rowell, G., xlviii, l
Rubin, S. S., 226, 230
Rude, S., 238, 254
rumour(s), xxiii–xxiv, xli, 3–6, 9,
    16–19, 264 *see also*: paranoid
Ryan, A., 258, 276

Salovey, P., 266, 276
Sanson-Fisher, R. W., 145, 150

Scanlon, C., xxv, 152, 154, 157, 163–164, 169, 171
scapegoat(ing), xxv, xl–xli, xlv, 5, 17, 19, 80, 83, 89–90, 94, 98–108, 138–139, 185, 205, 211, 222, 237, 249, 264
Scheidlinger, S., 5, 22, 218, 230
Schermer, V. L., xxviii, 272, 275
schizoid traits/schizophrenia, xxxvi, xlv, 39, 133, 147, 163, 211
Schleiermacher, F., 178, 194
Schneider, S., xxi–xxii, xxx, 219, 230
Schultz, S., 257, 275
Schuster, M., 258, 276
Seibold, A., xx, xxix
self, xxxvi, xxxviii, 9, 70, 115, 147, 266–268
    actual, 8–9
    -concept, 8–9
    -conscious(ness), 243, 248
    -esteem, xxxii, 259
    -management, 175, 181, 185–186
    -reflection, 264, 267, 272
sexual see also: abuse, trauma
    liaisons, 97, 101, 104
    victimization, 113, 116
sexuality, xxxii, 48, 101, 109, 116, 120
shame, xxxiii, 14, 18, 60, 72, 93, 117, 124, 158–159, 167, 169, 187, 189, 191, 198, 200–201, 204, 207, 226
Shariat, S., 258, 276
Shayit, K., 228, 231
Shephard, H. A., 235, 253
Shibutani, T., 4, 22
Sievers, B., 49, 64
Silovsky, J., 257, 275
Silver, R. C., 258, 276
Sinason, V., 114, 125
Slade, M., 142, 148
Smith, E., 258, 276
Snyder, C., 268, 276
Sobsey, D., 114, 125
Solnit, R., xliv, l
Solomon, Z., 223, 228–229
Sonne, J. C., 120, 126
Sontag, D., 261, 276

Spillius, E. B., 141, 150
Spitznagel, E., 258, 276
splitting, xix, xliii, 9, 30, 46, 55, 71, 109, 111, 113, 116, 123–124, 138–139, 159, 161, 163, 165–166, 169, 178, 185, 192, 205, 216, 220, 222–225, 228
Stacey, R., xlii, l, 6–7, 22
Steiner, J., 62, 64, 160, 171
Steinke, P. L., 175, 194
Stiers, M., xxii, xxx
Stokes, J., 143–144, 150
Stoller, R., 48, 64
Stone, W. N., 7, 21
Suomi, S. J., 68, 86–87
symbol(-ism), xxxvii, xlvi, 66, 109, 122, 137, 155, 164, 177, 189, 200, 260
systems-centred training (SCT), 233–239, 241, 243–251, 253
Szmukler, G., 142, 150

Target, M., 70, 87
terrorism/terrorist, xxvii, xli, 76, 219, 228, 257, 259, 261, 266, 268
    9/11 attacks, xxvii, 255, 257–262, 264–266, 274
theory of living human systems (TLHS), xxvii, 233, 234, 236
Thomas, A., xx, xxx
Thornicroft, G., 142, 148
transference, 200, 225, 271
    counter-, xxii, xlv, 137, 249
trauma
    chosen, xliii, 164, 204, 216–217, 226
    cumulative, xxv, 95, 195, 199–200, 202, 205, 207, 210, 212
    group, xxxv–xxxvi, 93, 247
    organizational, 35, 120, 124, 224–225
    post-, 29, 35, 256–257, 259, 271, 274
    sexual, 113, 115, 117
    social, xvii, xliii, xlviii, 93, 216
traumatic
    event(s), xxvii, xxxvi, xliii, 95, 112, 176, 215, 218, 221, 224, 239, 244–246, 250

experience, xviii, xx–xxi,
xxvii–xxviii, xxxiii, xxxv,
xxxvii–xxxviii, xlii, xlv–xlvi,
29, 49, 61–62, 67, 69, 71, 84,
93–94, 103, 111–112, 118, 147,
159, 193, 220, 224, 226–227,
233, 251–252
situation, 35, 108
traumatization, 27, 35, 70, 167, 199,
205–206, 217
traumatized
group(s), xviii, 205
organization(s), xviii, xxi–xxv,
xxvii–xxviii, xliv–xlv, 20, 108,
114, 124, 190, 220, 222, 226, 228
patient(s), xviii, xxiv, xlv, xlvii, 83,
122
people, xvii, xxxvii, xxxix, 218, 251
social system(s), xli, 90, 97
societies, xxiv, xxvi, xl, xliii–xliv,
xlviii, 218–219, 222, 226, 228
traumatogenic process(es),
xxiv–xxvii, xxxv, xxxvii, 25, 35,
67, 71, 89, 92, 107–108, 177, 221,
228, 233, 251, 253
Treasure, J., 67–68, 86
Triest, J., 220, 230
Truffaut, F., xxii, xxx
Tugade, M. M., 266, 275
Turquet, P. M., xxxv, xxxix, xlvi, l, 7,
22, 40, 43–44
Tustin, F., 73, 87

unconscious
life, xxii, xxiv, xlv, 85, 89, 107, 215
of groups, xviii, xxiii, xxxiii, xxxv
of organizations, xxii, 85, 221, 226
social, 105–106, 176–177, 201, 203,
207, 209, 216–217, 220,
224–225, 228
USA, xviii, xxvii, 17, 21, 47, 90, 94,
106, 256
New York, 256–258, 260–261

violence, xli, 99, 103, 134, 136–137,
152–159, 164–165, 168, 174, 217
Vivian, P., xxviii, xxx
Vlahov, D., 258, 275
Volkan, V. D., xlix, l, 117, 126, 164,
171, 204, 209, 211, 214, 216, 218,
226, 230

Wagner, D., 257, 276
Watts, D., 142, 148
Waugh, C. E., 266, 275
Weinberg, H., xxi–xxii, xxvi, xxviii,
xxx, xlvii, l, 216, 218, 230–231
Welldon, E. V., xlv, li, 118, 126
West, B., 258, 276
Whyte, L., 144, 150
Wilke, G., xxvi, 196, 213
Wilkinson, S., 164, 167, 170
Willi, J., 39, 44
Williams, C., 196, 213
Winnicott, D. W., xxix, xxxiii, xlii,
xlvii, li, 195, 206, 210–211, 214,
267
Winther, G., xxiv, 166
Wood, D., xxiv, 162
Woods, J., xxviii, xxx
worker's block (WB), 255–259, 261,
263, 266–267, 269–272, 274
world
external/outside, 70–71, 73–74,
160, 208, 216
inner/internal, 70, 137, 208
social, 159, 165

Yalom, I. D., 272, 276
Yanay, U., 228, 231
Yeats, W. B., 161, 171
Yergin, D., 91, 110
Young, J., 153, 171

Zhou, M., 258, 276
Zinkin, L., 38, 44
Žižek, S., 153, 171